I NEVER KISSED PARIS GOODBYE

By the same author

Christine: A search for Christine Granville, O.B.E., G.M., Croix de Guerre

Edwina: A biography of the Countess Mountbatten of Burma

Edited by Madeleine Masson

The Compleat Cook, or Secrets of a 17th-century Housewife, by Rebecca Price

I NEVER KISSED PARIS GOODBYE

Madeleine Masson

Hamish Hamilton: *London*

First published in Great Britain 1978
by Hamish Hamilton Limited
90 Great Russell Street London WC1B 3PT

Copyright © 1978 by Madeleine Masson

British Library Cataloguing in Publication Data

Masson, Madeleine
   I never kissed Paris goodbye.
   1. Paris—Social life and customs
   I. Title
   944'.36'08150924   DC7 37
   ISBN 0-241-89872-2

Printed in Great Britain at
The Camelot Press Ltd, Southampton

Contents

	List of Illustrations	6
	A Letter to My Son, 1977	7
1	Paris—June 1940	9
2	Début of a Colonial Child	14
3	Enter the Baron	25
4	The Nest of Vipers	37
5	Enter a Marquise, with Dagger	58
6	The Enchanted Tower	77
7	In Search of Proust	96
8	Sergei and the Babuskas	118
9	Ex Africa Semper Aliquid Novi	124
10	Lament for Lucy	147
11	These Foolish Things	153
12	An Unofficial English Rose	183
13	Nat-Nat, Bright Angel, and Other Sacred Monsters	200
14	Murder was His Business	219
15	In Search of Vincent	246
16	The Writing on the Wall	253
17	Frère Jacques, Frère Jacques	263
18	Experience is What Happens to You	293
	Index	300

List of Illustrations

(between pages 96 and 97)

1. Myself in 1935
2. Lala—my mother
3. Géa—Georges Augsborg *Photo Marpège, Lausanne*
4. Colette at her desk in the Palais Royal

(between pages 128 and 129)

5. Suzy Solidor, with 'Kaboul'
6. My brother Jacques, 1940
7. Géa's drawing of myself with Tabou at a roadside café, *Reproduced by courtesy of Mme. G. Augsbourg*
8. Home in Johannesburg, 1942

A Letter to My Son, 1977

Beloved Merrick,

You are twenty-two years old, and at the beginning of what will, I trust, be a full and happy life. I am in my sixties, and although I hope to be around for a long time yet, I have begun the sensible task of putting my affairs and papers in order.

This is to spare you a wearisome task, and which might lead to some curious surprises when you discovered that the comfortable, cosy materfamilias, who had been part of the furniture of your childhood, adolescence and young manhood, was once as young, vital, selfish and intent on living life to the hilt as you are.

Furthermore, since it has become the fashion for authors' children to write fully and frankly of the lives and loves of their parents, I have forestalled such an urge on your part, by writing my autobiography, and painting my own portrait, 'warts and all'. This fragment I dedicate to you and to my future grandchildren, as a social document which records faithfully a small but important slice of the history of our times, in which I was not only a spectator, but also a participant.

It is a far cry from the France of the thirties and the war-torn years of the forties to the Britain of the seventies, from the young red-haired Madeleine to Merrick's grey-haired mother who sits writing these words in a little house in the Sussex sailing village where your father and I have for many years lived a peaceful and orderly existence, the *tempo rallentando* of which would have astonished us had we known what our future would be when we met a moment of crisis in both our lives in 1951.

It was fortunate for you and me that I did meet, and eventually marry, the remarkable, courageous and witty naval officer who brought much-needed sand and ballast into my life.

Thanks to him, you were brought up conventionally, with discipline, a decent regard for law and order and respect for your country. Friends who had known me in my 'salad' days were surprised to discover that I had become a devoted wife and mother. Sometimes I overdid the maternal role, as when you and I were walking in Hyde Park on Nannie's day out. Hoping to grapple you to me with hoops of steel, I thought I would entertain you with stories of my childhood; but very soon you became bored and restless and, pulling away from my hand, ran off and played with your little friends. I should have realised that the young are nearly always embarrassed by the memories of their parents, which do not in any way relate to their own very important here and now.

There was also a period when you were at public school, and it became evident from your conversation and that of the friends you brought home, that your parents had been cast in the role of antique waxworks in a museum for geriatrics. The fact that your father and I were as passionately in love as in the early days of our courtship did not cross your mind, and had this been suggested to you, you would have been deeply shocked. As far as you and your group were concerned, anyone over the age of twenty had one foot in the tomb. The generation gap was wide and deep. I have tried to diminish it by writing this book in which I have explained something of the background and influences which shaped my formative years. I wanted to take you with me through the various stages of my evolution, so that later, in your own development to maturity, you may understand, as I now do, that the real, the only fruits of the spirit are love, joy and peace.

I make no apology for anything described in these pages. I have enjoyed my life and all my varied relationships; and the most surprising fact is, that, old and passée as I may seem to you and your contemporaries, my darling, I still appreciate and value to the full all the miraculous pleasures that life has to offer, and I hope I always shall, until my final descent into the 'dazzling darkness'.

Bosham, West Sussex. August 1977

I

Paris—June 1940

It was a beautiful day in June 1940. I pushed open my bedroom shutters and looked down at the rue Jacob. It seemed singularly silent, and although it was not Sunday, most of the shops were closed. Géa came in wearing his hobnailed boots and old mountaineering cloak. His candid, wide blue eyes, the innocent eyes of a child in the seamy face of an adult, were anxious.

'I am going to get on to a train. Please come back with me. My father and Anna will look after you.'

'You're the one that has been called up, soldier boy. What would I do hanging about Switzerland while you do your duty? This is no moment to go skiing, or looking for edelweiss.'

Géa looked baffled. He had never understood my peculiar sense of humour. He said, 'But you will be in danger, real danger if you stay here. Please come with me.'

I snapped at him. 'I've no intention of staying here. But before I do anything I've got to find out where Jacques is.'

'He can look after himself. He's a man.'

'He's only a boy, and he's my brother, and I care about him. As soon as I know what his plans are, I'll be off. I want to go home, to my own home and people. Back to Africa.'

'I thought Paris was your home?'

'That's what I thought too. Now I'm not so sure. Maybe home is where my roots are.'

'How will you get out of France with a French passport? And Africa is so very far away.'

'I'll get there in the end. Remember me? I'm a born survivor.'

The doorbell rang. My secretary, Kathe Muller, came in sniffing in her usual irritating way.

'I know I'm early, but it was such a lovely day that I walked from home. Shall I help you with your packing and papers?'

Géa had always disliked and distrusted Frau Muller. Mostly, I suspected, because she had, for so long, been my confidante. He turned on her.

'You're very calm for an émigrée who is about to be overrun by the master race. Or are you cooking up a warm welcome for the Boche? I've often wondered about your activities, Frau Muller, I really have.'

'You thought I was a spy?' She looked coy and flattered.

'I wouldn't be at all surprised to find that you are a sort of Quisling, the Mata-Hari of Passy, perhaps.'

'Géa! How can you be so suspicious and unkind?'

'Well?' His voice was challenging. 'What is your reply?'

'Only that I am a Jewess.'

'This is a stupid and odious conversation,' I said angrily. 'It was more than kind of you to have come early, Frau Muller. I have a mass of papers to sort. Will you phone the office and find out whether they want me to come round? My instructions were to get myself to Cap-Breton as soon as possible. The Agency have managed to get a house there for their staff. You're welcome to come with me or to join me there later, if you can.'

Frau Muller pursed her thin lips. 'You are too kind, but no, I remain here. I have my reasons, but I shall be here when you return.' She then disappeared into the study.

The concierge, Madame Perronet, sidled in with some letters.

'The door was open. I thought you might like to have your post before . . .'

'Before what?'

'Before this afternoon.' She meant, before you go. Her eyes fastened on the open suitcases. I was not fond of Madame Perronet, a true descendant of the 'tricoteuses'. In her flat, nasal voice she said. 'They say that the Germans will be entering Paris at any moment . . .' It was as if she were shouting, 'A la lanterne', or its modern counterpart: 'To the concentration camps'. By then, every Jew in Europe knew all about concentration camps, and if the details had not yet been clearly spelled out, the name of camps such as Dachau had the same effect on anyone with Jewish blood as the word 'abattoir' may, for all we know, have upon cattle. A blind terror that chills the blood and turns the bowels to water.

Géa almost pushed Madame Perronet into the hall. Kathe Muller came in with a thick sheaf of typescript.

Paris—June 1940

'Shall you take this?'

I looked at the manuscript of my new book with deep distaste. It was a novel about a Norman peasant girl who went out to South Africa in 1900 and became a great financier. I was already bored with my heroine, Isabelle, and was delighted to jettison the half-written book. Years later the manuscript caught up with me and was published in London. It was still a bore. But 'Isabelle' was Frau Muller's favourite character. Although she was an efficient secretary she was a trifle quirky about my heroines. I could not cure her of the habit of changing the colour of their hair and eyes. She disliked blondes and I did not care for brunettes. I did not mind these changes so much when I was writing colourful novellas for women's magazines, but I hated her tampering with my 'serious' prose. Lala, my mother, had 'discovered' Frau Muller in a bookshop and had given her to me as a rather strange legacy. Because she was fond of me and believed in my talents as a writer (she was the only one at the time) she insisted on following me into my new life, when I left my husband, the Baron. The fact that I could not pay her wages did not particularly worry her. She was faithful, discreet and she stuck like a burr.

Madame Perronet poked her nose round the door, her face alight with malice.

'Old Monsieur Laperche from downstairs says the roads are so jammed with refugees that nobody can get away, so he has decided to stay. He's so old that nobody will bother him, but if I were you Madame I should really begin to worry.'

Géa came out of our bedroom holding a pair of skis.

'I must take these. They're brand new and may come in handy.'

'Surely your sketchbooks would be more useful?'

He looked obstinate. 'Sketchbooks are easy to come by. These skis were specially hand-made for me by my cousin Léon, you know, the hunchback at Sion. I owe it to Léon to take the skis back to Switzerland. Have you sorted out what you want to take with you?'

'Not yet.'

We looked at one another. The flat was filled with the flotsam and jetsam of both our lives. Although we had not long lived together, we had managed to accumulate a good many books, pictures, photographs and small personal treasures like my collection of Madonnas in china, glass, wood, crystal and metal.

'When fleeing from the enemy it is always well to travel light,' said Frau Muller.

'O, you deadly Cassandra,' said Géa.

She tossed her head with its rigid old-fashioned Marcel waves. The only uncontrolled thing about my secretary was her appetite for male flesh. She gobbled up spotty boys as I did hot chestnuts. Her sexual extravagances were expensive and she had to work very hard for the money she spent on gifts for her Jojos and Titis, the little Parisian toughs she met in the course of her nightly duties as Madame Pipi in Princess Babouska's night-club in Montmartre. My tutor, Serge Cheremeteff, had helped Frau Muller to get the job with one of his many White Russian relations. It was a satisfactory arrangement, except that the long hours made Frau Muller so sleepy that she often nodded off at the typewriter when I was dictating.

My lover Géa and Frau Muller did not get along very well, and from the beginning he begged me to get rid of her. He said she gave him the creeps, with her blue marble eyes, perpetual catarrh and floury-white make-up, but I was sorry for her and grateful to her for her loyalty and devotion, so I refused to part with her.

It was impossible to reason with Géa. Once he had decided on a certain line of conduct, he kept right on until he was satisfied he had succeeded or failed in whatever it was he had set out to do. He was the only completely 'original' man I had ever met. Until I discovered him I thought all men came in the same mould as my father, brother and husband. Also, I had never before met a truly dedicated artist who believed sincerely that God had given him his gift.

Géa, when I first lived with him, was not making much from the sale of his pictures. This was hardly surprising as he was on an umbrella kick. He refused to paint anything else and our flat in the rue Jacob was filled to suffocation with brollies, mainly large, black cotton peasant *parapluies* with stout handles, which, he said, reminded him of market places in the rain and stirred up the necessary inspiration within him to trigger off an attack of painting fever which might well last all day and all night for weeks.

Life with Géa, though financially insecure, was never dull.

Now, on this lovely day in June it looked as if we had reached the end of the road and that I should have to leave Géa and all that life in Paris meant to me. Since the day I had decided to settle in the most beautiful city in the world, I had never imagined myself living anywhere else.

I went to the window again and looked down at my little universe, at the quiet street, and across the way at the Square Furstenberg, with its plane trees shading Delacroix's studio. The small sunlit square with its plane trees in their iron corsets, a typically French invention, were the essence of the Paris I loved.

At last I turned back to go on sorting my possessions. Each object was symbolic of a milestone in my life in Paris; in my development as a woman and a writer. Here were letters and photographs of my family, of Chris with Simba in his arms, of the Baron and of my home in Normandy. Why, I wondered, had I kept the photographs of Renaud posing affectedly, as was his wont, in front of the camera? Even now I did not tear them up. Filled with nostalgia for the past I put them gently back in the album.

2

Début of a Colonial Child

It was almost six years since the day that Lala, my mother, and I had arrived in Paris and moved into an apartment in the rue de la Faisanderie, to prepare for the arrival of Papa and my only brother, Jacques, who was at boarding school in South Africa where we lived. We were going to have a family holiday together in Paris. Generally, Papa was too busy making money for us in his Johannesburg office to spare time for a family reunion in Europe. In any case, he preferred to take his Continental vacations alone, or in the company of one of the attractive mannequins who always accompanied him to Vichy or La Bourboule or whichever spa he had chosen for a 'cure'.

Lala was an inveterate traveller, and from the age of four I was always included in her European journeys. She felt guilty at leaving Papa with his nose to the grindstone, and as, at that time, I was an only child, I think having me with her salved her conscience. So, from a tender age I became part of what her critics called Lala's travelling circus; composed as it was of our Nannie, known to us as Nursie, Lala's devoted slave, and an escort of young men she picked up on her travels who acted as couriers, guides, and chauffeurs to my delicious mamma. She never moved without innumerable trunks filled with linen, pictures, books, bibelots and cushions, for she said she liked her hotel rooms to reflect her personality and to have individuality.

Sometimes I was left with Nursie, who was a Cockney, in a London boarding-house or seaside hotel, but, more often than not, Nursie and I were comfortably installed in the quiet back bedroom in the French, Swiss, Italian or Austrian palace hotel of Lala's choice.

I was left pretty much to my own devices, and when Nursie was 'maiding' Lala, I wandered about the hotel grounds, or spent long, blissful hours curled up in vast chairs in dismal, ornate hotel salons, reading Tauchnitz novels, which were generally housed in glass-fronted bookcases together with a collection of solemn and unreadable tomes bought for their bindings.

I counted liftmen, hotel concierges, porters, chefs and chambermaids amongst my friends. All of them spoilt me, so that in no time at all I became a precocious little pest. Finally Papa, at the insistence of his French relations, put a stop to my European progresses and, to my great chagrin, I was then incarcerated in an English-type boarding school in Johannesburg, my home town.

Father was born in France and when quite young was sent out to Portuguese East Africa to represent the family bank. He was transferred thence to South Africa, where he met Lala, a ravishingly beautiful creature with Viennese antecedents. After a brief engagement they married. Everyone seemed to think that both parties had made a good match. But Lala always felt she should have married a career-diplomat, or a millionaire, while Papa was often enraged by Lala's extravagant and seemingly frivolous attitude to life.

Fundamentally, however, my parents were united, and cared deeply for their two children, my little brother Jacques being much younger than myself. As the only son he was, of course, the apple of the patriarch's eye, and so far as Lala was concerned, the child who had inherited her smile and her great grey eyes could do no wrong. As I felt the same way about the little boy who clung to my hand and endlessly repeated the words 'metoo, metoo', whether I was being given castor-oil or chocolates, I can truthfully say that I had a happy, secure, sunlit childhood, wanting for nothing, and loving my parents, particularly Lala, who, when I was little, was the sun, moon and stars in my small world.

We often came to Paris where Lala generally lived on terms of armed neutrality in an hotel near Papa's family who disapproved of her on the grounds that her extravagant way of life was ruining 'poor Emile', my Papa. Thanks to the good offices of my statuesque Aunt Gabrielle, I was finally packed off to the ultraconservative and snobbish convent school near Paris which she had herself attended, and where in company with a select band of young ladies, I learned to love Jesus, have visions, drink 'abondance' (wine and water mixed) and almost perish of a neglected appendix which finally burst and nearly killed me.

Lala loved French clothes and hats, perfume and food, but her happiest moments were spent in Florence where she bowled the Italians over in droves with her peachlike beauty. She, like Papa, enjoyed taking cures, but for different reasons. She liked the relaxed social atmosphere of the famous cure-places such as Marienbad, Bourboule-les-Bains and Montecatini in Italy, where you were treated like a hot-house flower, and where a wardrobe of beautiful new clothes was part of the cure.

After our family holiday, which to everyone's surprise was a success, Papa and Lala prepared to return home in time to get Jacques back to school. They had, of course, expected me to accompany them, but by this time I was enjoying Paris far too much to leave, and after a row of monumental proportions, I put an advertisement in the Paris edition of the *New York Herald*, offering my services as a bi-lingual secretary willing to travel. Mrs van Hoorn in the Swiss clinic where she was being treated for the serious thyroid complaint which would later kill her, chuckled when she read my advertisement, and immediately sent me a telegram inviting me to an interview a week later in her apartment on the Quai de Conti.

I was enchanted with this news, and waving the wire triumphantly at my parents, finally cajoled them into letting me at least keep my appointment with Mrs van Hoorn. Lala offered to escort me to see for herself whether my future employer was a respectable woman, or was part of a White Slave Organisation which would drug me senseless before turning me over to the captain of the ship which transported nubile European females to North African ports where they were purchased by wealthy merchants who subsequently sold them to brothels, or to lascivious Arabs who installed them in harems, never to be seen by any other male eye again. Lala had a vivid imagination and a fund of cautionary tales, most of which, I believe, were based on real happenings.

My interview with Mrs van Hoorn was brief. The flat was immense, luxurious and was beautifully decorated in tones of smoky grey, blue and Chinese yellow. Elodie van Hoorn looked as unlike the concept of a Southern belle as possible; she resembled a pekinese, with a small flat nose and protuberant pale blue eyes. She was dressed always in black by Lanvin, and the thin sliver of red ribbon that was the Légion d'Honneur was her only adornment.

Début of a Colonial Child

When we were working she took her ease in charming, floating négligées made by Fortuny. Her small plump hands with their shining pink nails were very pretty, as were her tiny, dainty feet in their black, patent-leather pumps. When I arrived on the scene, she was working on her second book, a biography of Charlotte Corday, a gentle, admirable creature who had managed to summon up enough patriotic adrenalin to stab the revolutionary Marat in his bath.

Years later, when we had become friends, Mrs van Hoorn told me how amused she had been by my self-assured manner which, as she well knew, masked a fit of nerves which dried my mouth, swelled my tongue, and made my palms sweat. I was in such a state that when my future employer asked me a few leading questions, I could only babble like an idiot, assuring her that I could do shorthand—untrue—Lala had booked me for a course of *sténotypie* and bought me a small and very expensive machine which I left in the métro after three lessons. Typing, true. I *had* finished the typing course. She also asked whether I had ever done any research in the Bibliothèque Nationale? I nodded violently and she plunged me into utter confusion by saying, 'In that case you can start making good use of your ticket immediately. Come here tomorrow at nine sharp and we'll go through my notes. Your working hours will be from nine to six, depending on my moods, and I am a fanciful creature.' I was then ceremoniously escorted out by the butler through a hall flagged in black and white marble. Only when I walked gaily along the quais, stopping at all the bookstalls, did I realise that Mrs van Hoorn had made no mention of a salary.

I was in such a state of euphoria at having landed my first job that I rushed into the nearest café to telephone Lala. As I was collecting a *jeton* at the counter, I noticed a tall young man having what seemed to me a very late breakfast. His back was towards me but there was something about the set of his head and shoulders which excited my curiosity. I went and sat at the table opposite. With lowered lids, the young man was moodily stuffing croissants into his mouth. Then he raised his eyes. I had heard of love at first sight, it was one of the main subjects of discussion in every dormitory in which I had slept; but I was unprepared for the reaction inside me, which almost knocked me off my chair.

So violent was the seismic shock wave through my system that I actually grabbed at my flat little stomach with both hands. Lifting my head, I looked long and hard into the sea-green eyes of François d'Harcourt. This naval officer with the butter blond hair and the sensitive lying mouth was home on leave. He lived with his widowed mother in Neuilly, and, at first, he loved me as wildly as I loved him.

First love, like the first lilies-of-the-valley, the first wood strawberries, and the first real kiss has a unique, an unrepeatable flavour, and I remember vividly every detail of that first encounter and have never to this day forgotten how the universe rocked and whirled when François gave me my first French kiss.

*

Before returning to South Africa, Lala had made elaborate arrangements for my future welfare by finding a wealthy but utterly dreary family with whom I was to live. After a week of dining off scraps on a tray in my room, without a hot bath or a kind word, I packed and left. François had found me a new home. It was the Pension des Marronniers, just around the corner from his mother's apartment.

The pension was set well back from the road in a cobbled courtyard which was picturesque, but death to anyone wearing anything but sabots. I liked the house, a pavilion which had seen better days and badly needed a lick of paint. But I appreciated its air of romantic decay, and was enraptured by the large back garden in which a few tables with red-and-white checked tablecloths were set out under two large horse-chestnut trees. God knows whence these two magnificent trees drew the nourishment which made them, each spring, into a great fiesta lit by pink and white candelabra. I liked to think that their roots were watered by one of those underground springs on which the *Lutetia* of the Romans had been built.

Madame Rose Tricon, the *patronne*, was a large, busty woman, with long false eyelashes which had a tendency to fall off at the most inconvenient times. She told me that she was one of the first women in Paris to have eyelashes made from the hairs of her current lover's legs. 'Imagine, *ma petite*,' she said, batting two black centipedes at me, 'imagine to yourself the voluptuousness of giving him Japanese kisses with his own hairs.' Madame

Tricon, or Madame Rose as she preferred to be called, was vague, kind-hearted, randy and totally impractical, and was for these reasons perpetually on the verge of bankruptcy.

She offered me a small, clean, cheap, room overlooking the garden. The furniture was ramshackle, but there was a small cabinet-de-toilette with a flowered wallpaper which pleased me. I had just begun putting my belongings away when there was a tap at the door, and in bustled an elderly creature in a shapeless voile garment. She wore, looped round her neck, a long chain of blue beads, one strand of which terminated in a locket which lay on her flat bosom. On her sheep's face was a wide and amiable grin, and her soft fluffy snow-white hair looked like 'apple snow' pudding.

'I'm from Tunbridge Wells,' she said in a genteel accent, extending a pudgy hand. 'I teach English to the "Froggies". I thought that as this was your first day here you might feel strange, and would like to have a nice cup of tea with me in my room. My name is Margaret Feathers, Mrs Harry Feathers, but everyone here calls me "Muzzie".'

I did not like tea, and I did not much care for Muzzie, but as she was so insistent, I left my unpacking and followed the old lady down the corridor to her room, which was half the size of mine. It was a chintzy nest seemingly contrived mostly out of old packing cases.

'I've a lot of lovely furniture in store back at home,' said Muzzie, bustling round and producing a tray and cups from a curtained recess, 'but when my late lamented, Mr Feathers—he was with Cook's you know for years, one of their Head Couriers, well, when he passed over, very sudden it was after supper one night when I'd taken so much trouble over the steak and kidney pudding, he had a delicate tum and couldn't be doing with French cooking all that garlic and herby stuff, well, as I was saying, one moment he was there, and the next he had gone. . . . I came abroad to get over it and stayed here at the Pension. Madame Rose was so kind to me that somehow I didn't feel like going back. She and the Padre, the English priest here, found me so many pupils that I settled down quite happily, although there are times when I get homesick.'

She rattled on breathlessly as she set out the tea things.

'I'm sure you'll love being here, such a nice set of folk, most of them. Of course my best friend is the Countess.' She rolled the title on her tongue like Napoleon brandy. 'She's the real thing, not one of your jumped-up parvenoos. But she doesn't mingle with everyone. She keeps herself to herself. If we get on well together, I'll ask her if I may bring you to her. She's a real aristocrat, Russian, *White* Russian of course, and so well connected, one of her friends is a close relative of the Czar that was. The Countess' son is married to an American lady, a millionairess; but the Countess has her pride and hardly accepts any help from her.'

Handing me a cup of tea, she opened a battered Huntley and Palmer biscuit tin and peered inside.

'Have a ginger-nut or a Marie, English biscuits are so much tastier than those things the froggies pass off as biscuits. Now, dear, I am going to talk to you seriously. You're full young to be in Paris alone, and even though you are a Colonial girl, I think of you as British and want to protect you.'

'From whom?' I asked, with opened wide, ingenuous eyes.

'I'm very broad-minded, dear, but I do have my principles, and my advice to you is to give a very wide berth to that Hungarian woman.'

My curiosity was aroused.

'What Hungarian woman?'

'She's away at the moment. But she has rooms here. Yes, three rooms. Imagine being able to afford to keep on *three* rooms when you are staying elsewhere?'

'She's probably wealthy.'

'She's no better than she should be, if you ask me. Red hair, very showy in her dress. An actress or worse, I shouldn't wonder. The only decent thing about her is her dog, and even he is peculiar. He has one blue eye and one brown eye. Frost his name is. Very foreign.'

'What is the lady's name?'

'She says it is de Polnay. Madame de Polnay. She'll be back soon. Just you mind me, and keep away from her.'

By now I was determined to meet the Hungarian lady who, as it turned out, was to become a great and beloved friend.

As I finished my tea, Mrs Feathers patted my knee and said, 'You must tell me all your little secrets. I'm like a mother to lots of the young people who stay here.'

I immediately determined never to tell Muzzie anything about my private affairs and to do everything in my power to avoid her. My youth and lack of experience blinded me to the pathos of the homesick old exile. Only now do I realise how cruelly and intolerantly I dismissed her. My nostrils were as yet unconditioned to the stink of genteel poverty bravely borne, or heartbreak gallantly concealed by this old woman who I later discovered had been repudiated by her son, her only living relative.

Some weeks after my arrival at the Pension a summons to visit the Russian Countess came in the form of a note scrawled in purple ink on crested writing-paper. I was invited to visit her at exactly 4.30 p.m. When I arrived, it was to find Muzzie dancing with impatience outside the door.

'Come along, do,' she said. 'The Countess cannot bear to be kept waiting, and she is strict when it comes to the manners or young people.'

Scratching on the door, Muzzie waited, like a well-trained poodle for the word of command. A deep booming voice bade us enter. I opened the door on to a large room dominated by a vast bed. In the bed, sitting bolt upright, was a grotesque huddled figure with a totally bald pate. The Countess crooked a scraggy finger at me. In her chalk-white face bloomed a pair of eyes of a deep violet colour. So remarkable and youthful were these eyes that one was immediately entrapped into their depths.

'Pass me my wig,' snapped the Countess to Muzzie; 'no, not that one, stupid, the red one.'

I looked with amazement at a row of wig-stands, all bearing wigs of different colours and made up in a variety of styles. Muzzie handed over the red wig, which the Countess pulled down over her bald pate. Now she resembled portraits of the ageing Elizabeth the First of England. Under the thatch of red hair, the beautiful eyes sparkled maliciously.

'So you're the little colonial? Where are your parents? Why have you come to Paris alone? Have you a guardian? In my day no decent girl of your age would have been permitted to live in a city like Paris. Perhaps you have run away from home? If so, I advise you to run back, and quickly. You are not safe here, not with that mouth and those eyes. Sit down by me. No, not on that chair, you'll disturb Sasha.'

I saw then that the overstuffed chair by the bed was already occupied by a large and unattractive tomcat, and that on the Countess' bed, blending with the moth-eaten fur cover, lay three more cats. Since the windows were hermetically sealed, the horrible smell that had assailed my nostrils from the moment I came in was now explained.

'You can go now, Feathers,' said the Countess, summarily dismissing Muzzie. 'I want to talk to the girl, and your whinny gets on my nerves.'

Muzzie departed, after having cast me a glance which expressed admiration and respect for her high-handed, nobly born friend.

'That's more peaceful,' said the Countess. 'Mrs Feathers is a good, kind creature, a splendid character really, but boring. Now tell me about yourself. No lies and no evasions please. I shall know whether you are telling the truth. I always know.'

The fact was that the Countess did know whether one was lying. She had second sight and could read palms and hearts. In the course of time I became accustomed to the terrible stink in her room and visited her frequently, rejoicing always in her tales of the Russia of the *ancien régime*. It was she who brought Serge Cheremeteff into my life; she said my mind needed cultivating, and that he was the person to do it. She was right. Serge, like Lucy, was to become one of the key people in my development. Even when I left the Pension I continued to visit the Countess. I saw her frequently, until one day her wealthy daughter-in-law fetched her away and put her into a magnificent home for the aged, a gilded cage in which she rapidly faded and died.

*

Now began a sunlit period. I had a love in my life, an interesting job and I was young and in Paris. My first close contact with the French mind made me desperately anxious to become integrated in the French current of life and thought. New ideas engendered by reading the works of French philosophers, poets and novelists exploded like catherine wheels in my brain.

I was enchanted by the beauty and lucidity of the French language, and the fact that many of the writers whose books had been such a revelation to me were alive and writing in the city I loved gave me the feeling of belonging to a great literary fraternity to which I might one day be admitted.

The great ghosts of the past were part of my daily life. Villon had darted down these narrow side-streets; Baudelaire's mistress had bought her groceries in the same dark little *épicerie* in which I bought my biscuits. The proprietor had initialled slips to prove that the dark lady liked hot spicy foods. Here was the fusty, insulated flat in which Marcel Proust had lived and died.

The boozy, rheumy-eyed Verlaine, the 'pauvre Lelian', had sat in the sun outside the same café in which I now drank my *café-crême*, and the feet of the proud, damned young archangel, Arthur Rimbaud, had trodden these very same pavements.

Nor was access to historical Paris denied me. Here I lived only in the company of the great. This quarter in which I strolled with my love was still the Paris of Henri IV who built the Place Royale, now the Place des Vosges, and still the most beautiful square in the world.

François shared my love of Paris and we wandered, hand in hand, through its parks and palaces, museums and art galleries. He had little more than his naval officer's pay, and I was not exactly rich, though Mrs van Hoorn's cheques, if erratic, were princely for that epoch and I was also getting an allowance from my parents.

We ate in small bistros, toasted one another in wine, and spent hours in cinemas. There was no place where we could be alone together to release our tensions, and in the long hot summer we became so frustrated that we began to bicker. I was conscious of a great longing to lie with this man, and with him discover that shimmering, mysterious alluring world of sex of which I had heard so much and experienced so little.

Although François told me he had never been in love before, he never allowed his desire for me to get out of hand. Indeed, with the exception of the prolonged and passionate kisses we exchanged, together with moist and sweaty fumblings of my person, I remained sublimely ignorant of matters sexual. François was taking no chances, and while he told me he hoped to spend the remainder of his life writing poems to my eyebrows and to my 'beautiful, passionate lips', he never discussed his future, or our future together.

It had early been established that he was the only son of a doting mother with a weak heart, and small means. Herself the daughter of a naval officer, she had married into the 'petite noblesse', and seemingly had never recovered from the shock of finding herself addressed as *Madame la Vicomtesse*. She had great ambitions for her good-looking son and it had taken twenty-three years of concentrated effort on her part to ruin his sweet, affectionate, but weak character. François was an egoist, completely dominated by his fragile maternal parent whose sempiternal widow's weeds blinded him to everything but her distress at the idea of his becoming seriously attached to any female but herself.

I never met François' mother. On the day he was to introduce me to her as his intended, she had a heart attack, or a maternal *crise du coeur*, and then a second more serious one, which necessitated François taking her away to relations in the Dauphiné to convalesce. François did not have the courage to tell me, face to face, that he had accepted his mother's pressing demands that he should give me up. She had more than once told him that she would never accept a daughter-in-law who was not a born Catholic.

François wrote me a constipated little farewell note, full of clichés in which he said that his duty to his 'sainted' mother overrode all other feelings. When I had finished reading this letter, my world fell to pieces, and I tumbled into a deep pit of despair from which I was not to emerge for five years, when I fell in love just as desperately all over again.

3

Enter the Baron

The night François d'Harcourt delivered my congé, Mrs van Hoorn was giving one of her musical soirées. She had a succession of protégées. The star of this particular fiesta was a singer called Bianca Albini. She was Neapolitan and a bundle of nerves. I had the task of keeping her calm until she was due to sing. It had not taken Mrs van Hoorn long to graft other more social duties on to those of literary secretary. She relied on me to stage-manage her soirées by attending to all the minor details, such as ordering the flowers and the buffet, produced by Poire et Blanche. I loved flowers and gloried in the beautiful and expensive out-of-season white lilac, prunus and great bunches of spring flowers (flown from the South of France) which adorned Mrs van Hoorn's salon.

Bianca Albini was a good mezzo-soprano, but she was far from being the *casta diva* she thought she was, and kept throwing tantrums just for the pleasure of upsetting those around her.

As I lay on my bed, clutching François' abominable note in my hand and with my heart in shreds, I knew that I must appear at the Quai de Conti, if only to keep Signora Albini out of her patron's hair until it was time for her to take to the boards, which in this instance, was a raised platform at one end of the great room whose long windows overlooked the Seine.

By the time I arrived the household was buzzing. The butler Hodges was in disgrace because he had forgotten to order sufficient ice; Kate, the lady's maid, was suicidal because Mrs van Hoorn's new gown was too tight, so, fighting back my tears, and a violent desire to be sick all over the Aubusson in the hall, I ranted and raved until order was restored.

By the time Elodie van Hoorn emerged encased in black velvet, with a train, all was sweetness and light in the salon, perfumed, as I had been taught, with the scent of Guerlain's *Plantes Marines*, which I produced by heating this liquid in a spoon over a tiny, highly dangerous spirit stove. In the meantime, Signora Albini was on her knees in my little office, telling her beads as she always did before a performance.

The salon looked like an engraving of an eighteenth-century music room, with its great lake of shiny parquet, the rows of small gilt chairs and the Trianon-blue curtains billowing in the breeze off the river, and the scent of the white lilac blended with that of *Plantes Marines*.

I was wearing an unbecoming black dress, which suited my state of mind. My lids were pink and swollen, as was my nose, and my shock of auburn curls was more disordered than usual. I caught sight of myself in a mirror, shuddered and stuck my tongue out at my untidy image; then, as the realisation of my loss swept over me again I retired behind one of the voluminous curtains in the room set aside for the buffet, and stood there with tears pouring down my face.

Intrigued by the sight of a pair of size six bronze sandals behind the curtains, the Baron Renaud Marie de la Minaudière, who was nothing if not curious, twitched the curtain aside and discovered me, red-nosed, sniffing and gulping down my sobs. Later he told me that I had looked such a pitiful little freak that he longed to pet and comfort me, as one does a stray, sad dog, and while Signora Albini next door was making the crystal droplets in the chandeliers vibrate with the hard jet of her rendering of *Butterfly*, the Baron was trying to coax me into a better frame of mind.

He fed me with lobster patties, *barquettes* filled with caviar, and forced me to drink a fair number of glasses of champagne, so that by the time the applause from next door announced that the concert was over, my agony was allayed by a spurious sense of well-being and by the curious notion that I was being a great social success. The Baron had, by this time, fallen desperately in love with his little waif and later told me that as I munched my way remorselessly through the assorted canapés, he was evolving a plan of action which should bring me swiftly to his bed.

The last of the de la Minaudières looked like the young Fredric March. From his murderous but illustrious Italian ancestors, the Borgias, he had inherited a classical cast of visage. His nose was perfection, his brow lofty and his eyes dark, liquid and shaded by long silky lashes. His skin was a pale amber and his black hair was sleeked down close to his well-shaped head.

There emanated from his person an aura of breeding and well-being. It was obvious that here was a man of the world, a creature of leisure whose only problems were the set of his jacket and the colour of his tie. His big powerful hands did not seem to belong to his slender body; they were the hands of a navvy with spatulate fingers. In fact he hardly ever used his hands except to play the piano, which he did pleasingly, but with little talent.

He was a natty dresser. His suits were made by Anderson and Sheppard in London, and his fittings were a matter of real moment to him; his shirts and dressing-gowns came from Sulka, his shoes from Bunting and his hats from Lock. He smelt of freshly laundered linen and *Fougère-Royale*. It took him three hours to dress each day with the help of his rogue of a valet.

The Baron was lazy, amoral, deeply religious, sentimental and selfish. He had the gift of tongues and had picked up an astonishing number of foreign languages, including a smattering of Russian, and a fluent knowledge of English. He admired the British monarchy unreservedly, and was proud to number a Stuart king among his ancestors.

Renaud was superficially the prototype of a certain type of young French aristocrat as described in the novels of Gyp. He seemed to me at first to be a straightforward enough personality, but I was later to discover that his character was infinitely complex.

Although he observed the rituals and traditions of his caste and felt as strongly as did his family that the 36 quarterings intact of which they so constantly boasted lifted him above the ruck of ordinary mortals, there was in him a maverick streak. From time to time he impudently defied the immutable family laws of the *ancien régime* by committing some act which put him temporarily beyond the pale and finally contributed to his becoming completely *déclassé* in the eyes of his peers.

Marrying me was one of the greatest revolts he ever staged against the Establishment which had, until then, governed his life and actions. It was totally out of character for a man who had been born and bred in a family which for centuries had given its daughters to the Church, and its sons to the well-dowered daughters of members of the clan, actually to wed a young woman who was not only a *foreigner* in the most pejorative sense of the word, but who also had Jewish blood.

Strangers were seldom welcome in the town houses, manors, châteaux and lives of most families of the *ancien régime*. Many were descendants of the *aristos* who had perished under the blade of the guillotine. Each year the descendants of those who had died attended a macabre party known as 'The Victims' Reception'; a roll-call of those present was a carbon-copy of the names of their ancestors who had attended the balls and fêtes given by Louis XVI and Marie-Antoinette. Like the Bourbons, the Baron's family had forgotten nothing and learned nothing. Their social guide was still the *Almanach de Gotha*, and their daily visit to their father confessor was as important as the enemas they so frequently used.

Being an only son, the Baron had been lapped in the love and admiration of his mother and sisters. Bitter, narrow-minded, and sexually frustrated as she was, Madame Mère doted on her boy who, beautiful as a marble statue by Donatello, resembled her patrician male family forebears.

The General, Renaud's father, was a peppery old character who had a distinguished career in the Army, one of his closest friends being a former classmate, Philippe Pétain, whose obiter dicta he used to quote with tiresome reverence until the Fall of France, when he forbade any member of his family to mention the former hero of Verdun.

The General retired with a profusion of medals and a jaundiced view of his son, whom he suspected of being a spineless mollycoddle. The Baron was certainly pampered, but he was not a mollycoddle, and there were steely depths to his character which were to surprise all who thought they knew him well.

Renaud was incurably lazy, with a total aversion to discipline in any shape or form; the fact that he had managed to scrape through his schooldays without being expelled says much for Madame Mère's subtle manipulations of the Jesuit faculty at which her son cut his scholastic teeth.

He was just sixteen when he was handed over to the Marquise de Rastignac, his mother's closest friend, to serve his apprenticeship in becoming a man. Madame Mère's choice of a teacher to initiate her loved one into the mysteries of sex was inspired. Laure de Rastignac, an orphan and great heiress, had been married off at the age of fifteen to a Marquis who preferred the more hirsute charms of his cowmen to those of his wife. Having provided the Marquis with an heir, she made the best possible use of her secluded life in the country by debauching and being pleasured by all the virile young males in the neighbourhood.

When the Marquis, who had old-fashioned ideas about the role of a wife, found out what was going on, he exiled her to their Paris home, forbidding her ever again to see her child. Though saddened at being separated from her boy, the Marquise was delighted to be in Paris, which admirably suited her temperament, since it afforded her a wider choice of lovers. The Marquis joined his wife only once in the entire year; this was so that they might attend 'The Victims' Reception' together.

The Marquise had been educated at the Convent of the Sacred Heart, where she shared her dreams and secrets with the dark, spidery little Italian princess who was to become the mother of the Baron. The Princess was far more intelligent than her beautiful blonde friend, so she knew early how to manipulate her in such a way that ultimately through her she could control her own son's destinies.

Once the Marquise had initiated the Baron into the joys of copulation, strangely she kept her ravening sexual appetites and endearing tricks for him alone. From the time the Baron first became the Marquise's lover, until the day when he found me lurking behind the curtains in Mrs van Hoorn's supper room, he had been faithful to his first love, and even when his sylph, as he called her, had vanished, lost forever in the ample curves of the middle-aged lady who replaced his slender love, he clung to her, as Balzac clung to Madame de Berny. The Marquise gave him something of the warmth and tenderness denied him by his own mother, and gradually, through the years, she grappled him to her with the insidious silken hooks of habit. She smothered him in an ocean of tender care and concern which began with choosing his ties, servants and furniture, and ended by dominating his thoughts and senses. Also, and perhaps most important of all, she made him free of her great fortune which he helped her to administer. So long as this happy state obtained, Madame Mère was content. The Marquise was as malleable as wax in her fine Italian hands, and through her she was informed of all that was happening in the life of the son she loved with a fierce and devouring love.

*

The first time I saw the Marquise was when, unexpectedly, I was invited to luncheon by Mrs van Hoorn. As a rule my midday meal was served in the tiny study by the benevolent Hodges, or even by the grumpy old lady's maid, Kate. Both her servants were loyal to and loved their exigent but generous mistress. Elodie van Hoorn was a very social lady and she did not believe in the lower orders having a life of their own. She hailed from the Deep South, and the stories she told me of her family saga made *Gone with the Wind* seem like a penny novelette.

The Marquise's finest hour, *L'heure bleue*, was *her* hour of triumph. From 5 to 7 p.m. was visiting time for French lovers; and in love nests all over the country, and in Paris particularly, men were taking down their trousers and heading for the Louis XVI style bed where lay *la petite amie* in a frilly négligée. Tearing off this garment was part of the ploy. I could never visualise the Baron's Laure frivolling naked on what the Baron called with some respect *the battlefield*. For this lady, who to me resembled a Roman matron, had a misleading air of impenetrable virtue. Her clothes appeared welded to her massive frame, and her large handbags and tiny feet were as much a legend in Paris as was her vanished beauty.

It was only when I saw the portrait, by Boldoni, of Laure de Rastignac painted in the early days of her marriage that I realised why she had been nicknamed the 'Swan'. Atop a long and very sinuous white neck was a small proud face with a coiffure of burnished chestnut hair bound with a pink ribbon; her features were delicate, her skin like porcelain, and her eyes were a true lapis-lazuli blue. She was painted in a white satin and lace tea-gown whose ruffles foamed to the floor, showing only the tips of her little kid slippers.

When I first met the Marquise at Mrs van Hoorn's luncheon-party, she was fifty-eight and seemed to me a crumbling ruin. All that was left of her beauty was her long neck and the slender legs and feet which seemed unable to bear the weight of her big body. So she contantly stumbled and lurched forward, scattering hairpins and holy medals as she crashed into the furniture. It never occurred to me, then or later, that this ageing, adipose woman with her faded eyes and pouched cheeks could ever rival my fresh young charms; but she could and they did. It was she who finally wrecked my marriage to her lover.

*

During the whole course of Elodie van Hoorn's *soirée musicale*, the Baron never left my side, and I was grateful to him for being so kind and attentive. It did not strike me that this 'elderly' but handsome man could be seriously interested in the brokenhearted young woman whom he was trying to restore with food, drinks and merry quips. I had not confided to him the secret of François' treachery, though I hinted at a dark and tragic association with a royal personage who had to choose between his throne and myself. The Baron was not taken in, but at the end of the evening, he insisted on driving me home in his grey Duisenberg automobile.

All through that long hot lovely summer of my eighteenth year, the Baron was assiduous in his courtship of Mrs van Hoorn's little secretary. Each day when I left the Quai de Conti for my luncheon break he was there, waiting for me, out of sight around a corner. As I had only an hour for my meal we could not go very far afield and most often he took me to the Tour d'Argent, where he tried to initiate his *petite sauvage* into the rules which govern *le bon manger*.

I was a recalcitrant pupil. The sight of *canard pressé a l'orange* made me feel nauseous. I was unhappy at the sight of the blood mixed with gravy, and the thought of the poor duck (though dead) being pressurised for my pleasure made me feel guilty. I did not really enjoy eating flesh or fowl and quite ruined the Baron's pleasure in his food by nibbling with little enthusiasm at the exquisitely prepared dishes presented to me.

Yet I knew something about food and wine. Lala was a *cordon bleu* and wine was a religion with Papa. When I was seven, he took me on a tour of the battlefields of Verdun, combined with a visit to some of the wine-growing châteaux of Burgundy with which he did business.

The battlefield seemed to me to correspond to the *morne plaine de Waterloo*. I never forgot the sight of the scarred and pitted earth, the trenches and the rusty debris of long departed armies still lying about the field of battle, splashed with Flanders poppies stained, I was told, with the blood of the soldiers who had died there in the name of freedom.

Nor did I ever forget the warmth of that first sip of Burgundian wine, like a dark red rose petal on my tongue, before caressing its way down my young gullet. The tasting took place in the ancient *Hospice de Beaune* and later there was a luncheon in a château where, stuffed with the specialities of the region, washed down with vintage wines, I fell asleep with my nose in my plate of *profiterolles au chocolat*.

On that occasion, Papa and I forged the first link in the slender chain of our mutual interests. The study and appreciation of French wines were his delight. They became mine mainly because I hoped to please him, and because knowing something about *crus* and the jargon of viticulture made me feel superior to my young friends who had not progressed beyond the fizzy drinks stage. Finally, my interest in wine enchanted the Baron, who was as passionate about the product of the grape as my papa, and this was in fact about the only thing these two men in my life had in common.

But Papa was not a *gourmand*. The scent of fresh truffles did not give him a *frisson*, as it did the Baron and Madame Colette.

If you do love it [the truffle], then pay its ransom royally—or keep away from it altogether. But once having bought it, eat it on its own, scented and grainy-skinned, eat it like the vegetable it is, hot, and served in munificent quantities. Once scraped it won't give you much trouble; its sovereign flavour disdains all complications and complicities. Bathed in a good, very dry white wine—keep the champagne for your banquets, the truffle can do without it—salted without extravagance, peppered with discretion, they can then be cooked in a simple, black, cast-iron stew-pan with the lid on. For twenty-five minutes, they must dance in the constant flow of bubbles, drawing with them through the eddies and the foam—like tritons playing around some darker Amphitrite—a score or so of smallish strips of bacon, fat, but not too fat, which will give body to the stock. No other herbs or spices! And a pestilence upon your rolled napkin, with its taste and odour of lye, last resting place of the cooked truffle! Your truffles must come to the table in their own stock. Do not stint when you serve yourself.... Do not eat the truffles without wine. If you have no great Burgundy of impeccable ancestry to hand, then drink some wine from Mercurey, full-bodied and velvety at the same time, and drink only a little, if you please. In the region where I was born, we always say that during a good meal one is not thirsty, but 'hungry' for wine.[1]

*

Sido was the first book I read by Colette, and as with *War and Peace* and *Madame Bovary*, both of which gave me a soaring temperature, the story of Colette's childhood with her parents in the old house in the Burgundian village threw my mind into some kind of convulsion from which it has never to this day quite recovered. For I knew as I gobbled down the homely descriptions of the family, the garden and the adorable Sido that this was great writing and that the hand that had penned these pages was that of a genius. Colette's writings opened wide the casements of my mind upon an ocean dotted with the sails of the great barques of literature, and having the good luck early to discover Colette the writer, I was no less fortunate in meeting Madame Colette the woman.

In those days it was unusual for a famous writer to dabble in commercial ventures. But Colette, who was unconventional and in advance of her time, startled her Parisian aficionados in 1932 by opening her Institut de Beauté in the rue de Miromesnil. This salon was dedicated to the cult of beauty by means of natural organic unguents and lotions compounded with fruit, vegetables and flowers. Even her closest friends were a little shaken at the audacity of Colette actually selling a mash of strawberries and cold cream, while the *literati* were horrified that the white hope of French literature should stoop so low as to sully her hands by messing around with beauty preparations and with people's faces. Colette herself wrote: 'For my friends and myself I used to boil the flesh of quinces and the mucilaginous envelope of their seeds. I beat the cold cream and pressed out the juice of cucumbers.... Why not? The Duchess Sforza, born Antokolski, set me an example when she fitted up an ancient apothecary shop....'.

[1] From *Prisons et Paradis* (*Earthly Paradise,* Secker and Warburg, London, 1966).

At first, Madame Colette, blissfully unaware of her critics, was delighted with her new career. She wrote all her own prospectuses and instructions for use. She even drew her own caricature on the cover of her boxes of powder. I had read of the official opening reported in the press as a major Paris event. I did not believe that I could actually make an appointment to have one of Madame Colette's treatments.

When I went to the salon my knees were trembling. I could not credit the fact that at last I was going to see my idol, the author of such masterpieces as *Chéri*, *Le Blé en Herbe* and *La Naissance du Jour*, besides *Sido*. I was going to see Shelley plain at last. And see her I did, the darling woman. She looked after me herself; and as I sat in a comfortable chair in a cubicle enveloped in a blue wrapper, Madame briskly rubbed all manner of deliciously scented creams into my face.

I looked at her in the mirror. The thin young writer, described by Cocteau as 'a fox terrier in skirts', had been replaced by the well-rounded curves of serene middle-age; but the triangular, cat-like face, thin lips and long, gold-flecked sapphire eyes outlined in kohl, the coiffure with the frizzy bang which covered the high noble forehead, were as I had always imagined them.

There was an immediate rapport between us. She instantly christened me 'Irish Crosby', I who was neither Irish nor Crosby. She said she regretted not being able to speak English fluently, but while she was vigorously kneading my face, she recited an English poem made up by one of her three-year-old nieces. The fact that the child had picked up her German governess' accent gave a peculiar piquancy to the poem which Colette had entitled 'Hymn to Summer', and which she insisted was 'not the revelation of a precocious genius, but a first song'.

> Heer iss the summer, it iss wery varm
> And the sun sheinz like a crate pig star
> And the moon is lightink us up there
> All through the night.

Sad to relate, I left the Institut de Beauté looking like a young lady in a brothel picture painted by Toulouse Lautrec; but I was puffed up with pride, for Madame Colette had invited me to call upon her at the Hotel Claridge in what she called her 'eyrie'.

At that time she had a suite of rooms at the top of the hotel in the Avenue des Champs-Elysées. This consisted of 'two small communicating rooms, a bathroom and two small twin balconies beside the gutter'. Here, high above the traffic, she worked her particular magic, transforming the banal hotel rooms into the charming and familiar décor made up of her own pieces of furniture, such as the little squat armchair and an austere bookcase and all the *lares* and *penates* that accompanied her on her many perigrinations from nest to nest.

Madame Colette liked all growing things and certainly she had green fingers, for on the little balconies in the clouds she managed to coax geraniums and creepers to bloom, as well as a few strawberries anaemic as slum children.

From Madame Colette, now the most sophisticated and chic of Parisiennes, there still emanated a breath of the countryside which had cradled her youth. Her rich rolling Burgundian accent was like the wine of that province; and there was about her always the delicate aroma of lavender and thyme, of new-mown hay and of freshly-baked bread. She used to say that, like the snail, she carried her house on her back. Her husband called her both home-loving and adventurous. He wrote, 'She was a product of the French soil at its purest, French to her finger tips and a provincial above all. She loved moving house, but it was that she might immediately build another nest and establish her province there. She was a provincial in her art of living, her household recipes, her tidy cupboards, her provisions, her punctuality, her proverbs, her boxwood and lily-of-the-valley, her Epiphany-cake, her mulled wine, wood-fires, chestnuts and slow bakings under the ashes....'[1]

Although Madame Colette liked the notion of foreign travel, she rarely left France. But so vivid was her imagination that she ranged the universe by means of the maps, letters, cards, books and gifts showered on her by those who knew how much she appreciated the shells, stones, and exotic trivia sent her from faraway places.

Through the years I kept in touch with Madame Colette, and never failed to send her cards and photographs of the curious places I visited in my journeys into the blue. She knew little about me. Ours was never an intimate friendship. I was always a

[1] *Close to Colette*, by Maurice Goudeket (Secker and Warburg, London, 1957).

little awed by her genius, but she never failed to greet me warmly whenever I came to Paris.

My last memory of her is visiting her when she was nearly eighty, propped up in her bed, in her 'raft' near the open window from which she could observe every facet of life in her beloved Palais-Royal. I had brought her some shells from the beach at Malindi, in East Africa. She was delighted with them and held them up to her face, rubbing her cheek against their smooth surfaces and testing them delicately with her tongue. I stayed only a few minutes, for it was evident that talking tired her. I left her, the captain of her 'raft', riding at anchor beneath her *fanal bleu*, the lamp with the blue bulb and shade that illuminated her nights. I knew I should not see her again.

4

The Nest of Vipers

The Baron's courtship lasted six months before he formally asked me to marry him. During all that time he spun a glittering picture of the glamorous and interesting life that would be mine if I became his wife.

Most young girls are snobs. Nearly all of them are romantic ninnies. I was both. I was a small-town South African who was being offered Prince Charming on a platter, decked with yachts, châteaux, sable coats, jewels, town-houses and a coat-of-arms equal to that of the Valois. It never entered my silly, empty little head that châteaux, yachts and town houses need a substantial income to keep them going. Money had never played a very important part in my life. There had always been enough to get me anything I particularly wanted and the 'nuts and bolts' of everyday life were a closed book. I had never heard of income tax, and I thought that water and electricity were laid on by Divine Providence. It might have been well had Lala seen to it that I took a course in domestic science, but she always said I was 'bookish' and bad with my hands, whatever that meant, so I was spared the usual apprenticeship given to young ladies to make them into good managers, housekeepers and mothers.

I was flattered by the Baron's attentions. I liked going out with him. I noticed with satisfaction that attractive and elegant women envied me my escort. The next time Papa came to Paris on business, I brought the Baron to see him at the Ritz. The two men disliked one another on sight; and Papa, having lectured me on the stupidity of marrying a man of forty-odd, who seemed to have no visible means of support and no occupation, forbade me to see him again and once again urged me to return home where I belonged.

There was a defiant streak in me. Papa's fiat infuriated me, and I decided I was no longer a child to be pushed around. Also I knew that Lala, who was as romantic as I, liked the idea of my entering the sacred portals of the French aristocracy and thus I could count on the support of one of my parents.

The day Papa returned to Johannesburg I told the Baron I would marry him. He seemed overjoyed and presented me with an engagement ring which he said had belonged to his great-grandmother. The emerald had been reset by Bulgari, and my fiancé had removed it from the Marquise's jewel case. As he had given it to her in the first place, I suppose he thought he was entitled to pass it on to me.

No sooner were we officially engaged, than the Baron asked me to come away with him for the week-end. He wanted me to go to Ouistreham to see a boat that was for sale. It did not enter my head that this might be a ploy to get me out of Paris and into his bed.

We arrived at Ouistreham, north-east of Caen in Normandy, on a dark and stormy evening. The Baron had reserved accommodation in the only inn of any consequence in what was, at that time, a small fishing village frequented in summer by a few pioneer families who had built primped-up little villas on the other side of the port.

The inn was little better than a *bistro*. It was the *local* of the fishermen, who were congregated round the *zinc*, or playing *belote* or dominoes at little marble-topped tables.

The patron had a swivel eye and an ingratiating manner; whenever he spoke to the Baron he would give a curious little jerky bow. I was treated to a leer and a series of bows. He was, I think, surprised at having to take my suitcase up to the single room that had been reserved for me. Even by country standards, this bare and chilly room, its rickety bed covered with a dubious cotton counterpane, could hardly have inflamed the senses, had one been madly in love, which I was not.

The idea of what might befall me in that narrow cot terrified me. Girls of my generation, though fairly emancipated in some ways, still had their heads stuffed with a mishmash of ill-digested facts about sex, which were a hangover from the days of the Victorian nursery and schoolroom.

I was certain that if I allowed the Baron to 'have his way with me', I should certainly end up with a baby or with one of those dread diseases which I had heard Nursie discussing with her friend Hilda Leathers one evening on Durban beach ten years before. The taste of the Sharp's Kreemy Toffee she then gave me to stick my jaws together is still on my tongue as I write these words.

Fear was the secret weapon by which adults ruled children in the good old days. Fear that made you sweat and tremble; fear of the bogies that lurked in the dark; fear of what *they* would say if you did not behave; fear of reprisals if you did nasty things. Nothing was ever brought out into the open light of day. Not even the most enlightened mother told her daughter the true facts of life. There were hints, genteel laughter, and veiled references to what the birds and bees did in the pursuit of happiness. Babies had several curious methods of arriving in the world: by stork, in the doctor's black bag or being dropped by angels under a bush.

I personally crashed from one crisis and mystery to the other, and the truth about menstruation and masturbation, not to mention copulation, came as a great shock to me. I must have been excessively dim not to have connected the cautionary tales I had heard over the years with something that would one day directly concern my ego and my body.

L'Auberge du Chien Vert had the special ambience which would later be the hallmark of a certain type of French film produced by masters such as Réné Clair and Claude Renoir; from books like those being written at that very moment by the future lord of suspense, Georges Simenon, who was bobbing about in his fishing-smack, *L'Ostrogoth*, on the choppy waters of the harbour down the hill.

Over an excellent dinner which began with a herb-scented pâté, followed by a succulent steak with golden, glistening chips, and ended with a melting Pont l'Evêque cheese, the Baron explained that his reason for coming to Ouistreham was to look over *L'Ostrogoth*. If she came up to expectations, he proposed buying her as the corner-stone of his fishing fleet. He had never before mentioned a fishing fleet; but he said that, in one of what he called his flashes of inspiration, he had seen himself heading a great and powerful fleet of fishing smacks which would supply all the fish-markets along the Normandy coast. I was awed, both by his command of a subject of which I knew absolutely nothing, and by the authority with which he pulled a shiny little notebook from his pocket. Papa had been mistaken in his assessment of my fiancé, I thought. Here indeed was a captain of industry, a man who thought in millions. I was deeply impressed.

'Maître Pelissier and I have done some very interesting calculations,' he said, opening the notebook and showing me pages covered with columns of figures. At that point I did not know of the existence of Maître Pelissier. Later I was to discover that he was part of the Baron's *entourage*, a shady country solicitor who sailed so close to the legal wind that his shiny, pointed nose was as red as if it had been singed.

The fact that Renaud knew absolutely nothing about boats or the fishing industry did not deter him from rushing headlong into his newest enterprise. He could always fire anyone with whom he came in contact with the real, almost fanatical enthusiasm with which he greeted each new, crazy project.

The fishing fleet was only one of a series of business ventures with which the Baron had tried, unsuccessfully as it happened, to beggar his partner, who was none other than his long-suffering mistress, the wealthy Marquise, the lady with the swan neck and tiny tottering feet.

*

My bedroom window overlooked the sea and a vast phallic symbol in the form of a lighthouse. Each time the beam flashed in my direction, it illuminated the bare little room furnished mainly by its narrow bed and night-table which housed a very pretty flowered chamberpot, considered to be an indispensable part of the furnishings of any bedroom when the *vataire*, as in this case, was in a remote part of the building.

The room was chilly. I undressed and washed in the tiny *cabinet-de-toilette*, a curtained recess which contained a basin, sloppail and china bidet that matched the chamberpot. The water in the jug under the thin towel was tepid. I put on my nightdress, said my prayers and got into bed. I lay there for some time in trepidation, wondering what I should say and do when the Baron came in to claim my body.

I was woken by a tousled maid carrying my breakfast tray. She plonked it down on my lap and opened the shutters which I had finally closed in an effort to shut out the penetrating beam from the lighthouse. The sun poured into the room. I was hungry and full of joy at being alive and young and in the midst of a great adventure.

On the tray was a note from the Baron. It read: 'I spent the night thinking of you. I burn with love for you. Meet me on the quay at ten o'clock. I kiss your hands and your little bare feet.' Heady stuff for the romantic young creature I was then.

On that crisp September morning, with the tang of sea and the scent of apples in the air, I fell in love with Normandy. At that time I knew nothing of her ancient farmhouses, of the foam of pink and white apple-blossom which was an annual miracle of spring. I was aware only of an extraordinary sensation of unity with my surroundings, a feeling I achieved only rarely with the ones I loved the best. This was certainly not a physical sensation, for it was, too, a flow of pure joy from the deep springs of the spirit.

The Baron in cream gabardine trousers with a blue reefer and peaked cap was waiting for me on the quay. He was examining the *Ostrogoth* from afar, while making notes in his book. To my untutored eye the boat looked both heavy and clumsy, and exactly like a fishing smack, which of course is what she was. There did not seem to be any movement aboard, but as we grew closer to the companion way that led down to the saloon we heard the staccato rat-a-tat of a typewriter.

The owner of the yacht, Georges Simenon, wearing the striped jersey of the French matelot, was pounding away at an ancient typewriter. He had a pipe in his mouth, and he was being cheered and inspired by a comely little wench in very tight trousers, whom he introduced as 'mon petit mousse'. The 'cabin-boy' whose tight round little buttocks obviously interested the Baron, said not a word throughout our visit, but made certain that Georges' glass was constantly replenished from the bottle of Calvados beside his manuscript on the table.

Georges Simenon was at that time a rosy, chunky young man on the threshold of a brilliant career, not only as the creator of Maigret, but in the considered opinion of Gide and of T. S. Eliot as one of the finest prose writers of this century. He was then, I believe, busily writing serials for a local newspaper for a few *sous* a line. His companion, besides providing him with calvados and coffee was also, he told us, his literary critic and adviser. A simple little village lass with a well-developed sense of the dramatic; if *she* understood his current serial, he knew that it would go down well with his readers.

I do not think that Monsieur Simenon was impressed by the Baron's knowledge of the sea and ships, or with his business acumen either. The Baron made it a point of pride never to haggle or bargain. Since his own money was never involved in his business transactions, he could afford to be generous. Thus the sale of the *Ostrogoth* was soon concluded. We returned to the auberge with Sim, as he asked us to call him, and the bargain was celebrated by a memorable luncheon which lasted well into the afternoon.

I disliked spirits and partook sparingly of wine, but Sim and the Baron grew ever more friendly and conspiratorial over several bottles of wine and endless tots of *Calva*, the real stuff which is as colourless and potent as aquavit and vodka. Finally, I got bored with this male chauvinistic drinking spree, and went to my room. My last view of this unusual pair was seeing them lurching off, with linked arms, in the general direction of the quay.

*

I could never analyse my real reasons for marrying the Baron. The fact that he was a member of one of the oldest families in France flattered my ego. Also, I wanted to prove to François and his mother that, though I had not been considered good enough to marry into their family, I was being asked to marry into one whose lineage was as old as that of the Kings of France.

Papa, as I have said, was not impressed by the idea of the Baron as a son-in-law and refused us his blessing. His jaundiced view of Renaud was not unconnected with the fact that Tante Gabrielle had told him of his liaison with the Marquise. Lala on the other hand was quite carried away with the more amusing and social aspects of my nuptials and was excited by the thought of getting my trousseau together. Cynical Tante Gabrielle, who was an even worse snob than I, made arrangements for a posse of Belgian nuns to embroider coronets on my French knickers, cami-knickers, petticoats and linen.

From the moment I became the Baron's fiancée, I was passed around his family like a bundle of soiled linen. Meeting Madame

Mère, the General and the last remaining sister—the others were all immured in convents—was a traumatic experience.

It was easy to see whence the Baron had obtained his classical good looks. His mother's profile was perfection, though her lips were so thin that only a faint pink line indicated their whereabouts. We sat in the salon of their gloomy apartment sipping porto and eating little sweet biscuits, while Madame Mère took me apart, feature by feature. The General was obviously puzzled by his son's choice of a bride, but imagined that I must be a great heiress. The sight of Lala's jewellery made a great impression on everyone.

The Baron's relations lived in the Faubourg St Germain as their ancestors had done. Some occupied enormous fusty, dusty rambling apartments, while others of the clan lived in considerable style in beautiful old houses set well back from the street behind *porte cochères* with double doors which in the old days were opened to their fullest extent to allow carriages to enter the cobbled courtyards.

Generally speaking, the exteriors of these houses were shabby and neglected, with peeling paintwork; but inside there were wide entrance halls paved in black and white marble, sweeping staircases lined with tapestries, and everywhere the flotsam and jetsam of good and bad taste accumulated through the centuries. In most cases the long French windows of the salon opened on to a paved garden decorated with urns, statues, and trees in tubs.

Most of the elderly aunts, uncles and cousins had little interest in what went on in the world beyond their double doors, or in the march of progress. Like flies caught in the amber of an ancient tradition, they frowned on all that was new or different.

Only in a few cases had a young fledgling escaped the stifling and repressive atmosphere of the Family; no matter how successful his life thereafter, he had to suffer the full censure of the clan. There were no marks for being different. Originality, so far as they were concerned, was a sign of insecurity and of bad blood. Although the Baron was the heir, the future head of the Family, and was, as such, sacrosanct, the entire clan was appalled when he announced his intention of marrying me.

Had I possessed two heads, I could not have made a greater, or less favourable, impression than when I was first invited to meet the assembled aunts, uncles and cousins. After examining me minutely from top to toe, they proceeded like piranha fish to strip me down.

'She will run to fat,' shrilled the Princesse de Clèves.

'Poor thing, she has all the least attractive characteristics of her race,' squeaked the Duchesse de Montespan, through her harelip.

'Their children will be hideous,' piped Adeline de Ligny.

The uncles were more clement. 'She has beautiful eyes,' said one, 'and lovely hair' murmured another.

'*Elle est bien potelée*,' snuffled an old cousin.

'Renaud is a clever fellow. I bet he won't be bored with that fiery filly around,' said the Marquis de Montespan, avoiding his wife's eye.

'They think you don't understand French,' said Renaud helpfully. Only his eccentric old Aunt Régine, the richest of them all, took me to her bosom.

'Never mind them,' she said, offering me a jewelled box filled with snuff. 'They're a nest of vipers, all twined round one another for warmth. You'll bring a breath of much needed fresh air and strong bourgeois blood into this decadent lot, if you survive the attentions of Renaud's dear Mamma who is not named Lucretia for nothing.'

Père Joseph Taillois, Renaud's father confessor, lived in the rue d'Assas, which is where I first saw him in the sombre little *parloir* in which the fathers met their flock socially, as opposed to hearing them from the confessional box.

No member of the Baron's family had impressed me. Père Joseph did. He looked like a painting by Velasquez. Everything about him was elongated: his fine, high-bridged nose, his long fingers and long, beautiful hooded grey eyes. His voice and his hands were remarkable, and he used both with great effect. He was a man of tact and sensitivity. He immediately understood my character and motivations and admired me for what I then was: a normal, healthy, extroverted young animal, avid for life, adventure and love.

He understood why I should never be welcome in the Baron's family circle, and he did his best to dissuade me from marrying the man whose spiritual mentor he had been from the time of his First Communion.

Loving me, Père Joseph was none the less most definitely on the other side, and he pointed out that with my background and upbringing it would be impossible for me to fit into the rigid pattern of the Faubourg St Germain world. He pointed out that I should be even more unhappy living the château life to which all daughters and daughters-in-law were doomed for at least three months a year.

For a moment, while he was telling me of the life that awaited me if I married Renaud, I had the impression of a steel trap snapping shut in my heart. It was an alarming sound, and one I have ever since associated with intimations of danger.

'My daughter,' Père Joseph said, 'you would not wish to change your religion, would you? A good Jewess would never wish to abandon her faith.'

'But, Father, I was brought up in the Protestant faith. See, here is my certificate of baptism. I belong to the Church of England and don't mind swopping over.'

A fanatical light suddenly invaded the hooded grey eyes. He held the paper at arm's length. One of his eyelids twitched slightly, a signal, had I but known it, that he was getting irritated by what he thought was my levity in approaching the subject of religion. He never got angry. But I was.

'Look here, Father,' I said. 'I may have Jewish blood, and be unable to claim 36 quarterings intact—whatever that may mean—but my family are a damned sight more warm, generous, human and lively than Renaud's collection of degenerate family skeletons. Don't think I don't know about Duke Charles who married a milkmaid by whom he'd already had six children; and what's so grand about Uncle Nando who thinks he's a sheepdog and chases ladies around his salon? And what's so moral about Cousin Robert who was found dead-drunk on his wedding night in La Paiva's bathroom?'

Père Joseph's eyelid had stopped twitching, and suddenly he began to laugh, great gusts of laughter which shook his slender frame so that I thought he might fall off his chair. In the end he agreed to give me religious instruction in the Catholic faith, and when I left him he traced the sign of the cross on my forehead.

*

One of the most rewarding bonuses in getting married was the frenzy of shopping which preceded the event. I had never been really indulged before, for my wardrobe consisted in the main of practical garments which did little for my figure, and nothing at all for my morale. I was not particularly interested in clothes, mainly, I imagine, because Lala's elegance tended to make anything I wore look dowdy and provincial.

My mother was a compulsive shopper, and in this instance she identified completely with me so that I had an elaborate trousseau of cobweb-fine lingerie and a cupboard full of *haute-couture* gowns and coats for which I had to endure many long and boring fittings.

Some of the clothes came from Schiaparelli. The admirable Elsa deigned to take a personal interest in my going away outfit, which was of grey flannel with a jacket trimmed with red frogging. I thought I looked rather like a porter in this outfit. Lanvin created my wedding gown and Rose Descat the cap of pearls and orange blossom which covered my curls. The wedding veil was of Mechlin lace and the Baron presented me with a parure of pearls to wear on the great day.

On several of our shopping expeditions I ran into Barbara Hutton who was just about to marry Prince Mdivani, the first of her husbands. The Woolworth heiress was, in those days, a plump, very pretty girl with blonde hair and cornflower eyes. Although we never did more than exchange remarks about the collections we were being shown, I always, throughout my life, felt sorry for this rich, unhappy woman who collected husbands as I once collected little silver boxes.

Not only did I have to run the gauntlet of the Baron's family, but I had also to submit to a thorough grilling on the part of my father's family who were also divided on the subject of my marriage. Statuesque Tante Gabrielle was in favour of the match; her husband, Oncle Paul, Papa's brother, sided with him in condemning my decision to marry a man twice my age who seemed to have no ambition and no visible means of support. My two cousins, their sons, were far too busy with their own affairs to pay much attention to what their wild little South African cousin was about.

One of the clearest memories of my childhood was visiting Oncle Paul and Tante Gabrielle in their apartment in the Avenue Hoche. Not long ago Cousin Laurent and I, now both middle-aged, made a strange pilgrimage to this house, just for the pleasure of riding in the lift which was part coffin and part

The Nest of Vipers

jewel-casket. Just as in my childhood, it still creaks and is manipulated by ropes and pulleys. As in the past it jerked its way to the fourth floor, where it stopped, with a thud, just below the lift door, and I experienced the same thrill of excitement and terror as I climbed across the gap.

Behind the wide entrance with its handsome bronze door furniture was the long gallery in which I had had my first glimpse of Tante Gabrielle in a long pleated négligée by Fortuny, sitting in a chair by the window, with her newly born son Laurent, in a wicker cradle by her side.

Tante Gabrielle was a Junoesque creature with eyes the colour of ripe horse-chestnuts. With her bee-stung mouth, Titian hair and arms like Parian marble, she was arresting and vivid. She was immensely proud of her shapely arms, which Rodin had likened to those of a Greek statue. As a result of this observation, she discarded long sleeves, and thereafter, for the rest of her life, proudly displayed her bare arms and fine plump shoulders. She was intelligent, malicious and scheming, and she was jealous of my pretty mother. They did not get along at all well, but because the brothers, their husbands, were devoted to one another, the two women observed an armed truce whenever my parents came to Paris.

Tante Gabrielle was shocked by my sturdy bare legs, smocks and freedom of thought and action. Little Laurent, her favourite, was the most pampered child we had ever known. Tante Gabrielle had wanted her second and last child to be a girl, and when Laurent was born, the determined lady, subconsciously perhaps, decided to mould the child into becoming as like the female companion she wanted and needed as was possible.

By the time Laurent was ten he was accompanying his mother to all her fittings. He chose her hats and some of her gowns. One of his hobbies, which she encouraged, was collecting first editions, which he carefully catalogued in a precise hand, in a leather bound volume, sitting at his superb little desk designed by a pupil of Reisner, in his sitting-room, luxuriously furnished in Louis XVI style alongside his mother's boudoir.

While I was an avid, even a compulsive reader, and had long since discovered the pleasure of owning well-bound books, Laurent's rooms gave me claustrophobia. Indeed the whole grand house with its 'gold' salon and lighted vitrines filled with *objets de vertu* nauseated me, and I deeply regretted the homely atmosphere of the Avenue Hoche whence the family had moved to the grander purlieus of the Avenue Malakoff.

Tante Gabrielle and Oncle Paul entertained their friends to luncheon parties, followed by 'un bridge', which meant the entire ground-floor salon was filled with small card-tables covered with velvet cloths. I remember vividly the aching boredom that used to overwhelm me when I was brought over to 'play' with Laurent, while my parents made up a four at one of the tables.

Sometimes we were taken to the Champs-Elysées or to the Parc Monceau. I remember one afternoon when we were sent off with my Nursie and Laurent's Nounou. Laurent wore a white ermine coat and matching toque, white leggings and buckskin boots, and around his neck, on a silken cord, hung an ermine muff of spotless white, with just one black tail. That muff was to me an object of extraordinary and irresistible beauty, and I longed most passionately to possess it.

When we reached the Parc Monceau, Nursie and Nounou allowed us to bowl our hoops briskly down the snowy paths while they joined their peers who, as always, were laughing and gossiping in a group. As soon as we were stationary I offered to swop my new toys for Laurent's muff. He said coldly that he did not care for my toys, and did not wish to lose his muff. He ran away, I ran after him, tripped him up and removed the muff by brute force. Laurent bellowed for help and there was an ugly clash between Nursie and Nounou. The muff was again placed around the neck of its owner and I was marched back to the house in disgrace. Strangely enough, when Tante Gabrielle heard of the *fracas* she forced Laurent to give me the muff as a gift, and the subject of '*Le manchon*' has remained a family joke and a password back to our childhood.

*

It was at this time that I made a new friend. This was the Lucy de Polnay against whom Muzzie had warned me when I first moved into the pension. She was tall, elegant and slender, with rich red hair, green eyes, and a skin as white and soft as kid. Against that shabby background she stood out like an orchid in a bed of pinks. In spite of Muzzie's evident disapproval, Lucy and I became inseparable. I was flattered that this sophisticated lady should want to be with me. Lucy teased me, called me 'Little Dorrit', and loved me like a younger sister. We had two years of friendship and laughter before she was taken from me.

Lucy de Polnay was Hungarian. She was the daughter of a business man whose wife had died soon after the birth of her fourth child. Lucy was brought up by a series of English nannies and governesses. She spoke flawless English and her knowledge of the classics was astonishing.

When she was seventeen, her father's business failed, and in order to get the capital needed to refloat his vast enterprises, he bartered his daughter to a Latvian timber magnate, an aged roué, who locked his young bride in a wing of his castle, until such time as her will should be broken. Lucy was a spirited creature and after a year of captivity she managed to escape. She went home, but her father threatened to hand her back to her husband, so she fled again, this time with a young diplomat who brought her to Paris where he was *en poste*.

I was never certain that Lucy was not 'embroidering' the story of her life, but many years later I met a talented Hungarian-born writer who assured me that the account Lucy had given me of her background and adventures was substantially accurate.

There were many lacunae in the story after she came to Paris as the mistress of the diplomat; but it seems pretty certain that she became a successful *demi-mondaine* and was kept by a succession of wealthy, intelligent men. After a famous writer came a well-known scientist and then a business tycoon. After that her luck began to run out, and when I first met her she was on the slide which had brought her to the Pension des Marronniers and would eventually lead to her suicide.

Lucy was an enchantress. She was also a terrible liability. But she had the gift of laughter, and although Lala did not altogether approve of my new friend, whom she said was 'fast', whatever that may have meant in Edwardian jargon, she was none the less beguiled by Lucy's undeniable charm and beauty.

As I did not wish to join Lala at the Ritz she decided to come to the *pension*. In a short while, to my surprise, the *pension* and its seedy inmates seemed to fascinate her, and she became friendly with a curiously ill-assorted family who had the table next to us in the dining-room. The little group consisted of a pale, resigned-looking, middle-aged woman who spoke little and ate less; she always wore black and her face was innocent of any make-up. With her was a young girl with high cheek bones, a full, sultry mouth, and a sinuous, expressive body which drove the males in the room into silent frenzies of desire, and a young man who was rosy, cheerful and handsome with curly dark hair, and a gay ringing voice. His name was Guy Davin.

It took us some time to work out their relationship. I finally discovered, with Muzzie's help, that the girl, Natasha, was Russian, that she was 'engaged' to the young man, and that the grey-haired respectable matron was the young man's mother; they were staying at the *pension* while their own house was being repainted.

All three, it appeared, were mad about bridge, as was my Lala, so in no time at all a foursome had been established, and night after night Lala would join her new friends in the Green Salon. I detested all card games and spent most of my evenings with the Baron, so it was not until he went away for a few days that I was made aware of the sinister by-play going on in the bridge room.

I came quietly into the salon so as not to disturb the players, and sitting down in an armchair, I opened my book. The young man and Lala were partners and my chair faced that of Guy Davin. I was not much concerned with what I was reading as I was thinking of details connected with my wedding.

Suddenly I looked up and saw Monsieur Davin staring fixedly at his partner. I was used to men staring at her pretty face, but Davin's eyes were fixed, not on her roseleaf skin, but on her bosom, down which cascaded three rows of magnificent pearls. Pinned to her shoulder in the style of the thirties was a large and ornate Cartier clip, a recent anniversary gift from Papa. There was something avid and icy in Davin's eyes which chilled me, and later, when I went to say goodnight to Lala, I tackled her about her acquaintances.

'What do you know about these Davins?'

'What do you mean? They're pleasant enough and they enjoy a game of bridge as much as I do. Certainly Madame Davin who is an excellent bourgeoise does seem to resent that lovely vampire, her son's fiancée.'

'Why do you think she's a vampire?'

'I know the type. When she's sucked him dry, she'll throw him away like an empty orange.'

The Nest of Vipers

'Even when they're married?'

'She won't marry him, not that one. But why this inquisition?'

'I didn't like the way he looked at you.'

Lala laughed. 'Come now, darling, you'd be the first to be upset if men no longer liked looking at me.'

'Davin wasn't admiring your looks. He was much more interested in your jewellery.'

Lala tapped my book. 'You read too many thrillers.'

'Please,' I insisted, 'please be careful, there's something evil about that young man.'

Lala, having bedded her pearls in a jewel case, snapped the lid shut, lighted a cigarette and got into bed.

'Sit down. Let's have a cosy. Did I ever tell you about the man who offered me the drugged cigarette that time I was travelling to Stamboul on the Orient Express?'

*

One afternoon just as I was setting out to take my typewriter to be repaired, Monsieur Davin and I collided at the front door. Politely he took the typewriter case from me.

'Allow me, Mademoiselle, this is far too heavy for such a fragile young lady to carry. Are you taking it for an airing?'

'I'm taking it to be repaired.'

'Permit me to escort you both. My car is at your service.'

I looked into his pale blue eyes and was afraid.

'Thank you, I can easily get a taxi.'

'Never, *charmante mademoiselle*. Come.' Gently he pushed me out of the door and, tucking his arm in mine, led me into the street towards his long, low red sports car. Once inside I resigned myself and told Davin where the typewriter repair shop was. It was straight up the Avenue de Neuilly, in a side street. It was quite near the *pension*, but my chauffeur had ideas of his own, and he swung away from the traffic-laden avenue to the Bois de Boulogne. He said nothing, but, all the time he was chanting a queer little song, all about 'les Bois de St Cucufa' in a light and pleasant baritone.

My distrust turned to anxiety as we drove deep into the heart of the Bois, but ignoring my feeble bleats, Davin drove faster and faster. For a second I contemplated jumping out. Then my common sense reasserted itself. The Bois was filled with sunshine and with people. The young man would not, I said to myself, dare harm me here in broad daylight with hundreds of witnesses all around. Nor did he stop or even endeavour to touch me. He simply drove me by a circuitous route to the repair shop, where he deposited me, with a little bow and a mocking grin on his face.

A few days later, to my great relief, the Davin family moved back into their house and though, in spite of my pleas, Lala went there to play bridge with them, she eased quietly away from them. Suddenly her enthusiasm for the *pension* also waned and we moved out to a suite at the Ritz. I was in our sitting-room having breakfast one morning, when Lala came rushing in with the *New York Herald Tribune* waving like a flag. She put it down in front of me and there, in banner headlines, I read, 'Murderer of wealthy American arrested last night', and the copy was accompanied by a smudged, unflattering, but unmistakeable photograph of mother's recent bridge partner, Guy Davin.

For some years Davin, the spoilt only son of respectable parents, had led a double life. Always desperate for funds, his liaison with Natasha had precipitated his downfall. In order to gratify her exorbitant and expensive demands he got deeper and deeper into debt. Finally he turned to petty crime to help out. He stole cars, made them over, and resold them.

Natasha wanted a mink coat and Guy could not raise the necessary funds. He stole and sold his mother's jewellery, but the sum he got was not sufficient. Natasha threatened to leave him. At this point Davin met a wealthy American tourist called Wall who was anxious to buy a car. Wall flourished travellers' cheques and a wad of dollar bills under Davin's greedy nose. Davin offered to sell the American a car he had just stolen. To gain the American's confidence, he offered to test-drive the car in the country.

Nobody knows exactly what happened during this sinister outing. A garage attendant remembered Davin because, when he stopped for petrol, he was singing an old-fashioned song 'Les Bois de St Cucufa'. Soon afterwards Wall's body was found riddled with bullet holes and partially burnt in a dried-up river bed.

Davin covered his victim with mud and went home. When his mother saw his bloodied clothes he told her that he had murdered Wall. Having disposed of his shirt, the meek and gentle little woman deftly unpicked the hems of the new drawing-room curtains, rolled Wall's travellers' cheques and dollar bills inside them and carefully sewed them up again.

The police did not take long to find Davin. They walked in on him when Natasha in the nude was trying on her new mink coat. He was condemned to life imprisonment on Devil's Island. I saw a newsreel of the convicts walking to the ship that was to take them out of normal life to the other side of the world. Guy Davin was among them. The *forçats* in their ugly prison garb shambled along with lowered heads. On the opposite side of the road, which was as near her only child as she was allowed to get, walked the Widow Davin, trailing her weeds like her grief, along the wet pavements. I believe that Somerset Maugham used Davin's crime as the basis for a novella.

*

I remember little of our first wedding ceremony. There were two, civil and religious. My dress was a foam of white organdy edged with Chantilly lace, and the scent of the lilies-of-the valley of my bouquet mingled with that of the incense in the church. Papa was not present. He remained in Johannesburg, pleading pressure of work. Lala cried quietly throughout both ceremonies. Her mascara always ran, making her look like a panda.

The reception was a classic affair with dozens of strangers all eyeing me with malicious interest. I saw little of my bridegroom, who, a model of decorum, was circulating among the aged relations, screeching into their ear-trumpets, and bringing them plates of delicacies from the buffet.

There was a claustrophobic feeling about the whole day. Cousin René, himself but recently married, impudently invited me to go to bed with him; and Cousin Laurent spent far more time than was decent stroking the silky hair of one of my little pages.

I was again conscious of the extraordinary beauty of Cousin René's wife, Edmée, with her shining cap of blue-black hair, enormous eyes and pouting mouth. I thought she looked like a dark red rosebud. She was heiress to a great Jewish fortune, which is why Cousin René had chosen her as his bride. Cousin Laurent, watching René striding about the room, told me that his brother, who since the age of fourteen hadn't been able to keep his hands from straying—he had once locked himself and a maid in the lavatory for hours—had been hard put to control Edmée, whose dusky incandescent beauty was early to turn to fat and who turned out to have an insatiable appetite for carnal pleasures.

Many aged aunts, uncles and cousins came and pecked at my cheek and I can still remember a feeling of repulsion as dry, cracked lips brushed my face, and the shudder that shook me when Uncle de Montespan kissed me full on the mouth, pressing his damp moustache against my lips.

We were to spend our honeymoon in Venice in a palazzo lent to the Baron by one of his Italian relations. In accordance with my wishes—since I had at that time a great cult for Queen Marie-Antoinette, and a passionate interest in every detail of her life and death—we were, however, to spend the first night of our honeymoon 'resting' in the Trianon Palace Hotel at Versailles. This would enable me, next morning, to pay a fleeting and nostalgic visit to the Petit Trianon.

A model of its kind, the Trianon Palace is one of the great European hotels of the past. Set in fine grounds, it was then all plush, gilt and glittering chandeliers and was devotedly run for the convenience of its wealthy aristocratic patrons. The staff was tried and tested, the service impeccable, and the suites, particularly those overlooking the park, were furnished in eighteenth-century style. Only the plumbing was modern, although the sunken marble baths with their silver taps had been installed at the turn of the century.

I was enchanted with the flower-filled suite and with the discreet attentions of the chambermaid, who addressed me respectfully as Madame la Baronne. Although I knew I was now a grown-up married lady and that the gold ring on my finger was real, I also felt as if I were taking part in a charming masquerade and that, as soon as the curtain was lowered, I should return home to Lala and to my narrow little white bed. I could not believe that the elegant, polite, stranger who was studying the menu and wine list with grave attention was my husband and that later he would turn into the lusting raging monster all men were supposed to become on the nuptial couch.

I only had a vague notion of what was meant by the words, conjugal rights. I thought I knew all about love which was to me a most uncomfortable sensation, rather like indigestion, which lodged in the middle of your chest and made you acutely uncomfortable. I also thought I knew what desire meant, for the thought of François' nearness still made me shake. I had had a fair amount of experience of being cuddled and fondled by a variety of breathless young men who seemed to have trouble controlling the never-mentioned, hardly imagined, protuberances in their trousers, but I had never thought that one of these protuberances might, at some time, come into contact with my naked person, for I had absolutely no idea what a man and a woman did together under the sheets. I had a notion that whatever the performance was, I might not enjoy it, since I had gathered from careless talk and girlish chatter that whatever a male did with that protuberance was likely to cause dire physical discomfort, inevitably followed by the birth of a baby, which was more uncomfortable still.

Suddenly I was absolutely terrified by the thought of what must inevitably follow upon the delicious meal the Baron was now ordering with such care. I looked at him searchingly. He seemed to me to be already flushed; in fact I had never seen such colour in his pale olive cheeks. I decided that it must be due to passion building up and that I was in for a pretty stormy passage.

We dined in the suite. The Baron said he did not want to share our first few hours with strangers. I would have welcomed a battalion of soldiers. I tried to distract my partner from his lecherous thoughts by a boring monologue on the beauties of the Château de Versailles, particularly the Queen's *petits appartements* which I knew well. He said nothing so I babbled on, insisting that we delay our departure for some days so that I could again visit the hamlet built by Mique and Hubert-Robert in which the Queen could play at being a shepherdess. The Baron did not seem responsive, and I noticed with trepidation that while he only picked at the exquisite food, he drank down great gulps of the Montrachet he had ordered, which was not his usual way of enjoying a good wine.

I kept looking at the time. There was a pretty little clock on the marble mantelpiece crowned with putti, ribbons and doves, and I was wearing a wedding-present, a watch set in brilliants. Both clock and watch were in perfect accord, and it seemed to me that never had time gone more quickly. After a large helping of pistachio ice-cream, and hoping to postpone the evil hour to bedtime, I suggested a stroll in the moonlight.

The Baron shook his head, and pulling aside the curtain, pointed out that it had begun to rain, then, giving me a curious lopsided smile, he finished off the wine. Now totally unnerved, I locked myself into the bathroom where, to steady myself, I decided to wash my new doeskin gloves.

I had never before possessed a pair of gloves of such supple beauty, nor had I ever washed so expensive a pair. I felt that only my new cake of Guerlain soap would do justice to the occasion and soon I was happily engrossed in my laundering operations. While gently squeezing the suds from the finger of a glove, I happened to look up from the marble basin into the mirror above, and my eyes widened as I contemplated the face of the victim who was so soon to be immolated on the altar of lust. My springy copper curls which had been straightened for my wedding by the famous Antoine, were now standing up wildly all over my head and my round face was shiny; so what, I wondered, could a sophisticated man of the world who looked like a film star possibly want with the dithering plain little creature reflected in the looking-glass?

Finally, soaked in scent, and attired in my sacrificial robes, with a coronet embroidered over my thudding heart and the limp wet gloves like new-born lambs in my hands, I opened the bathroom door and peeped into the nuptial chamber. My spouse was lying on the large ornate bed with its gilt corona and taffeta curtains. He was wearing white silk pyjamas. On his thin feet were parma violet slippers with yet another coronet embroidered in gold thread. He looked even more flushed than when I had left him, and his eyes glittered wildly in the roseate glow of the bedside lamp.

Carefully I draped my damp gloves atop the radiator to dry. Then kneeling down beside the bed, I said my prayers, the baby prayers I had said all my life, for I reckoned that I should have need of the protection of Matthew, Mark, Luke and John to bless the bed I was about to lie on.

No sooner had I shed my negligée and slipped between the sheets than the Baron's hand sought my breast. It was so hot that it nearly scorched me. He lay beside me breathing stertorously. I was waiting with tensed muscles, closed eyes and rising hysteria for him to leap upon his prey. Instead he began to moan and then to babble. I sat up, switched on my bedside light and looked at my loved one. His face was now deathly pale. His nose was pinched, his eyes were closed and a nasty gluey sweat was pouring down his face.

I summoned the hotel doctor. Despite the lateness of the hour he arrived wearing a frock coat and striped trousers. He kissed the air above my fingers and sent me into the drawing-room while he examined the Baron. When he came out his voice was chilly.

'Your husband has typhoid fever. He is very ill. We are taking him to an isolation hospital where he will be well nursed. He will, I hope, recover. You will accompany him to the hospital where you will have to remain under observation until such time as we are certain that you have not caught the malady. The chambermaid will pack for you. Please dress now. You will remain incommunicado, as we do not wish this terrible news to penetrate further than this room. As you can imagine, it would create a panic, and it would take only a few minutes to empty the hotel of all its patrons.'

Four husky night-porters carried the now unconscious Baron in an ottoman, through the back entrance of the hotel, into an ambulance disguised as a laundry-van, which was always at hand for just such emergencies. A male nurse sat by the Baron's head. The doctor handed me in, saying with a leer,

'This is certainly a strange way to begin a honeymoon, but if you are too impatient...' Then the door was banged shut and we were on our way, rattling over the cobble-stones as if we were in a tumbril.

5

Enter a Marquise, with Dagger

When the Baron had fully recovered, which took some time, we set up house in a splendid, chilly apartment with a marble-paved entrance hall and miles of beautiful parquet flooring in the rue du Bac. The long windows of the *salon* gave on to the inside courtyard, which meant that we were privileged to get only a modicum of light, whilst the bedroom, bathrooms and kitchen quarters were plunged into perpetual Stygian gloom. I had never had a home of my own to run, and while I had subconsciously absorbed some of my mother's precepts on housewifery in general, it took a considerable time for me to understand the principles that govern the smooth management of a household. I had, of course, no experience of hiring or firing staff. Our servants had all been with us since my babyhood, so I found myself alternating between the *persona* of a half-witted child-bride in need of a nannie, and that of a female Simon Legree with a tongue like a razor. The right way lay somewhere between these two extremes, but it was some time before I discovered the golden mean.

The Baron was not much use when it came to dealing with domestic problems. That side of his life had always been run for him either by his mother or his mistress, both of whom were what the French called *d'excellentes femmes d'intérieure*. I thought the Baron unreasonable and exigent. He was, in fact, reasonable and tolerant, and while his house was run like a switchback railway, he did his best to educate my tastes in food and wine.

Initially my staff were always in a state of flux. We had a succession of insolent *valets-de-chambre*, pert, light-fingered housemaids, and temperamental or alcoholic cooks. As I never bothered to take up any references, the criminal population of Paris sent representatives flocking to answer my advertisements.

I never knew to whom I owed the solution of my domestic problems. The Baron must have discussed our difficulties with his mother, the Marquise, Père Joseph or all three, for one day a new cook called Ernestine Lescot arrived, and from that moment my troubles were over.

She was a tiny wiry creature with a will of iron. A Parisienne born and bred, she refused to accompany us to the country, saying that the propinquity of 'wild beasts', as she called cows and horses, brought on her 'itch'. She was an incomparable manager, thrifty, neat and almost too parsimonious, and though she did not have the culinary genius of Madame Hauchecorne, whom I was to discover later in my married life, she was a good and often subtle cook. Her only real failing was a fondness for garlic, which she chewed constantly, as Americans chew gum.

Ernestine ruled the kitchen with justice tempered by fits of irritation. She had a lover, a sturdy dark gentleman with long furry sideboards who worked for the office of Posts and Telegraphs. He was a messenger boy, who delivered *petits-bleu* around Paris.

A *petit-bleu* was the equal of the casual phone-call of today. For a few *sous* you could scribble a message and be certain that it was delivered almost within the hour. Ernestine's 'mec', Ramon, came from the Basque country. He had large velvety eyes, like pansies, and seemed to spend a great deal of time in my kitchen, helping Ernestine to carry her shopping bags up the back stairs, and chatting to her while she peeled the vegetables and prepared her sauces.

It did not take the wily Ernestine long to get me to sack the Baron's supercilious valet whom she replaced by her Ramon. At first he was quite useless, and the Baron was vastly irritated when he found his new body-servant had no idea of what valeting a gentleman meant. However, a crash course with a friendly gentleman's-gentleman in the building proved that Ramon had brains as well as brawn, and when Rosine, my own maid, complained to Ernestine that her 'mec' tweaked her breasts each time he met her going about her business, I was subtly encouraged to dismiss her.

Her place was taken by Lilli, a cousin of Ernestine, whose Mafia-type family seemed able to provide the solution to almost every problem in my domestic life. Clock repairs were carried out by cousin Hippolyte, a hunchback who came down from the heights of Montmartre where he lived; painting and decoration work was carried out by a blond giant called Victor, and when I gave dinner parties, twin nephews, Mimile and Bébert, with identical dimples, would wait at table.

It was some time, however, before I felt sufficiently organised to give my first dinner party. In the meantime, pampered and surrounded by servants, I was lonely for friends of my own age with whom I could laugh and chatter and exchange impressions of my adult life. Lucy was away in Portugal, and I had no wish to involve anyone from the Pension des Marronniers in my new life.

In those days social life was governed by a certain formality. Nothing was casual and one did not easily enter into new relationships. There were certain conventional visits and dinners which had to be endured; but any impromptu moves to improve communications or widen one's circle were frowned upon by the Baron's relations.

Mrs van Hoorn had been somewhat miffed at my marrying the lover of one of her closest friends, so for some time I was exiled from her salon, lest I poach any more. As for the Baron, he saw no reason to change the routine and habits of a lifetime. He never spent a whole night in my bed, but left me always before dawn, to return to his own quarters, where he remained incarcerated until it was time for him to go into his 'cabinet-de-toilette'. He did not believe in daily baths, maintaining that water washed away the essential oils of the skin, and that fundamentally the British (being South African born, I was loosely lumped under the aegis of the British flag) were a dirty people, who liked to lie soaking in water polluted by their own bodies.

It never took the Baron less than three hours to complete his toilet. I must admit to having been a trifle envious of the panoply of ivory and silver-gilt objects on his dressing-table. The use of many of these tiny scalpels, files, tweezers and curved spoons had to be explained to me. The tiny spoons were for extracting wax from the ears; while some of the scalpels were used as nail diggers. There were also battalions of jars, bottles and boxes of pills and medicaments, for the Baron was something of a hypochondriac, and always insisted on taking his temperature after having made love. In fact he was a perfectly healthy man.

In the early days of my marriage I was, as I had always been, an early riser. In Africa I had so much to do that there was never enough time, so I woke early not to waste a moment. Breakfast on

Enter a Marquise, with Dagger

the *stoep* with Papa was the charming overture to an action-packed day. I believe that the brilliant sunshine invested everything with a sparkle that seemed absent from European mornings, particularly in cities on which the sun shone seldom and late.

I missed the sun more than I missed my parents, more than my friends, for without its warmth and glow my world was dim and drab, so I stayed in bed most of the morning, reading, scribbling and chattering on the telephone.

I did not wake until Lilli had opened the shutters, passed me my bed-jacket and put my tray on my knees. My breakfast consisted of an enormous glass of orange juice, a croissant, a crisp roll and a miniature brioche baked specially for me by a local baker, yet another of Ernestine's clan. There was a jar of honey and a pat of country butter, the whole of this calory-rich fare being washed down by a cup of excellent *café-au-lait*.

At first the Baron had initiated me into the joys of sharing his morning chocolate. This concoction was brought foaming in a silver jug and poured into a magnificent Sèvres cup. A tiny lace-trimmed napkin was used to dab the dreamy foam from my husband's lips. This drink was made from blocks of rich, pure chocolate specially and painfully ground by hand each day. After a week or so of drinking this rich brew I became nauseous at the sight of the chocolate-pot, and returned thankfully to my orange juice and coffee. My habit of drinking quantities of orange juice all through the day puzzled both the Baron and the servants, who saw it as an eccentric extravagance peculiar to foreigners such as myself who took two baths a day, refused to feed their pets on kitchen scraps but bought them better meat than that given to most Christians and did not themselves do the daily marketing.

It had never entered my head to accompany Ernestine and Ramon on their shopping trips to the rue de Buci. We had never, in those days, heard of deep freezes, and even if we had, Ernestine would have refused to give one house room. Happily for me she had a fixation about using nothing but fresh vegetables and fruit: I never saw a tin of any kind in the kitchen.

Like all good French housewives, Ernestine shopped from day to day. Nothing was wasted or thrown away. My little maid Lili, who had fallen out with Ernestine over a split commission of the cook's perks—a custom picturesquely called in French, *faire danser l'anse du panier* (to make the handle of the shopping basket dance!)—maliciously suggested that I might enjoy a visit to the market with my two servants, if only to see for myself why the weekly household books were so high. I thought this an excellent idea; and thereafter, much to Ernestine and Ramon's chagrin, accompanied them frequently to the local markets and to the *Halles*, the 'belly' of Paris, which teemed with the fruits of the earth, and presented a holocaust of slaughter of flesh and fowl from whose dangling carcasses I tried vainly to avert my gaze.

Ernestine was not squeamish. With little cries of pleasure she would dive into a hideous mess of bloody flesh and entrails, emerging triumphant with bits of this and that beast which would later appear on the table cunningly camouflaged in veils of delicate sauce piped with truffles, or set like precious stones in blocks of glistening aspic. It was after my eighth visit to the *Halles*, where Ernestine went into raptures over the remains of a sucking pig with a blue rosette between its ears, that I became a vegetarian.

At some time during his long convalescence, the Baron compiled a list of shops used by the family. I found this list the other day in a bundle of letters from my mother. Obviously I had sent her a copy. Reading through the list, I remembered myself skipping gaily—I was never able to walk sedately as a grown-up married lady should—through the provision shops he had so carefully listed.

Many of them had an historical background to rejoice any student of domestic life in Paris in the late eighteenth century. Debauve and Gallais, whence came the Baron's blocks of chocolate, was a case in point. The first Monsieur Debauve was one of Louis XVI's apothecaries. Deprived of his best client by the guillotine, he entered into partnership with a Monsieur Gallais and in 1800 they opened the shop which, to this day, specialises in a great variety of fine chocolates, particularly their 'crottes au chocolat', flavoured variously with coffee, praline or nougat.

The best cheeses in Paris came from Androuet in the rue d'Amsterdam. A keen housewife could spend a lifetime learning the art of choosing with which cheese to complement a particular dish. 'Nose' came into it, I remember, and 'pressure' which must be lighter than a butterfly alighting on a flower!

When homesick for my native land I would go to Hédiard, where I could snuff up the scent of the exotic fruits in which they specialised, and where pineapples, lichees and loquats were as common as apples. Once I came across a mango. It was unripe and cost a fortune. Cradled in a bed of cotton wool I took it home and put it in the airing cupboard to ripen. It never did, but when I peeled it, my extravagance was rewarded by the well-known tang of turpentine that emanated from the pulp.

Once when we were away, a box of chincherinchees, a flower indigenous to South Africa with small creamy blooms, was sent me by Lala. The servants opened the box, saw the long green swollen stems and came to the conclusion that this was a special type of hot-house asparagus. On our return, Ernestine cooked and served a great dish of the flowers with a butter and parsley sauce.

Fauchon in the Place de la Madeleine was, and is, the Parisian equivalent of London's Fortnum and Mason. I bought my snails from a shop called 'Escargots', founded in 1894. Only two types of snail were available, both French. The 'Burgundians' came from Savoy, the 'Greys' from the Vaucluse. I never had much stomach for these rubbery delicacies, but Ernestine and the Baron relished them, and we kept the same snail shells for use time after time.

Tanrade in the rue Vignon enchanted me, as it has so many writers and poets. For over two hundred years the households of the great and the famous served ice-cream and sorbets made from Tanrade's exquisite *purées*. Their *sirops* were unique. One was made with raspberry vinegar, while another was a compound made with flower from the orange trees at the Château de Versailles. Yet another speciality was 'lait d'amandes', said to have been Marie-Antoinette's favourite beverage.

*

Each morning when I had scanned the newspapers which included the New York *Herald Tribune*, I read a few pages of one of the volumes of Marcel Proust's work. I had set myself this task which gave me not only infinite pleasure and a panoramic and encyclopaedic knowledge of a vanished society, but also a blinding headache; the print in my copies of Proust's monumental opus was exceedingly tiny, and it never entered my head to go to

Galignani's, our bookseller in the rue de Rivoli, to see whether I could purchase an edition with large print.

The Baron was amused by my literary enthusiasms and bragged of them to the Vipers, who were unimpressed by what they said was yet another unattractive aspect of my make-up. Young married women of good family were not supposed to read Proust, much less to like his scarifying observations on a world to which he, like myself and for the same reason, had never really belonged.

The Baron teased me about my 'literary' loves. One morning, taking *Sodome et Gomorrhe* bound in purple morocco (a gift from Cousin Laurent) from my hands, he kissed me and said, 'My Aunt Vigier de la Tour knew Proust's parents quite well, and I have often chatted to Olivier, the head waiter at the Ritz who used to look after him. I'll take you to lunch there tomorrow if you like?'

Aunt Vigier de la Tour was surprised at my interest in the scribe. 'His father was an eminent physician, you know. Such a charming man. A pity Marcel was so unhealthy. His mother always said he was "delicate", but you know what that means. I've never had time to read anything he wrote, though I believe his books had quite a vogue. You should talk to my niece Thérèse de Carpentras about him. They were quite close at one time, I believe. Thérèse had a literary salon where poor little Proust met some of her friends.'

It took me some time to wangle an invitation to visit Madame de Carpentras, who lived on the Ile St Louis, the Parisian Venice which, like its Italian counterpart, is renowned for its views over the water and its lovely old houses. A single street runs from end to end of the island. At its eastern extremity is the magnificent Hotel Lambert, with its 'hanging gardens', and at No. 17 is the Hotel de Lauzun. It seemed extraordinary to me that ordinary mortals like myself might actually live in this splendid place whose tip, like the prow of a great ship, projects into the Seine.

Thérèse de Carpentras' Annamite servant let me in. She received me sitting in a bed of red and gold Chinese lacquer. She retained the fine bone formation and peerless long eyes which had made her one of the most beautiful women of her time. Now her face was lined and haggard, her hair like tufts of soiled cotton-wool, and her fingernails definitely needed attention. She wore a lacy woollen shawl over a nightgown of finest baptiste trimmed with lace, and long diamond earrings glittered and sparkled each time she tossed the dishevelled cotton-wool curls.

Except for a desk and a beautiful little *canapé* like the one in David's picture of Madame Récamier, the bedroom was bare; the floor was covered with a deep drift of old newspapers; and Madame de Carpentras, snug under her vicuna rug, was writing a poem on the back of a bill.

Although she was eccentric, she was far from crazy and seemed uncannily able to divine my thoughts.

'You're wondering why I'm sitting in bed here in this freezing house? It's a long story. Let us simply say that, as a result of bad advice—my lawyers should be lynched—I have sustained crippling financial losses. As I have sold nearly all I possess to stem the tide—one has certain obligations, you understand— there is now nothing left for me but to bury myself in the depths of the country. For I am told that I must economise. Indeed, living in Paris is very expensive. Do you know how much it costs to have my meals brought over every day from the Tour d'Argent?'

I said I thought a large sum might be involved, since this restaurant was one of the finest in the world.

'Maybe so,' she said, 'but it's cheaper than keeping a staff of useless cretins sitting around eating their heads off at my expense. Don't you agree?'

I said I agreed.

'Poets,' she continued sadly, 'do not flourish well in the country. Poets such as myself, I mean. There's a whole old-fashioned school of poets who positively revel in rustles in the bushes, bird-song and the sound of running water. Running water always affects my bladder. . . . Now, why have you come to see me? Yes, of course, Blanche wrote to me about you. You're the little outsider who set the Vipers by the ears. Marrying you was by far the most original act Renaud has ever committed. But he's much too old for you.'

Then, with a flash of penetration, she said, 'My poor child, you're lonely. Young and lonely, what a combination. How old are you? Eighteen. *Bon Dieu*, they will certainly devour you. You must meet my daughter Marie-France, an adorable creature. She will be your friend. She is quite unlike me. So calm, reasonable

c

and well balanced. Gracious, I do tire myself. What did you want to see me about?'

'About Proust.'

'He's dead,' she said sharply. 'He had terrible asthma.'

'I know. He interests me. I'm trying to be a writer. At the moment I'm collecting impressions from people who knew him.'

'A sort of literary scavenger. I do hope not. Why don't you write about yourself, as poets do, as I do?'

'Tell me about Proust?'

She smiled, showing small, uneven yellow teeth.

'He had exquisite manners. But he was so sensitive that one had one's time cut out not to offend him; he took offence so easily. A sharp word could literally devastate him. I think I am right in saying that his close friendships were, how shall I put it, a trifle unusual. His illness kept him shut away in that dreary flat he moved into after the death of his parents. I don't think he cared much about his surroundings. He cared about people, their lives, their secret motivations. I think you could say that he himself was a secretive man.

'He loved social life, but he had to ration his activities. His visits were conditioned by the state of his health, which meant that he might easily awaken you in the early hours of the morning. No matter what hour of the day or night, Marcel expected to be received with all the formalities and courtesies which he felt due to friendship. He had no sense of time. Fortunately I too was an insomniac, so I never minded his nocturnal visits. It was he who introduced me to 'les Boules Quies', those rather disgusting little wax balls coated with cotton wool you stick in your ears to shut out noise. I'm never without a supply. Look, over there on the desk, that little box. Do take it. It's brand new. I'm sure it will be a boon to you, as it was to me and to poor Marcel.'

'Thank you,' I said. 'But what did you and Proust talk about?'

'I can't remember. People mostly. He asked innumerable questions. He spent a whole evening examining one of my ball gowns. He wanted to know about the underskirts, and fastenings. All kinds of details. He was mad about detail. It's all in his books, you know.'

I liked Madame de Carpentras. Zany as she was, she had style and panache, and, true to her promise, she introduced me to her daughter who, in the course of time, became a dear and loving friend. Marie-France was a slim, cool-looking girl with a close cap of golden hair. Her long grey eyes, so like those of her mother, reminded me of city pavements glistening with rain. She seldom smiled. Taking care of her dotty and adored mother was her major preoccupation.

'You simply cannot trust her,' she used to say of her maternal parent. 'She does such extraordinary things, like trying to adopt the young men she picks up at parties and *thé-dansants*. Our own lawyers and accountants know most of her tricks, but one can never be sure that she might not find a solicitor to help with her crack-brained schemes.'

'What kind of schemes?'

'She's been trying to break the family trust for years. It's too long and complicated a saga to explain, but briefly, if mother had a son instead of a daughter, she could break the family trust and get at the capital. My father died a month before I was born. He had made provision in his will only for a male heir. Maman, who understands nothing about legal matters, thinks that by *adopting* a son she will be allowed to spend her capital. She's wildly extravagant, and mad about gambling. Even her very considerable income is useless. She's already sold most of the family jewels and heirlooms to get ready cash.'

'Do you mind, about the jewellery, I mean?'

Marie-France always weighed her words thoughtfully. When she had given my question her considered opinion, she said,

'No'.

There was a serene, nun-like quality about this girl, an aura of purity and innocence, emphasised and underlined by the small, all-white apartment she shared with a fluffy Angora cat with china blue eyes. All the upholstery, curtains, lamps and ornaments were white; and white too the narrow, virginal bed in which Marie-France lay, with her arms folded across her breast like the carved statue of a medieval lady on a tomb. Not that she had much time to lie around meditating, for following her Mamma about kept her pretty much on the go.

This was the era of the *thé-dansant*. These establishments were, I believe, mainly designed to bring a little joy into the lives of mature, sex-starved and well-heeled middle-aged ladies. Such was the clientèle of the more exclusive halls of pleasure such as the one in the Champs-Elysées, which became the Mecca of many

English and American divorcées and widows, living alone in Paris on substantial funds.

Each of these salons had their *aficionados*, who came, every afternoon, decked out in their finest war-paint, scented, furred and bejewelled to dip and swoop and swoon with ecstasy in the muscular arms of their favourite *gigolo*. These gracile young men were a special breed. Trim, lithe, modelled on their hero Rudolph Valentino, they were generally impervious to the overblown charms of the old bags they danced with. At the same time they exercised their peculiar calling with kindliness and discretion.

They were not highly paid by the management, but there were perks, sometimes very valuable ones, such as gold cigarette cases from Cartier with jewelled initials; gold cuff-links, pearl tie-pins, heavy gold identity-bracelets, and crocodile wallets plumped out with banknotes or a substantial cheque.

Whenever I drive along the Champs-Elysées I am reminded of Marie-France and myself in her little white *Topolino* roaring down this superb avenue in full cry after Madame de Carpentras. We used to give her time to have a few tangos before descending on her and detaching her gently from her partner. She never made a scene, but willingly and trustingly accompanied her daughter, like a child happy to be fetched from the kindergarten by its nurse.

I had not really appreciated the depths of Marie-France's love for her mother. I thought of her only as being an exceptionally dutiful daughter; but when I saw her after Madame de Carpentras' sudden and dramatic death from heart-failure, I was shocked by her appearance. Her ivory and gold beauty was grey and tarnished. Although she was too staunch a Catholic to take her own life, she now had no reason for living, and quietly dedicated herself to death, the only fiancé she ever wanted. She died, as silently as she had lived, after being tortured in a German concentration camp a few years later.

*

During the first few months of my marriage I had no reason to feel anything except satisfaction at the way my new life was shaping. True, I was lonely for people of my own age, but the Baron was a kind and attentive husband and, for all I knew, since I was totally inexperienced in these matters, a superb lover. He was a quick and silent operator, rejoicing in rose-shaded lights, while I preferred the anonymity of the dark to cover what I privately considered an act which, performed in the light, might well embarrass both protagonists when they later came to their senses.

The Baron and I did not discuss sex. Middle-aged husbands seldom initiated their innocent young spouses into the slightly *louche* atmosphere of the brothel and *café-conc*. Renaud had rigid views on what subjects might be discussed between husband and wife; intimate little chats on sexual deviation were not among his conversational gambits.

The Baron chuckled at the risqué little sketches in *La Vie Parisienne*, but I was not encouraged to look through this magazine, which was taken straight to his room by Ramon. Female emancipation was never mentioned in our world, and if there were equivalents of the British suffragette, I never met them.

My husband was a creature of habit. Every afternoon when he was in Paris, the Baron went to the rue d'Assas to visit his father confessor, Père Joseph. He always brought me courteous little messages from the priest as well as pretty boxes of chocolate truffles from a little old *confiserie* on the corner of the rue d'Assas.

The Baron was never at home between five and seven-thirty. We dined punctually at eight and at five minutes to he always appeared in the salon, immaculate in a dark suit with the white high-winged collar he always affected, worn with a Charvet tie. His dark hair was immaculate, plastered close to his narrow well-bred skull. Full face there was something a little insipid about the perfection of his chiselled features and beautiful empty dark eyes with their rounded lids, like those of a Roman statue. His profile, however, was strong, clean and even noble. This he knew, and the right profile, the 'best one', was always turned toward anyone he wanted to impress. It left me totally unmoved.

Renaud was a vain man, an exquisite who took far longer to dress than I. When we first shared the matrimonial bed, I got a bad attack of the giggles when my liege lord joined me wearing a hairnet and carrying a black sleeping-mask. He was acutely sensitive to daylight, and even though shutters and curtains were always firmly closed, he complained that I kept him awake by reading far into the night.

On the morning of the day that was to revolutionise the course of my life, I lay longer in bed than usual. The previous afternoon

I had been to see my gynæcologist who had told me that I was two months pregnant. As the gaze of Madame-Mère and of the aunts and cousins always fastened like limpets on my flat belly, I was much cheered by this news, which I had suspected but kept to myself. I wanted to choose the right moment to announce the glad tidings. I visualised a cosy little domestic scene that evening. After a *recherché* meal by candlelight, we should adjourn to the salon, where I would nestle in my pretty brocade bergère, while the Baron stretched his long legs in their velvet slippers by the wood fire which burned logs of scented applewood.

I knew the Baron longed for an heir. He was kind to young animals, and to the few babies that came into our lives. For the first time since my wedding-day I felt that I now belonged to my husband in the total sense of the word. I hoped that he would react to my news as husbands did in the movies, by clasping me to his bosom, with tears of joy in his eyes. I also hoped that the next day I might be taken to Cartier's or Van Cleef and Arpels, to choose a little memento of this unique occasion.

What actually happened was totally unlike this day-dream. The idea of being pregnant made me think I should feel tired, so, deciding I must now indulge myself, I remained in bed after my breakfast tray had been removed and soon drifted into a lazy doze. This was interrupted by Lili's knock on the door.

'There's a visitor for Madame la Baronne. I have shown her into the salon.'

I knew at once that Lili had been impressed by my visitor, or else she would have been shown into the small cosy library we used as a living-room.

'What is the lady's name?'

'Madame la Marquise de Rastignac.'

Why, I wondered, as I got out of bed, had Mrs van Hoorn's friend come to visit me? Perhaps she had heard that I was lonely and had come to give me some more of the advice that mature French ladies seemed so anxious to pour out to young brides. I wished that the Baron had been at home to help me entertain this forbidding guest. All the time I was dabbing powder on my nose I was trying hard to remember what my visitor looked like. I had seen her so seldom. I knew, of course, that she and Renaud had been more than friendly when he was a young man. He had a great respect and admiration for her. He had told me so on many occasions. She was, he said, so *wise*. I supposed that she had decided to forgive me for having married her one-time protégé. Perhaps she and Madame Mère had decided that I should be graciously pardoned for having entered the charmed circle. I determined to be winning and sweet. To please Renaud I would make a friend of the lady who had once, so long ago, meant so much to him. Full of warm good fellowship I opened the door.

The Marquise was standing at the window, looking down into the great cobbled courtyard. As I came in, she turned, giving the impression of a rustle of silken skirts and taffeta petticoats. Even in the soft, filtered light of the afternoon, I could see that her face was like a map, criss-crossed with secondary roads. She was impressively corpulent; but she still held herself well, her small, proud head, pivoting slowly on her long, swanlike neck. She stood there silently, balanced on ridiculously tiny feet, in minute shoes whose counterpart are to be seen only in the Cluny Museum.

I have often wondered since what the Marquise was thinking as she stood, looking round the long pleasant room, with its pools of golden parquet, waxed to perfection by Ramon, who loved to roll up the rugs, and wearing felt pads on his house-slippers, dance up and down the room, whistling the tune of a *Java*, with his thin legs prancing beneath the striped apron that made him look like a demented wasp. Early one morning I had come by and heard a sweet, clear voice singing a popular tune, and peeping into the salon, saw Ernestine and Ramon entwined in a fierce and passionate embrace. They were dancing *bal-musette* style, and for a moment I envied Ernestine as she twirled and turned in the arms of her lover.

The Marquise's eyes were the colour of turquoise and hard as that stone. I stared at her, feeling as gauche as when I used to be carpeted by the formidable head-mistress of my school in Johannesburg. Then the Marquise smiled, and the spell of fear was broken, for I was reminded of Josephine de Beauharnais, Napoleon's dear love, whose teeth, according to an ungallant biographer of the period, were, like those of the Marquise, 'decayed stumps rotting in a swamp of saliva'.

I flashed my visitor a grin of dazzling brilliance. My pearlies, like those of most South African girls of my generation, were strong, white and in perfect condition. The Marquise said nothing, but her eyes probed me again as if I were a stall at a jumble sale; her gaze darting among the rubbish to see what piece of glittering junk had attracted her friend, the Baron.

While waiting for my guest to take the initiative and to explain the object of her visit, I remembered my manners, invited her to remove her coat and furs, and rang the bell for tea. Fortunately my staff, who, as I have said could be lax, had mastered the tea-routine, English-fashion, and Lili arrived, in her black afternoon dress with tiny lace cap and apron, pushing a loaded trolley, with Ramon in attendance with a silver tea équipage on a tray. I blessed the fitting at Lanvin that had followed my visit to the doctor, for elated, I had walked home, and had called in at Smith's in the rue de Rivoli to buy an English magazine, a Dundee fruit cake in a tin, and some scones.

Smith's must for ever remain a shining memory in the hearts of those who lived in Paris during the thirties. I am not sure when the Paris branch of this very British company opened. But by the time Paris had become my permanent home, Smith's, like 'Old England' and Kirby Beard, was the haven and refuge of British expatriates and distinguished homosexuals from the most elevated political and social circles. It was considered chic to use Smith's tearoom as a rendezvous. Here, in the long, low-ceilinged olde worlde room, above the bookshop, with views on to the Tuileries, and within spitting distance of the very spot on the Place de la Concorde where Marie Antoinette's neck was severed, one could meet one's friends, drink a pot of real tea (instead of the concoction of dried grass served as tea by the French), accompanied by scones, crumpets, or hot buttered anchovy or cinnamon toast.

When I first became an habituée of Smith's in Paris, the manageress had just emigrated from Gunter's in London. She had a wide toothy smile, masses of hair, and small bright eyes behind gleaming pince-nez. Her handmaidens were all carefully picked sensible middle-aged bodies like herself, who would never have credited the *mores* of some of their favourite patrons. Smith's was, now I think back, rather like a nursery in Belgravia with a posse of nannies perpetually in attendance.

The Marquise eyed the trolley with interest.

'How charming,' she said, 'how very *style anglais*.' Then, pointing her lorgnette at the silver équipage, complete with spirit-lamp, which I had recently purchased at a sale at the Salle

Drouot, she murmured, 'How traditional. I haven't seen an équipage like that since I stayed with the Duchess of Devonshire at Chatsworth when I was a girl. One of my ancestors, Corisande de Gramont, was brought up by the fifth Duchess, the beautiful gambler, and there has always been a link between the Devonshires and ourselves. The Duchess was a close friend of our late Queen Marie-Antoinette and did all she could to help her escape from prison. Have you ever stayed at Chatsworth?'

I had to admit that I had neither stayed at Chatsworth nor ever met their Graces of Devonshire. The Marquise arched her eyebrows and pursed her mouth.

'But you've been a guest at Badminton? ... At Belvoir, then?'

I shook my head. I did not at that time know that in order to qualify for admittance to the cabala, it was necessary to claim (and to be able to implement your claim) friendship with at least three great English families. This complicated game had clearly defined rules. An English lord counted ten points, and was equal to certain *ancien régime* French dukes. The Spanish aristocracy rated more highly than the Italian; close relatives of the Czar scored as high as the British Royal Family. Reigning royals (but it was imperative to have their signed photographs with a personal dedication) scored the highest points.

Having thus ruthlessly exposed me as a nonentity who knew nobody, the marquise proceeded to flay me by stripping me of all my illusions about the sanctity of marriage and of my role in the life of Renaud, my husband. The lady had a fluent and plausible tongue; besides, she was telling the truth. Even though I hated her I was forced to recognise the ring of authenticity in her voice as she proceeded to wreck my marriage.

She had come to see me, she said, to explain the Baron's motivations in marrying outside his class.

'We were all against it,' she said sweetly.

'All?'

'His mother and myself, but, as you have probably discovered, Renaud is a headstrong young man.'

I gaped at this obscene old woman who was talking about my middle-aged husband as if he were still the spoilt young adolescent she had first taken into her bed and into her heart. Though I hated her, I realised that she loved him deeply, as I could never love him. Even so I grew hot and restive at the patronising tones in which she pointed out that, as a raw foreigner from a country beyond the pale of civilisation, I could hardly be expected to know the *mores* that obtained in the more distinguished circles of European society.

'Of course,' she said, delicately sipping her tea, 'one is prepared to make allowances. Renaud has had many infatuations, many *passades*, women find him irresistible.'

'He didn't marry any of them legally or in church. Surely you must see that?'

'Of course I do, my dear, and that is exactly why I am here.'

I began to feel a kind of nausea rising in my throat as I stared at the large pale woman sitting opposite me who was threatening not only my marriage, but also my unborn child and its inheritance. She represented the leader of the pogrom, the one who had bayed that Dreyfus was guilty. She was the one who hated the whole Jewish race; who hated me not only because I was young and had taken her lover, but because I represented the future and a race of women who would finally overthrow the outmoded systems of the society of which she was a representative. Neither of us could have put our innermost feelings into words; but between us there was not only antagonism—there was naked, virulent hatred.

I determined that if she was going to stick me full of banderillas, I was at least going to be responsible for the *mise à mort*.

I said, 'Did my husband know you were coming here today?'

'No.'

'Why have you come?'

'I was trying to tell you. To help you to a better, more sophisticated understanding of Renaud's situation. You must by now have some idea of how much we mean to one another; but what I am sure you cannot know is how indissolubly linked we are by many ties, some of which must inevitably affect Renaud's way of life, and therefore your own.'

'I think my husband should be present at a discussion of this kind.'

She shot me a glance of admiration.

'*Touchée, petite madame*, first blood to you. But, all the same I do not think it would be advisable for you to speak of this interview to Renaud. Since I see you are an intelligent creature, let me be plain with you! Apart from a few unimportant lapses which I mentioned, Renaud has been mine since he was eighteen years old. I mean he has been my lover and my responsibility.

'He is a hothouse plant, he would not survive in the chilly winds of reality and he is incapable of fending for himself. I know this, but because I love him I am prepared to back all his fantasies and follies, even that of marriage to a person half his age and a total stranger to us all.

'Renaud is my life and I don't propose giving him up. Naturally I am prepared to be reasonable and to effect some sort of compromise to keep him happy and contented. After all, you do bear his name, which is that of an ancient and honoured line indeed with 36 quarterings intact, at least they were intact until you came into his life. I cannot imagine what will happen now, particularly as I'm sure your family have no armorial bearings.

'To come to the point: I am prepared to continue to give Renaud my full support providing you are reasonable about our relationship. After all, you must realise that he and I have been together for many, many years. During all this time my fortune, which is considerable, has always been available to my dearest of friends, as were my counsels which regulate his business life. I, of course, depend entirely on him for certain essential services'—her eyes were bright and malicious—'acts which keep our friendship as fresh and full-blooded as it was in the early days of our passion, and it was passion, I assure you.'

'I'm glad you find my husband's performance in bed to your satisfaction, Madame, and now, if you will excuse me, I should like to lie down. I am pregnant, you see, and as a grandmother, you will readily understand that I must obey my doctor's advice, which is to take plenty of rest. Besides, I am sure you will want to hurry home to report to Renaud, before he goes off to see his father confessor.'

With which I rang the bell and asked Ramon to see my guest to her car. She was completely overcome by my bombshell. The Baron had been at pain to convince her that I did not want children. My secret weapon had, in one blow, pierced her jealous heart. Looking back on that scene now, I feel a certain compassion for the poor woman, who realised immediately that the advent of a child would give me a great hold over her lover.

When the Marquise had gone, leaving behind her the sickly scent of the essence of violets she affected, I found my knees were trembling and that I was parched. I rushed into my bathroom, drank three toothmugs of cold water and was then violently sick. When the Baron came home to dinner, he found me on my bed, pale and exhausted. He knew, the moment he entered our apartment, that the Marquise had been there. Her perfume had betrayed her.

He sat on a chair next to the bed stroking my hand. He was tender, compassionate, understanding and furiously angry with the Marquise. I hated him. The encounter with his mistress, and the realisation of what her hold over him meant appalled me. For the first time I understood how we were able to live in such luxury.

I insisted then on knowing the true state of his finances, and to my surprise he told me the truth. He had a small income from a family trust and his family owned a great deal of land, but he was entirely dependent on the Marquise's goodwill.

'I am her financial adviser,' he said grandly. 'I handle her portfolio. She has never had much of a head for figures, poor lady, and everyone has always tried to exploit her. I have greatly increased her capital, so it is natural she should wish to show her gratitude by involving me in her affairs. I do wish you wouldn't bother your dear little head about such matters. Just trust me.'

I turned my head away so that he should not see my tears. I knew that I should never be able to divorce him from the world of fantasy and from the fine web of lies she had spun about him. He had betrayed me and I knew too that he would continue to do so. That for all his protestations of love and fine speeches about changing his life, he would never leave his woman, for she was his woman. The pattern of their lives together was set. I was the foreigner, the outsider, and from that moment I knew that my escape from Renaud and from the Nest of Vipers was only a matter of time.

6
The Enchanted Tower

Three days after my interview with the Marquise, I was seized with appalling pains. Ernestine sent for our doctor and when the Baron came home, all was over. It was the only time I ever saw him moved as real men are moved. I was deeply distressed by the loss of my baby. I had been looking forward to having a child to care for and to take away the terrifying sense of loneliness which so often encompassed me. I had made plans for the coming of the child, and now could not bear to go near the rooms which I had destined to be the nurseries. I had written to my own Nursie who was now married, and living near London, to ask whether she knew of a good English nannie.

The Baron was very cast down and blamed me for not telling him earlier of my condition. It did not seem to enter his head that he and the Marquise between them were responsible for the loss of the longed-for heir. When I grew more rational about my loss, I was relieved; for I realised that had I had a child by Renaud, I should have been forever bound to him by the ties of religion and sentiment.

It was the first time in my life that I had suffered in an 'adult' way and from an adult complaint. Now none of the remedies of my childhood—Lala's cool hands on my forehead, the low, melodious murmur of the voices of the African servants floating through the open windows of my sick-room—were available to soothe and heal me.

I was suddenly the victim of a body which refused to obey me but followed strange dictates of its own. Being a grown-up married woman was, I decided, an unpleasant state. Suddenly, the snatches of conversations, the winks and nods which had been part of the behaviour-pattern of adult conversations I had overheard as a child, made sense. Nursie's concern for Lala as she grew larger and larger with the great belly that contained my brother. The winks and whispers when Nursie and her friend,

Hilda Leathers, looked at wedding pictures of one of Lala's diminutive cousins to a bridegroom of monumental proportions.

I was disgusted with the whole messy business of procreation, and decided I was not yet ready to bear children, and that when I finally achieved this state of grace, I should not give them the Baron as a father.

Daily I grew more listless and anaemic, lying stretched out for hours on a chaise-longue in my room, an unread book in my hand, and with my eyes fixed on the sky that in no way resembled that of my native land. I was homesick. Finally the doctor became alarmed at my general debility and must have alerted the Baron, for one day he announced in jocular vein that we were going to spend the whole of the summer on the family estate, where Madame Mère herself could nurse me and bring the roses back to my cheeks.

My heavy heart sank even lower as I envisaged myself entrapped in the dreary web of the Queen Viper. I saw myself strolling aimlessly and endlessly in the formal grounds of the château, in which even the trees wore iron skirts; and I revolted at the thought of sitting through endless meals with Madame Mère's gimlet eyes probing my face with the 'Borgia' look.

I told the Baron quite plainly that I preferred to die quietly in Paris rather than spend my summer with his family, and one day he arrived with a large bunch of gladioli, a flower I do not like, and announced that he had just rented a villa at Deauville, where he hoped his little invalid might happily convalesce in the merry company of his friends—the horde of international celebrities who had made Deauville the summer watering-hole of their choice.

I hated the Villa des Fleurs on sight. It was new, pretentious and rather twee, ornate, with a superabundance of false beams and geraniums, which did little to hide the defects of jerry-building. While the Baron was at the bar of the Normandie with his friends, I hired a car and went off exploring on my own. I obtained a list of properties and visited a great many houses and estates. I was just about to give up the search, when the chauffeur suggested I might like to have a look at the Manoir de Rollo which he knew had been for sale for some time.

The *manoir* was some miles from Honfleur. It was hidden behind waves of overgrown greenery. It consisted of a semi-ruined pavilion flanked by a sturdy-looking tower capped with a pointed bonnet of greyish-blue slate. The tower had been built in the sixteenth century, and the pavilion was an eighteenth century addition. According to some surviving architectural sketches, the Manoir de Rollo seems originally to have been much more elaborate consisting of four pavilions, one at each corner of a square central court. Three more towers were to have been added to the one already in existence.

Another dwelling, across the courtyard, had once been a small farmhouse. This had been converted and equipped with a modern kitchen and bathrooms. The thatched roof needed attention, but everything else was in good repair. A cow-byre had been converted into staff-quarters, but little had been done to make servants comfortable. The tiny rooms were chilly with the original floors intact and uncovered. Everything was slightly stuffy and shabby, but the tower, melancholy as it was, was roomy and magnificent.

The Manoir de Rollo pleased me. It also presented me with a challenge and I very soon determined to buy it. But my financial situation was involved. As the Baron's wife I was entitled to draw on his resources, but I was unwilling to benefit from his manipulations of his mistress' fortune. Of financial matters I had little or no experience, Papa having always refused to allow any female member of the family to poke her nose into his affairs.

When I married he settled a small sum of money on me, the income from which was intended to provide me with 'pin money'. This, however, was swamped by the Baron's *largesse*, for although he never gave me an allowance as such, he paid all the bills, and filled my bureau drawers with bank-notes and sometimes, as a surprise, with *Louis d'or*.

I wanted the *manoir* and intended to possess it no matter what the difficulties. I told the Baron I was determined on this purchase and asked him to help me with the legal formalities. I said I wanted a place of my own, and rather to my surprise, he agreed that I should do as I wished. It was only later I learned that we were married in community of property which meant that, according to French law, half of everything I possessed belonged to my spouse. Furthermore, I could not even sign a lease without his written permission.

The situation, however, was simplified by the unexpected news that the Baron's Great-Aunt Régine, who had just died, had left me a not inconsiderable sum. The terms of her will had infuriated the vipers, for in it, she said she was making me a bequest in case I ever came to my senses and escaped from the Nest. So, thanks to Great-Aunt Régine, I was able to modernise the tower and make some repairs to the exterior of the pavilion.

One of my friends, a plump, sad *castrato* called Mario Bellini, offered me his services as an interior designer; and between us we turned the tower and part of the pavilion into a retreat which combined the romantic streak in my nature with Bellino's mature good taste.

The tower had style and possibilities. It consisted of four rooms, two of them very large, linked by a fine circular staircase. We turned the upstairs rooms into a bedroom with an archway leading to the bath-dressing room; an innovation which, when it percolated through the grapevine to the local farmers and peasantry, gave rise to a good deal of gossip mainly connected with the large bath bought for me at a sale in Paris. The tub was of marble with silver feet and chiselled silver dolphin taps of delicate workmanship. This extraordinary object was purported to have belonged to Miss Howard, the English mistress of Napoleon III.

The ground floor became a library-living room. Both bedroom and library had impressively ornate marble fireplaces, and, since the property included two farms, several orchards and a wood, I was always supplied with logs of chestnut, beech and applewood, all of which burned sweetly.

I never discovered who built the tower originally. According to legend, it was constructed to house the Circassian mistress of the famous pirate, Jean-Francois Doublet, whose fine town house stood in the rue des Capuchins, Honfleur. Even the name of the *manoir* was lost in the mists of antiquity, Rollo having been a ninth-century Norseman who, after raiding Scotland and England, sailed up the Seine and took possession of Rouen.

It was certainly haunted, for many times at dusk, as I walked down the avenue of trees leading to the tower, I heard the sweet, clear tinkling of the notes of a clavichord playing an air by Lully; and, as I came closer, a soft effulgent glow that was not of this world would shine for an instant from the upstairs window.

Bellini installed electricity, central heating and a telephone in the main pavilion, though while I wanted the heating and telephone, I would have preferred the gentle light of the oil-lamps which were still in use in many country cottages. My favourite oil-lamp with a pink and white frosted bowl had come from Flaubert's home at Croisset.

It took time to turn the tower into a real home. At first I found it difficult to get staff. None of my people from the rue du Bac would emigrate to the country with me. They came in a body to visit the *manoir* and assess its potential; but, sadly shaking their heads, they returned hastily to Paris, unable to contemplate life in a hermitage several kilometres from the nearest café, and where the peasants went to bed with the chickens. '*La vie rustique ne me dit rien*,' said Ernestine, while Lili remarked that she couldn't sleep without the sound of traffic in her ears.

The local girls were frightened by tales of the ghostly clavichord player; even the Baron was none too happy in the tower bedroom, and was always relieved, when, after a brief love skirmish in my four-poster (he much enjoyed having the curtains tightly drawn, which gave me claustrophobia) he could take himself off to his own snug room in the pavilion.

Although he himself understood why I had been enthralled with the *manoir*, his family thought my decision to exile myself in the depths of the countryside in a 'damp, unattractive and semi-ruined' tower showed that the loss of my baby had unhinged my mind. In fact, as soon as I was settled in, I was conscious of a feeling of great relief. I was free of the Vipers, and away from their baleful influence; my brain began to function properly as a writer's should, recording sights and sounds which were squirrelled into the deepest recesses of my mind, to be pulled out, examined and appraised at leisure much later, like sound sweet nuts in the long winters of my discontent.

It did not take me long to fall in love with the serene, charming and green countryside of the Roumois and the Lieven. Parts of Normandy were still off the beaten track and seldom visited by holiday-makers. This was still Maupassant's Normandy; populated in the main by crafty, avaricious and credulous peasant-farmers, who lived in their picturesque, damp, half-timbered thatched farmhouses amidst their apple-orchards. Witchcraft was still practised by black and white witches, and spells and omens more popular than the preachings of the local curé or the remedies of the village doctor. It was still the lush pastoral Normandy of superb, regional cooking, of Flaubert and of villages and farms similar to that in which Emma Bovary was born.

Many of those the Baron referred to as the 'first families of' Normandy were still living in the same three hundred Norman country-houses, castles, manor houses and fortified towers built by their ancestors. Since he was their kinsman we were at first invited to dinners, luncheons, shoots and picnics, all of which were enjoyable, though too reminiscent of the family circle I had just left. Nor did it take long for the 'on-dit' to circulate that I was not exactly *persona grata* with the Vipers; soon the invitations became fewer. The Baron was in despair and accused me of sabotaging his social life. I could only agree and apologise. I told him to tell his friends that I was not yet fully recovered from my miscarriage, and that I was happy that he should go out without me. This he did, liberating me from a social round which would have had corrosive effects on the new life of discipline I was trying to impose on myself.

Solitude and study are not always good for the young, but these I craved at this particular time. I adhered to a strict routine; to a rule of life which began on Mondays, as soon as the Baron and his posse of elegant week-end guests returned to Paris.

In my library I discovered the true pleasures of the mind. 'Numbers imitate space,' said Pascal, 'and books imitate the universe of our thoughts, the heaven and hell of our minds.'

In my long quiet room with its panelled walls, coral-coloured velvet curtains, comfortable sofas and armchairs upholstered in English chintz, I sat at the refectory table which did duty as a desk, reading, taking notes, and reading, reading, reading.

I discovered Montaigne, Pascal, Descartes, Balzac, Dumas, Flaubert and the Goncourt Brothers, that quirky pair of gossips who provided tantalising and racy snippets about the members of the literary circle who frequented their famous 'attic'.

It was then that I first read Alain-Fournier's *Le Grand Meaulnes*, which, as a Japanese flower expands in water, blossomed in my mind, setting up chain reactions which have not yet, even today, completely died away. I also discovered that, inside the plump and pampered chrysalis who was the Baron's young bride, was another leaner, ironical and more aesthetic self. The 'vie intérieure' as described by Père Joseph bore absolutely no resemblance to my 'interior life', and when I tried to explain this discrepancy to the Baron, he became vexed and irritated at what seemed to him an indecent pleasure in my own company. He taxed me with 'shutting him out', and then I realised sadly that he had never had any real place in my heart. At the same time I knew that I had a debt to pay. I had married him for the wrong reasons, and since nothing is for nothing, I should in some way have to expiate my snobbish greed for material things.

It was difficult to explain to my husband that I had never in my life been left alone long enough to let my thoughts develop quietly along their own channels without extraneous pressures. The Baron asked me to keep a journal so that he could follow the pattern of my days while he was away from me. This I did, but it bored him so, that after a month he gave up reading it. I felt like quoting the famous page in Louis XVI's diary to him. On one of the days on which the full force of the French revolution erupted, the monarch wrote, 'nothing'.

The Baron need not have been concerned about me. A hundred and one details that needed my personal attention kept me occupied. Never before had I furnished a house from scratch; up until then the décor of my life had been more or less chosen for me and I rejoiced in each and every piece that I bought or was given me by the Baron.

Bellini left me for the United States where a Vanderbilt required his services. Although I missed the surety of his touch and his great knowledge of period furniture, I enjoyed combing antique shops and attending country auctions which still offered extraordinarily rewarding bargains.

I wanted the *manoir* to look like a home and not like a museum. Unlike their English counterparts, French country houses with a few notable exceptions were inclined to be stiffly formal and uncomfortably crammed with splendid, pretentious or boringly ugly bibelots and furniture. The gentry who lived in the type of property I had bought were totally averse to spending their good money on changing the background that had suited the way of life of their ancestors.

I used a great deal of printed cotton throughout the house. I loved this charming caprice that had dominated French fashions in the eighteenth century. I also used a great deal of French provincial furniture which was then looked down upon as being 'rustic', and not suitable for furnishing a salon. I replaced the ornate marble mantelpiece in my bedroom by a smaller graciously carved mantelpiece of pine; and over a splendid Provençal *bombé* chest with silver handles I hung a Spanish mirror of leather and beaten silver.

The locals were greatly puzzled by my pride in the floor of waxed brick I had covered with some late eighteenth-century Beauvais pile carpets which the Baron had abstracted from trunks in the attic of the family château. I had no idea of the value of these superb carpets, any more than I realised the worth of some of the other pieces imported for me by the Baron. One of his gifts was a *bonheur-du-jour*, fitted out with gold-mounted toilet accessories. It was signed by Leleu.

The fabric I used in the tower bedroom is still one of my favourite designs. It is a *toile* called *Les Délices des Quatre Saisons*, designed by Jean-Baptiste Huet, and features a series of tiny vignettes depicting elegant, but hardy eighteenth-century figures indulging in seasonal outdoor activities. Another pretty *toile* was *Le Couronnement de la Rosière*, depicting a village virgin being crowned with roses. I used this fabric in one of the guest rooms and it never failed to stimulate friends like Serge Cheremeteff to recounting bawdy anecdotes about village *mores* and *les droits du seigneur*, a custom which I felt he had much enjoyed on his estates in his native Russia.

*

The Baron enjoyed country sales and in imaginative mood he attended one, returning with a charming red and black trap complete with black pony, with a silver harness, which *équipage*, he said, was all I needed to complete my resemblance to Sophie in *Les Pètites Filles Modèles*. Most of the books in the series known as *La Bibliothèque Rose* were by the Comtesse de Ségur. Sophie was a spoilt and prankish child who once cooked and ate a pet goldfish.

The *manoir* was some miles from the wonderfully picturesque town of Honfleur, with its tiny port grouped around a dock, the *Leutenance*. Here are narrow streets lined with ancient dwellings, such as the Governor's house on the Square. The Church of Ste Catherine d'Honfleur, too, is unique for it was built in timber by the master-builders of the *caravalles* for the Honfleurais corsairs. This church is possibly the only one of its kind in this part of the world to have a free-standing steeple.

Wherever I walked or drove in my pony-trap, I found ancient and interesting places to visit. Honfleur and its surroundings gave me an awareness of the life and mind of the Norman peasant-farmer. My own tenants were typically canny, with small salty blue eyes and an annoyingly bland way of countering my questions with a 'Perhaps yes, or then again perhaps no.'

To the older generation of country folk, Paris was a haunt of vice, whence none might return unscathed. At the same time they had no idea of its vastness. One old lady, hearing I came from Paris asked whether I should ever return there. 'If you do,' she piped, 'I count upon you to bring Jules Goupil the salutations of his Great-Aunt Noémi. You'll have no trouble recognising him. He has the family nose and red side-whiskers.'

The first of my neighbours to capture my interest was Madame Hauchecorne. I was taken to visit her by my bailiff who wanted to show me how well she ran her farm. At first I was not impressed by her appearance. She was a small, dumpy middle-aged woman, with more than a passing resemblance to portraits of Queen Victoria. Madame Hauchecorne had a fine clear skin and the milky-blue eyes of a newborn kitten. She also had a tight determined mouth and made it clear that the sooner I took my baronial airs and graces from her kitchen, the better. It was, however, all I had dreamed a farm kitchen should be. I was enchanted by the worn flagged floor, the wide, soot-blackened fireplace with its trivet on which stood a seemingly bottomless enamel coffee-pot; the window-sill with its pots of bright geraniums, of chives and of basil. According to the seasons, there was inevitably a basket or two of livestock warming near the fire. Madame Hauchecorne preferred animals to human beings, and there were always two or three kittens chasing balls of wool or paper. Tiny chicks and kittens touched her, but the moment they became adult and lost their pretty ways, she chased them out to fend for themselves. She was totally unsentimental, and could never understand why I took such care of the two cats she gave me.

This strange woman lived by an unvarying routine. Every afternoon the kitchen was swept out, and the great old kitchen table scrubbed to ivory whiteness. After this exertion, Madame Hauchecorne took a brief nap and then changed her working pinafore for a black dress with spotless white cuffs and a wide white collar. She would come downstairs and immerse herself in her two favourite newspapers; the local gazette and a financial paper sent to her from Paris, in which she studied the share market.

It was the sight of the financial journal that aroused my curiosity. It seemed such an incongruous choice of reading matter for a middle-aged farmer's widow living in the depth of the Norman countryside. My next discovery was that the Widow Hauchecorne, as she was known locally, was reputedly the most ill-tempered but one of the finest cooks in the province. Intrigued, when the greedy old Curé de Pennedepie, a neighbouring hamlet, told me this, I asked our local doctor for further information about Mathilde Hauchecorne's culinary activities. I knew that old Doctor Carre-Lamedon enjoyed good wine, the company of attractive women, and the opportunity of talking about his far-off student days in Paris. So I asked him to dine, baiting the trap with his favourite dish and invited a pretty, addle-pated young woman-friend to join us.

It took some manœuvering to get him on the subject of Widow Hauchecorne. But, when I mentioned her name a second time, he looked at me with malice sparkling in his small simian eyes.

'*Alors*, our Mathilde intrigues you, and well she may, for darker horse never stepped than this seemingly respectable matron.'

The Baron, an attentive host, refilled the doctor's glass with Calvados.

'Mathilde was the illegitimate daughter of a farmer who lived some forty kilometres from here. We are about the same age, and went to the same village school. She was not a pretty child, and I remember her vividly, mainly because she seemed always to have spots and chilblains in and out of season. Although the farmer's wife, her stepmother, had agreed to bring up her husband's bastard with her own brood, she never lost an opportunity of teasing and taunting Mathilde about the accident of her birth. Finally the girl ran away with a one-eyed pedlar who was notorious in these parts for his unhealthy preoccupation with little girls. Mathilde slept rough with this man, in barns and when they could afford it in inns, where she earned their keep by helping with the washing-up and general chores.

'In time they reached Paris where Mathilde, tired of being mauled by her lover, ran away again. This time she was luckier. She was taken on as kitchen-maid in the household of Prince Andrei Kuragin who, having married a ballet dancer, was exiled by his cousin, the Czar, and lived in great style in a splendid Parisian mansion.

'Mathilde was fifteen when she first entered the Prince's kitchens and it took her three years to come to his notice. The Prince was an eccentric. One of his quirks was to dislike coming across any member of his staff carrying out their lowly duties, such as cleaning grates, polishing floors, carrying bath-water or similar tasks. All the servants had to rise at five o'clock in the morning, so that the whole house should be in perfect order to greet the master when he came downstairs at eight to practise the piano, which he played well enough to have won the admiration and commendation of Liszt, whose pupil he had been.

'There was no reason for the Prince and Mathilde, the kitchen-maid, ever to meet. But meet they did, in the sickroom of the Prince's adored only child, Vassili, who, having contracted polio in his youth, was an invalid, confined to his bed or his wheel-chair. The poor, pale youth had a very tenuous hold on life, and although the services of the finest chefs were employed to tempt his capricious appetite, he refused almost every food but gruel, until Mathilde came into his life.

'Little Mathilde, the scullery-maid, had become a superb chef. Yes, I use the word advisedly. She *was* a chef, unique in her own class. Her cooking was the talk of Paris. How had she come by this knowledge? Partly through shrewd observation, and partly through pillow-talk. She had become the mistress of a master pastry-cook who told her all his secrets; he realised that the rare flame of a truly dedicated chef burned in Mathilde's breast. In the great hushed house in the Marais it was no secret that Mathilde's extraordinarily varied repertoire of dishes was keeping young Vassili alive. She tantalised his palate, piqued his curiosity, and made each meal a memorable occasion.

'Soon Mathilde became the young man's day-nurse as well as his cook. To the surprise of his parents and doctors, the ailing Vassili took on a new lease of life. For the first time in years he became interested in the world outside his sickroom. Knowing that his days were numbered, he decided to travel, and with a retinue headed by the now invaluable Mathilde on whom he relied, not only to keep his gastric juices flowing but to amuse him by her practical, matter-of-fact approach to life, he set off on a tour of Europe which included a visit to his father's estates in the Crimea.

'From this journey, Mathilde brought back a jumble of impressions of birch forests, flowers, solitude and of an estate the size of a small town—which I don't think she ever sorted out in her mind. She also brought back an impressive number of gifts from her grateful patient. She showed me some of them. They included an emerald the size of a walnut, a sable *pelisse* which she kept smothered in black pepper and rolled up in tarred paper in her attic. There was also a tender and delicate Fragonard, which hung over her brass bedstead. She was also given the assurance of a handsome sum should she remain with the Prince until his death. She promised not to leave him during his lifetime. Nor did she. When he died, she packed her belongings and returned in triumph to her native village.

'The thin, sad, illegitimate girl had become a fine woman. She was on the plump side, you understand, and it was obvious that she was ripe for marriage. She had no lack of suitors. She had a great deal to offer. She was an heiress, and she was an inspired cook. What more could a man want?

'The fellow who won her hand was a nice enough chap. He was a farmer from Barneville-la-Bertran. She moved into his house, and soon you would never have known that she had been anywhere but to the village pump. Mathilde took to motherhood as a duck to water, and the Lord blessed her first with a son, Jules, and then with a daughter, Angélique. Her good man Louis died at the onset of the Great War. He did not have the privilege given to so many Frenchmen of being killed in action, for he died of blood-poisoning from a tiny scratch on the thumb received when fixing a barbed wire cattle fence.

'Mathilde Hauchecorne was a model widow. She devoted herself entirely to the upbringing and welfare of her small children, until a Belgian schoolmaster, a red-bearded fellow, a refugee from a German-occupied town, was billeted on her farm. There was a certain amount of talk, of course. Bound to be in a tiny village; but in the end she and her lover settled down to a pleasant and profitable form of co-existence. He was as hard a worker as Mathilde, I give him that; so with their joint efforts, the farm prospered as never before. Mathilde's children grew up. Jules went off to do his military service, and was kicked to death by a horse. Angélique was a buxom girl, quiet and pleasant, with the same eyes as her mother, and a mane of corn-coloured hair which she put up so that she looked like a walking wheatsheaf.

'One day Mathilde went to the cider press and there, rolling about on the floor in the fiercest convulsions of fornication, were her lover and daughter.'

*

At this riveting moment, the doctor's story was interrupted by a message that he was needed to pay an urgent call. So it was not until much later that I pieced together the rest of this remarkable human document.

Once I discovered that the Widow Hauchecorne was such an accomplished cook, I begged her to give me lessons. At first she refused, but finally she softened, and once a week I went to the farm, *Les Trois Merles*, to work with her in her kitchen.

I was always conscious of a feeling of pleasurable anticipation on approaching the modest, white-painted wooden gateway that led to the farm. It lay cosily tucked away behind high banks lined with fine trees. The *clos normand* itself was planted with apple-trees under which red and white cows, a pony and a donkey cropped the emerald green grass. On a small pond bobbed a flotilla of ducks. Most of the rosy brick of the wall-space had been used to support espaliered peaches and pears and climbing roses, of which the star was a glorious *Etoile d'Hollande*. Even the midden and the guard dog Pataud, who spent all day tied by a long chain to his kennel, seemed part of a bucolic paradise.

In her pleasant, sunny kitchen which lacked every one of today's aids to cookery, I was initiated into some of the secrets of *le bon manger*. Madame Hauchecorne was a strict disciplinarian, and insisted on my making the same dish or sauce over and over again until, having tasted it, she would give a grudging nod which was her method of signifying approval.

She said that I should never become a great cook because I cooked with my brain, and not with my senses. 'A "nose" is just as important in blending a sauce as it is in wine-tasting,' she used to say impatiently as I tried to scamp a boring culinary routine.

'Conjure up the dish in your mind,' was another of her saws. 'A sensitive palate and a profound knowledge of the seasons are part of the equipment of a good cook,' she would say, beating white of egg with a fork, with a touch so delicate that the egg would froth of itself into a faery wave. 'Believe in using the fruits of the earth and of the sea in God's good time. He never meant us to cheat nature by forcing fruit and vegetables; and in spite of their rarity value, *primeurs*, to my mind, never taste so good as fruit and vegetables picked at their seasonable and opulent best.'

The Widow Hauchecorne had an enviable collection of cookery books. One of them was her favourite. This was *Le Vray Cuisinier François* by François Pierre de Varenne.

First published in 1651, the book revolutionised French cooking. Until then French cookery, like that which prevailed all over Europe at that time, was heavily spiced and anything but refined. De la Varenne introduced mushrooms and truffles: dishes became more subtle, and butter took the place of oil in pastry. He brought imagination into the kitchen. Here is his recipe for *champignons farcis*:

12 *large mushrooms.*
1 *cup cooked ham, chicken or veal, or raw minced steak.*
2 *tablespoons minced onion.*
1 *slice stale bread, (crusts removed) crumbed.*
1 *tablespoon chopped parsley.*
Salt and pepper to taste ('ware of the salt in the ham!).
¼ *cup cream.*

Remove stems of large mushrooms. Peel caps, dip in melted butter and put aside for stuffing.
Stuffing to be made as follows:
Chop meat with mushroom stems. Combine meat-mushroom mixture with all remaining ingredients, *except* the cream, and cook for a few minutes in butter until well blended. Cool, or transfer to a cool dish before adding cream. Mix thoroughly with cream.
Fill mushroom caps with your stuffing. Bake in a pre-heated oven 425° for 20 to 25 minutes.

The ever-generous Prince Vassili had given Madame Hauchecorne a copy of the 1682 edition, and though the book was carefully bound in a protective covering of blue waxed paper, she made constant use of de Varenne's recipes.

On one occasion I was allowed to bring this book home to use the recipe for stuffed mushrooms which I have given above. My cousin Laurent, the bibliophile, was staying with me at the time and nearly fainted with excitement when I showed him the book.

'This belongs to an old peasant woman?' he cried. 'But dearest Cousin, I will have a modern copy of this work bound specially in red morocco and elaborately tooled in gold for your widow, if only she will sell me her copy. I am sure she has no idea of its value.'

'She knows', I said, taking the volume from him, for by this time I knew that Mathilde Hauchecorne knew to the last centime the value of every single one of her possessions. My plump little professor in *haute cuisine* prided herself on having invented several dishes. One of these was a *gratin* of mussels, mushrooms and shrimps. She seemed to have a great partiality for mushrooms, on which she was an authority, having a large coloured wall-chart, listing the various species on her still-room wall. And she used mushrooms in her dishes whenever possible. She also introduced me to sorrel which she used with distinction in her *carpe à l'oseille*. She extolled the virtues of the *cuisine normande* which was, she said, based principally on the lavish use of fresh cream, butter and cider. She taught me to make a *soufflé surprise*, subtly flavoured with calvados, and served with macaroons and apples. She was firm in her likes and dislikes, caring for only three of the great range of Norman cheeses. These were Pont l'Evêque, Livarot and Camembert.

By the time Madame Hauchecorne had taught me to make a *ragoût* of chicken in a bottle, a *foie-gras* sauce, and an omelette that was really *baveuse*, I felt that she, like myself, had begun to look forward to my cookery lessons. Now, when I had acquitted myself satisfactorily of whatever task she set me, she would smile, a singularly sweet smile, pat my shoulder and offer me a tiny glass of *calva* to drink with the cup of coffee with which she generally rounded off my lesson. The widow spoke little of her own affairs, though her anecdotes of her voyage through Russia had the clear, bright quality of the *Images d'Epinal* which enchanted the childhood of generations of French children.

*

Early one morning I went to market in my pony-trap with my little groom, Auguste, sitting beside me, puffed up with pride at showing off his smart livery with its silver buttons and shiny topboots. I always enjoyed the Honfleur market. The square was a confused mass of peasant women selling succulent fresh vegetables (the spraying of crops was, as yet, unknown in France), fruit, bunches of herbs, and cottage flowers. Some of the farmers still wore their traditional blue starched smocks embroidered at wrist and collar; wealthier ones wore beaver hats, while the women had on shawls and starched white caps.

Widow Hauchecorne had provided me with a list of items she needed for a dish we were going to make together. Having bought these I went on to the *patisserie-confiserie* on the corner, where I chose some *marrons-glacés* for which delicacy Madame Hauchecorne had a weakness.

Auguste loaded my shopping baskets into the trap and we drove out of Honfleur towards Barneville-le-Bertran. The high ground behind Honfleur and the Côte de Grace is covered with the beech-trees of the Forest of St Gatien. The pony trotted along at a spanking pace, while I sat peacefully enjoying the sight of the hedgerows and of the wild flowers most of which were unknown in my native Africa. My lesson was at ten-thirty sharp, and my teacher insisted on perfect punctuality.

'Les Trois Merles' was built atop a plateau-like field. Generally I took the long way round, driving sedately through the gates into the *clos*; but, on this occasion, seeing that I was short of time, I decided to take the short cut and to walk up to the farm through a copse planted with beech and oak. Nearing the copse, I sorted out the provisions for my lesson, halted the pony, and instructed Auguste to take the rest of my marketing home. It was a lovely day and I was looking forward to strolling up the gentle ride through the trees. I was half-way up when I heard the clicking of sabots. Turning, I saw a young woman walking towards me.

She was a fresh-faced girl of about eighteen, well-built and tall; she wore a faded blue-and-white gingham dress that was stretched tightly across her rounded breasts. A small gold crucifix on a chain round her neck glittered in the sun. Her legs were bare. I noticed the quaint, old-fashioned way in which her great mass of corn-coloured hair was pulled back from her forehead and was looped in a sort of tea-pot handle effect atop her head.

I waited politely for her to join me, but she seemed in no hurry, for she simply stood there, staring upwards towards the farm. Finally, I lost patience and went on my way. As I passed through the wicket gate that gave onto the field leading to the garden, I peered down to see what progress she had made. There was no sign of her.

I hurried to the kitchen, and, handing my purchases to the widow, observed that I had just seen a young woman making her way to the farm.

'I can't understand what she was at,' I said. She just stood there, gawping up at your chimneys. I hailed her a couple of times, but she didn't have the courtesy to answer.'

The widow thanked me warmly for the *marrons glacés*, but made no comment about her mysterious visitor.

Two weeks later, I was in the midst of a great jam-making session. The farm lad had brought in baskets filled with newly picked strawberries, which we washed and hulled. The scent of the bubbling syrup in the great copper pans was mouth-watering. We had bottled most of our first batch, when the widow noticed that we were running out of glass jars. As she was busy stirring, she asked me to fetch some jars from the still-room at the end of the passage. I went down the stone-flagged passage with a basket over my arm, collected the empty jars and took a look at the coloured chart of mushrooms, which was, I observed, damp and discoloured, peeling away from the wall.

As I hastened back to the kitchen, I noticed an open door leading to what seemed to be a bedroom. Being curious I looked in. It was a clean, neat little white-washed room, containing a few pieces of rustic furniture which included a narrow bed with a white cotton counterpane. Over it was a crucifix to which was attached a twig of crumbling box. On the rickety bedside table was a large framed, hand-tinted photograph. I picked it up and stared into the face of the girl I had seen that morning in the copse. She was wearing the same blue-and-white tight gingham dress, and a tiny crucifix hung from a chain around her neck. The colours were crude, but the blue eyes were singularly lifelike and appealing. The girl resembled Madame Hauchecorne.

Returning to the kitchen, I took my jars out of the basket and arranging them on the table, said in an off-hand manner, 'That's a nice little bedroom at the end of the passage. It has a charming view of the field. I happened to notice a photograph of an attractive young girl. Is she a relation?'

'That was my daughter Angélique,' said the widow coldly, and turning her back on me, she went on vigorously stirring her jam with a long wooden spoon. I did not mention this incident to anyone until on Sunday, when the old Curé de Pennedepie came to luncheon with us. After the meal, I cornered him and asked him point-blank what had become of Madame Hauchecorne's daughter, Angélique.

'The poor dear child has been dead these many years, God rest her soul.'

'She must have died very young?'

The old man fumbled his words. 'Yes, it was very sudden, very tragic, poor Angélique, poor little girl,' and before I could grill him further, he had trotted off to play his weekly game of chess with the Baron.

September that year was mellow and beautiful. I watched the men working the circular grooved stone of the cider mill, with the great stone crushing wheel on its wooden arm. Once the big tuns were filled, the men went off, and the cider barn was abandoned. I had taken up sketching, and one afternoon was sitting on a milking stool outside the barn with my pad on my knee. I was trying to draw the farmhouse, when suddenly the soft summer air became chill. I began to shiver. I looked round. Angélique was standing in the doorway. There was nothing unearthly about this phantom. This was a solid, hefty girl with well-developed calves. Her fair skin was powdered with golden freckles, and I saw that her eyes were the same kitten-blue as those of her mother. She stood there, staring at me, and then walked slowly back into the barn. I had no sensation of fear, only of intense cold, sadness and pity.

This time, however, I told the family doctor about my two visions. I expected him to say that I was neurotic, which was what he said of all women; but surprisingly, he said, 'Describe the girl you saw in the barn.' This I did, in detail.

'Are you certain you didn't see your first "vision" *after* having seen the photograph in Angélique's room?'

'Absolutely certain. I noted the date and time in my diary. Here is the entry.' Holding the red leather book close to his nose, for he was very short-sighted, he peered at the entries.

'I think it very likely you *did* see the ghost of Angélique Hauchecorne.'

'But why does she haunt the farm? What does she want?'

'Justice, I should imagine.'

'Justice? But why, and for what reason?'

'Oh you writers,' he said, 'you're all the same, nosing around like pigs in the humus for truffles. You're after a good story, same as the rest of them. Listen then, and I'll try to give you my explanation as to why Angélique's shade haunts the farm.

'As I told you, Mathilde was madly in love with her young Belgian lover and when she caught him, redhanded, so to speak, with her daughter, she took it very badly. Nobody knows what went on between the three of them, but the upshot was the hasty departure of the Belgian. Mathilde never mentioned his name again. God knows what life was like for Angélique. She never asked for help, although it was evident that she was bitterly unhappy.

'One night, a few months after Mathilde's lover had left, I was called out to attend Angélique who had collapsed with severe abdominal pains, diarrhoea and vomiting. I worked on her all through that devilishly long night, but, in spite of all my efforts, the poor girl died at dawn.'

'What was the cause of her death?'

'Mushroom poisoning. Her mother, that famous *cordon bleu*, one of the foremost authorities on edible mushrooms in this part of the world, had herself picked and cooked the fungi.'

'Are you saying that Mathilde Hauchecorne murdered her daughter in a fit of jealousy?'

'I'm saying nothing of the sort. You are a writer, so you must draw your own conclusions, just as I did.'

7

In Search of Proust

Much to the Baron's astonishment, I now began a series of detailed tours of Normandy. These were arranged for me by a new friend, Etienne de la Varande. Etienne and his sister, Denise, owned and ran an antiquarian bookshop called 'La Plume de Madame de Sévigné'. It contained a sensational hodge-podge of books, many of them English and valuable.

Denise was one of those duck-bottomed Frenchwomen with admirable breasts, sallow complexion, a moist forehead, lank hair and slightly gamey armpits. She was a painter of some consequence, specialising in views of Honfleur and its environs. She was devoted to her brother. Etienne was an English translator, for his passion, apart from myself, was the English language. Although his grammar was impeccable, his pronunciation was extraordinary, and when he spoke English he sounded as if he were talking through a mouthful of flannel. He was slim and wiry, with small, very intelligent green eyes, a bumpy forehead, reddish hair, and beautiful slender hands. He understood and approved my naïve, but enthusiastic approach to the *manes* of my heroes, Flaubert, Proust and the painter Boudin. Etienne and Denise shared a battered little Renault car which they had christened Rosinante, and it was in this car that I scurried about with Etienne as a guide to the more literary aspects of Normandy.

We began our tour with a visit to Rouen, which, of all others, was Flaubert's city. Etienne told me that it had had a special attraction for the Impressionist painters; that Monet had painted the Cathedral in every kind of light, while Pisarro immortalised the old rue de l'Epicerie, and Marquet enjoyed painting the quays. Ruskin, Proust's idol, had come to Rouen on his honeymoon. 'This is *the* place of North Europe, as Venice is of the South', he had written, an observation which delighted the French writers and painters who hastened to christen Rouen, 'The Venice of the North'.

1 Myself in 1935

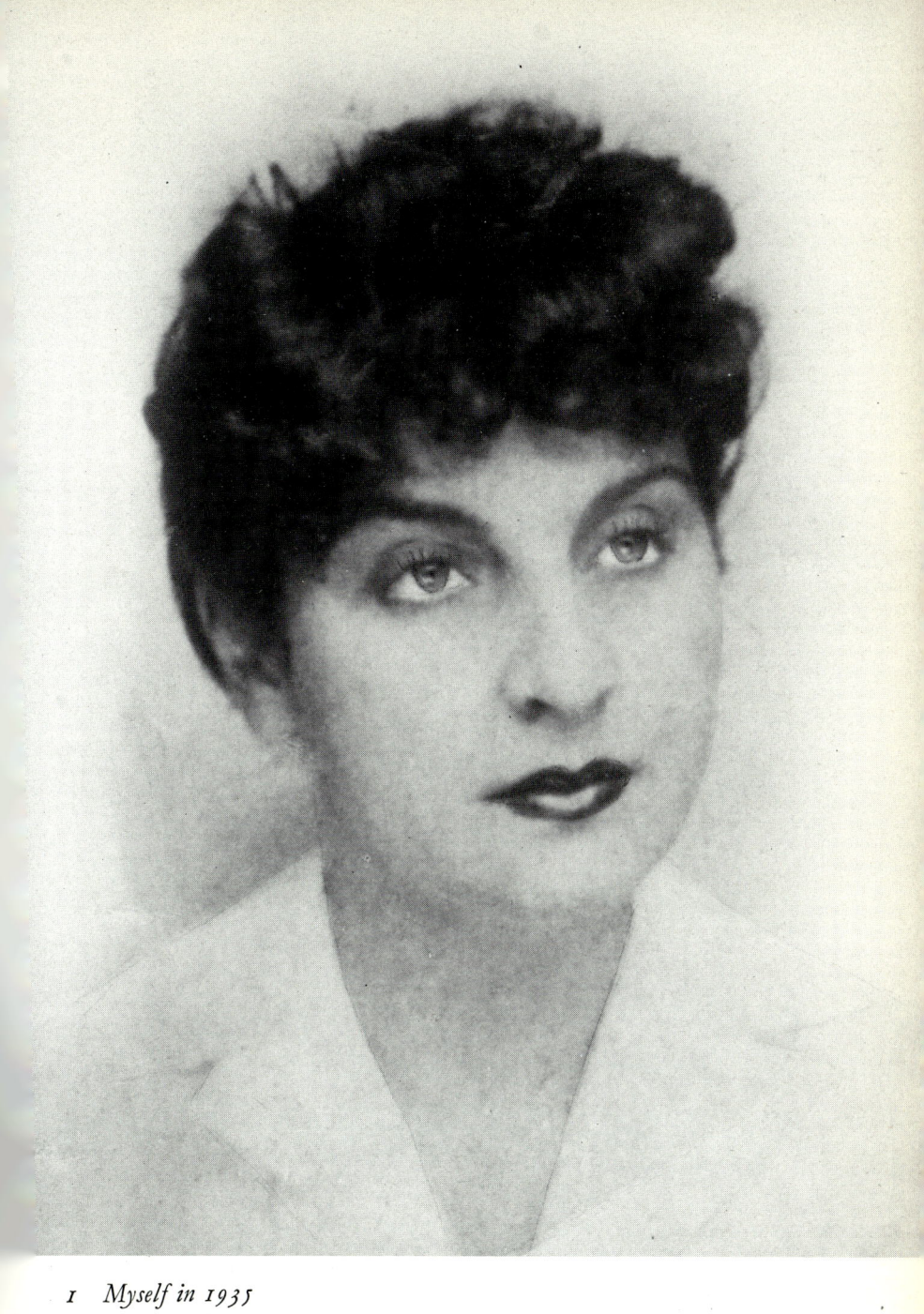

2 *Lala – my mother*

3 Géa – Georges Augsborg

4 *Colette at her desk in the Palais Royal*

I first came upon the Place de la Cathédrale from the rue du Gros-Horloge, and there before me was a vast frozen wave of stone. We went into the Cathedral by the main west door, which, according to Etienne, was the best way to appreciate to the full the magnificent simplicity of this place. He reminded me how Emma Bovary and her impatient swain, Leon, had been importuned by a fat and pompous beadle who was anxious to gain a tip by acting as their guide.... 'He pointed with his cane to a large circle of black paving-stones with no inscription or carving. "Here," he proclaimed majestically, "you see the outer casing of the lovely bell of Amboise. It weighed eighteen tons. There was not its like in All Europe. The workman who cast it died of joy."'[1]

The remains of a Gothic window is all that is left of the chapel in which the trial of Joan of Arc took place in 1431. She was canonised in 1920, and a plain railing in the Square du Vieux Marché is all that marks the place where the Maid was burnt.

It is only a few minutes' walk from there to the Hotel Dieu, the hospital of which Docteur Flaubert, Gustave's father, was Master. In the house at the end of the left wing the writer was born in 1821. I was anxious to see his house at Croisset, and I hurried back towards Rosinante, but Etienne held me back.

'Let us pretend that you are Emma and I am Leon,' he said. 'We shall make a grand tour of Rouen in a cab. Come on, it will be an experience you will never forget.'

There were a few cabs plying for hire near the square. Etienne hired one drawn by a plump white horse. Taking a copy of *Madame Bovary* from his pocket, he handed it up to the astonished cabbie. 'I've underlined the itinerary I want you to take,' he said, holding the page up under his nose. 'See, here it is in red pencil.'

The man stared at us. 'You want me to drive you to all these places? It'll cost you a fortune.'

'No matter,' said Etienne grandly, 'I am an English milord and this is my lady; we wish to go on a sentimental journey, a kind of pilgrimage of love, so *hue dia*, cabbie, let us be off'.

I leant back against the shabby seat which smelled of leather and polish, trying to imagine Emma and Leon clasped in one another's arms. Etienne lit a Gauloise, and the scent of black tobacco was

[1] *Madame Bovary* by Gustave Flaubert (Penguin. Translation by Alun Russell).

added to that of leather, manure and of my perfume, which, at that time was Guerlain's *Heure Bleue*.

The cabbie evidently thought we were mad, but was nevertheless faithfully carrying out Flaubert's printed directions. . . . We swung down the rue de Grand Pont, across the Place des Arts, along the Quai Napoleon, over the Pont Neuf, and pulled up sharply before the statue of Pierre Corneille.

By this time I was having some difficulty in controlling Etienne, who wanted to pull down the blinds and re-enact the famous love scene in the cab. What with pushing him aside, straightening my hat and trying to control my giggles, for the sight of Etienne in pursuit of love was slightly grotesque, I nearly missed the Carrefour La Fayette, and our dramatic gallop into the station yard.

By now the cabbie had got into the spirit of the game, and was out of the station, into the Drive, and trotting gently beside a screen of tall trees. Then he turned off towards the green by the waterside.

All along the river, on the pebble-paved towing path, went the fiacre, past the islands and a good way towards Oyssel. Then suddenly it switched off through Quatre Mares, Sotteville, the Grande Chaussée, the rue d'Elbœuf, and halted for the third time outside the Botanical Gardens.[1]

By this time I had had enough, and since I hadn't Emma's incentive for wanting to continue the journey, I made Etienne go back to where we had parked Rosinante. I was exhausted and felt slightly sick, but for a few moments I had experienced some of Emma's reactions as she lay gasping in the arms of her lover, 'in a carriage with drawn blinds, sealed tighter than a tomb and being buffeted about like a ship at sea'.

In the municipal library at Rouen are preserved a vast quantity of Flaubert's working notes. For *Madame Bovary* alone there are over 4,000 pages of foolscap written on both sides in the author's minute hand. Here, too, is the completed manuscript which I examined at length, page by page, as if to crack the code of Flaubert's genius.

There is nothing left of his home at Croisset but the pavilion, where, on Sundays, he watched through binoculars the faces of the

[1] *Madame Bovary, op. cit.*

bourgeois, who stared from the river-steamers hoping to catch a glimpse of the author of a scandalous book.

It was because of young Gustave's nervous illness that his father brought the property at Croisset, a few miles downstream from Rouen. It was an elegant eighteenth-century château with a garden running the length of the river, and an avenue of lime trees which perfumed the summer air with their sweet scent.

Croisset was to become Flaubert's permanent home, his hermitage, the place in which he lived out his life, and in which he finally died. Immediately after his death the house was sold by his niece and was pulled down. Only the little pavilion or summer house at the edge of the river remains; it has been turned into a Flaubert museum.

*

Etienne and Denise de la Varande lived with their old parents on the outskirts of Pennedepie. It was my first experience of life in an unpretentious country house, as opposed to a more formal existence in a château. Similar houses and families still exist throughout the length and breadth of France today. Certainly it had the charm of George Sand's house at Nohant in the Berry and, like hers, was filled with a pot-pourri of furniture in which delicate eighteenth-century pieces lived happily with others from the First Empire and from the reign of Louis-Philippe. The *salon* gave on to a terrace, reached from the garden by a double flight of wide stone steps topped by ornamental urns filled with trailing ivies and geraniums. The long room, with its original squares of shining parquet-flooring, had an engaging air of shabby elegance; the pretty eighteenth-century brocade curtains were in tatters as was much of the upholstery of the charming little *bergère* near the stone fireplace.

Tea *à l'anglaise* was served in my honour in Sèvres cups by a pink-cheeked country girl in a white apron. This was a house of contrasts. Madame de la Varande, my friends' mother, was a gentle, rather faded woman who wore loose, sack-like garments and a rusty straw hat trimmed with ruched ribbon, when she went out into the garden. Monsieur de la Varande looked like a French illustrator's idea of Mr Pickwick, with a velvet embroidered skull-cap atop his white poll.

Etienne had his own quarters in a wing of the house. His

rooms were crammed with books and papers. He slept in a monastic-like cell which contained only a narrow pallet, a chair and a table. Denise's studio was in an outbuilding in the grounds.

The only week-end I spent with the de la Varende family was memorable. Before retiring for the night we were each offered a candle in a silver candlestick. This was lighted by the *paterfamilias* as we filed past him up the staircase to our rooms.

I remember being almost hypnotised by the figures on the wall-covering, which was some kind of pastoral frolic, with lads and lasses endlessly repeating the same antics. My hypnosis was broken by the opening of a door in the wall, which was so cleverly masked by the material, that I had not realised it was there. Through this door came Etienne's respectable old father in a striped nightshirt with a woollen shawl draped round his shoulders. Behind his gold-rimmed pince-nez, his eyes were glittering with excitement.

We stared at one another in silence. My first inclination to shout for help was replaced by a wave of curiosity; so I waited to be told the object of this strange nocturnal visitation. The old man came straight to the point.

'Etienne was right when he said you were a very desirable young woman. You put me in mind of a ripe peach. But in fact I came here to allay your fears.'

'What fears?'

'This is a very old house. Filled with creaks and rustles... haunted too'—meanwhile he was coming closer and closer to my bed.

'You have very handsome slippers,' I said, sincerely admiring the *gros point* embroidery worked by Denise as a gift for her father's seventieth birthday.

'Yes,' he said, somewhat breathlessly, slipping them off to reveal a pair of puffy purple feet. He was, by now, so near that I could see the red veins in his bulbous nose, and the tight little mouth under the white moustache. By now I was furious with the old man, and when he put out a bony hand to touch me, I reared up like a snake and gave him a mighty push. I was a strong young creature and he fell over with a pitiful squeak. At that moment, Etienne, attired in a sort of monk's robe with a cord round his waist, appeared in the doorway. Somewhere, in the depths of my subconscious, I registered the unconventional attire of my nocturnal visitors. Etienne calmly helped his father to his feet, dusted him down, and, pushing him through the hidden door, locked it and took a flying leap into my bed. He did not stay long, leaving with a deep scratch—I wore my fingernails long in those days—down his cheek.

Early next morning, I was awakened by the elderly satyr's face grinning at my window. He was lodged in a large cherry tree whose branches had rapped against the panes during the night. He had been picking cherries, and, when I opened wide my casement, he handed me a *parure* of bright, large shiny cherries. To please him and show that I bore no malice, I hung them at my ears and throat. No reference whatever was made to his visit or that of his son, and my friendship with Etienne and Denise continued happily through the years.

The experience, however, ridiculous and inconclusive as it had been, did not leave me completely unscathed. Yet another illusion had been destroyed. I had always thought that old people at a certain age acquired serenity and wisdom and ceased to function sexually. As far as I was concerned, anyone over the age of forty was sexually a dead duck. I was extremely naïve and thought youth a talisman against all ills. I was not yet sufficiently aware to glimpse the grinning skull beneath the rosy skin, and although I was preoccupied with death in the most romantic, sentimental and theatrical way, being much addicted to buying death masks and meditating in cemeteries, I had no idea of the scarifying powers of its approach.

It was to take many years of tumultuous living before I could claim to have experienced the real pangs of love, jealousy or grief. Just as I have never been able to take in a diagram, a map or the instructions written on a packet, so was I unable for a long time to experience any deep feelings. As long as it took to mould and chastise my rebellious spirit, all my reactions to people and to situations were superficial and second-hand. I felt only what I thought I was expected to feel. I could identify closely with the trials and tribulations of any heroine in literature, or with any movie-star emoting in a film; but because of my inability to commit myself totally, I could not shed my inhibitions with my clothes, and cease being only a *voyeur*.

*

For a short time our activities centred round our yacht. The Baron had renamed her the *Ste Thérèse*. He was always trying to curry favour with the saints. At that time I knew very little about yachts and sailing, save that a boat was a status symbol. The *Ste Thérèse* was a good bourgeoise of a vessel. Beamy and comfortable, she was in fact a fishing-smack prettied up by the Baron. But she always seemed to me to be pining for the happy days when she had earned her keep trawling in the Icelandic fishing grounds, instead of stooging around with a crowd of cocktail-drinking landlubbers aboard.

We had a permanent crew. They were Norman fishermen who looked with deep suspicion upon the shennanigans of the owner of the *Ste Thérèse*. I cannot pretend that the Baron knew much about seamanship. He simply enjoyed the kudos of having a yacht and of dressing up in sailing gear, in an immaculate reefer, white duck trousers and peaked cap liberally besprinkled with scrambled egg. Levis and T-shirts had not appeared on our horizon.

The moment the sky darkened, or we were threatened by a slight swell, the Baron would order the captain to put back to harbour and to the safety of our *manoir*. After a suitable interval spent in my company, the Baron, his open-air life taken care of, would depart thankfully to Paris, to help the Marquise with her investments or to accompany her on her afternoon drive in the Bois in a vast hearse-like de Dion-Bouton automobile, while I was left to my own devices. It was during one of the Baron's absences that I asked Lucy to come and spend a week-end with me. Although Renaud did not approve of our friendship, I knew that she was one of the few people with whom I could be myself.

I met her at the station. She got off the Paris express looking like the splendid courtesan she was. She wore a leopard coat which set off the flaming copper bell of her hair, worn à la Rita Hayworth, whom she resembled. So high were her heels that she seemed perched on stilts. A chain of fine gold links encircled one of her slim ankles. By her side paced her magnificent collie, Frost, on a lead of gold links to match the anklet. Behind them, carrying her jewel-case, a gramophone and some records, walked Lucy's little Hungarian maid, Terka, in Hungarian peasant-costume. This colourful group was completed by an escort of porters piling a mountain of Vuitton luggage on to a barrow. As always, Lucy created quite a stir and I was relieved when I got the travelling circus into the car.

When we got home, and after Lucy had changed from her travelling ensemble to a tomato red négligée, we had 'English' tea in front of the fire in the living-room, with plum-cake from Smith's, sandwiches and piles of hot buttered toast, lavishly spread with *Patum Peperium* which Lucy adored.

Lucy was emotional, volatile, wildly extravagant and deeply sad at heart. She spent a great deal of time compiling a guide to the functions of the perfect mistress. At a time when sex was still a dirty word, she was more than explicit about extra-marital sex. She used to give me fascinating lectures on the boudoir tactics employed by the great courtesans, past and present. I listened with interest to the manifold ways of soothing a fractious lover; the correct massage for the relaxation of the benefactor, and the deep concentration needed to produce a rush of tears at the appropriate moment.

After tea I showed Lucy round the *manoir*, which she liked in every detail. We had an early night and next day I asked whether she would care to come with me to Trouville as the Baron had asked me to call in at the ship's chandlery where he had an account. I had a long list of bits and pieces wanted by the crew.

We walked along the quays bordering the river Touques. Trouville, unlike its flashy, more international neighbour, Deauville, still preserved much of the charm of the seaside town, which in the nineties had attracted so many writers and artists of note. Each year there was a migration of wealthy families from the cities to their large, ugly, turn-of-the-century houses, set in boringly well-tended gardens ablaze with red salvia, geraniums and pelargoniums. The French gardeners had little initiative, and each garden had its own green *pelouse* inset with *platebandes* of carefully dragooned plants. But Trouville had an atmosphere all of its own, an ambience of forty years before, and whenever I think about it, I see it in the autumn, limned in grey muted colours, or in the pale sunshine of spring with the figures on the pebbled beaches giving the scene the air of a Boudin painting.

I liked the chandlery with its invigorating smell of tarred rope and shelves full of shining, and to me, mysterious gadgets. Stepping into the shop from the glare of the summer sunshine almost blinded me. I closed my eyes for a moment, and when I opened them Louis de Rougemont, its owner, was standing before us. He looked like the illustrations of poor Emma Bovary's Rodolphe. Indeed, like Rodolphe, he was a member of *la petite noblesse normande*. Having spent most of his patrimony, he used what little capital remained to buy the chandlery. Louis-Charles was an attractive, virile male; within minutes of their meeting, he and Lucy were exchanging lascivious glances. It was a case of violent mutual attraction, and the strength of their desire was almost tangible. I knew the Comtesse de Rougemont was upstairs in their flat over the shop, with three of her children and that a fourth was due to be born within the month.

We drove home in almost total silence. When we reached the *manoir*, Lucy said, 'Can we have him to dinner please, pretty please?'

'He has a wife. She's heavily pregnant. They already have three little children.'

'Invite her as well.'

'Renaud will be furious.'

'Please do this for me. I love him.'

'Lucy you've only just met him.'

'That has nothing to do with it. This is the real thing. For him too. I know it. Feel here, feel my heart, it's jumping about.'

She pressed my hand against her lovely breast. Her heart did seem to be beating very fast.

'We'll have to wait until the week-end. Renaud doesn't like me to have dinner-parties without him.'

'The week-end will do very well. I've waited all my life for this man. A few days more or less won't make any odds.'

*

The dinner party proved a disaster. The Baron returned home early and was far from pleased to find Lucy installed in the guest-suite. He did not approve of the Comte de Rougemont, who, being in trade, was thoroughly déclassé. In the rarefied circle in which the Baron had his being, trade was on a par with the professions; and the family doctor and lawyer were admitted to the tables of the nobility only on rare and specific occasions—a dentist, with one notable exception, never.

The one exception was the Empress Eugénie's dentist, an American named Evans. When the news of the French defeat at

Sedan came through to Paris, a deputation from the Corps Legislatif urged the Empress to leave at once. She refused, but when the mob began rioting in the Place de la Concorde, and was joined by the National Guard, she knew the end had come.

With her reader, Madame Lebrêton, the Empress left the Tuileries and took a cab to the home of a friend. He was away. In despair, the Empress thought of her American dentist, Dr Evans. Though startled to find the Empress in his reception room, Dr Evans was equal to the occasion. He soothed her, fed her and made all the necessary arrangements for her departure. Within an hour the Empress, the dentist and Madame Lebrêton left Paris and drove to Deauville. Dr Evans and his nephew walked to Trouville harbour in search of an English yacht. They found Sir John Burgoyne in his yacht *Gazelle*, bringing his wife back to England after a prolonged holiday abroad. They were easily persuaded to take the Empress and Madame Lebrêton aboard and the yacht sailed, a few minutes past midnight. They were landed at Ryde at seven on the morning of 8 September, 1870, and left at midday via Portsmouth for Hastings to rejoin her son, the Prince Imperial, who was already in England.

My staff, too, gave trouble at my dinner-party for Lucy. Two of them were members of the crew of the *Ste Thérèse* assigned to domestic duties. They were mutinous, insisted on wearing their caps indoors, and when serving, leered down Lucy's inviting décolletage.

The Baron, who seemed to be taking a sinister pleasure in my discomfiture, sat silent and glum while we waited for Lucy to join us. The Comtesse had made little effort with her *toilette*, merely adding a sad little brooch made of authentic butterfly wings to her dowdy everyday dress. She was the daughter of a local grain-merchant and her dowry had saved her husband from bankruptcy. She had no small-talk, her teeth were bad, and she had brought her knitting.

During some uneasy preliminary small-talk, it was established, after some searchings into the genealogical branches of the Baron's family tree, that the Comte was a distant kissing cousin on the distaff side[1]; with this the atmosphere became a little less glacial. Dinner had been ordered for 8.30 p.m., but at this hour

[1] Almost anyone in France with an authentic title could find some way of claiming kinship with another title.

there was still no sign of Madame de Polnay. The Baron began to fidget and scowl. The Comtesse had almost completed knitting the sleeve of a tiny jacket.

At a quarter to nine, the sounds of a czardas on Lucy's gramophone were heard in the distance, to be followed, a few moments later, by the lady herself. Lucy held herself like an empress, white shoulders well back, small head crowning a long throat. Pausing for a second, so we could take in the full splendour of her shimmering Lanvin gown, she glided towards us, a long amber cigarette-holder in her hand.

Louis-Charles' reaction to this vision was instantaneous and embarrassing, for all of us saw with fascinated horror that he was quite unable to control his desire. Like many Frenchmen he evidently imagined that tight briefs would have been an affront to his virility.

I was furious with Lucy for making a spectacle of herself and involving us all in such a charade. I also wondered how she and Louis-Charles would get through dinner without exploding with lust. The meal was a long-drawn-out agony for us all. The food was cold, the service wretched. The Baron began to hum, a certain sign of tension. We had coffee and conversation faded away. Finally, Louis-Charles' wife began to yawn. Her husband gently pulled her to her feet and told her they were leaving. With a sweet, vacuous smile she followed him obediently into the hall, where the *valet-de-chambre* wrapped her in the cocoon of scarves and mufflers in which she had arrived.

Typically, the Baron made no mention of Lucy's immoral conduct. But, next morning, when I went in to see her, I tried to take her to task. She lay relaxed in bed in a satin bedjacket edged with swansdown which made us both sneeze. I sat curled up under a rug which lay over her feet. She looked like a large, contented white cat. She refused to listen to my admonitions and put her hands over her ears. So comic were her grimaces that in the end I began to laugh and, devoured by curiosity, gave up my role as a moralist to listen to what she had to say.

She told me that as soon as the house was quiet, she had slipped out and gone to the rendezvous fixed by Louis-Charles when he was lighting one of her cigarettes. They met by the Crucifix, which stood at the crossroads near the gates of the *manoir*. They decided to go to a *maison de passe* at Trouville, much frequented by sailors, but once they had met, they could not wait and coupled frenziedly and often in a wood on their way to the town. Lucy was nothing if not explicit.

'It was the fuck of a lifetime,' she said, sipping her coffee. 'I never felt the cold, though by that time it was freezing and I hadn't brought a wrap. I lay on a pile of damp leaves and went straight to Paradise. Louis-Charles is, as I suspected, a lover in a million, a man who uses his prick instead of words to get the message over.'

'What message?'

'That he loves me.'

I drank my coffee silently and speculatively, staring at Lucy with respect and envy. When she had finished her breakfast, she said:

'Now it's my turn to lecture you. It's all very well for you to retire from the world like Montaigne, when you have had all the experiences life can offer. But he was a man, and you are a very immature young woman. You have no right to shut yourself up with a lot of sub-human peasants who, from what you tell me, have much more fun in bed than you do. I'm worried that you might become a real recluse. Solitude can grow on people like poison ivy, you know. If this happens, think what you will have missed, what carnal experiences, what pleasures of the flesh.'

'I do have a husband,' I objected mildly.

Lucy cast here eyes heavenwards and puffed at her small black Balkan cigarette.

'Renaud is a poor lover, dear girl.'

'How would you know that?'

'Because I've been to bed with him. Don't start your moralising bit again. You know how I am. Anything in trousers will do if I am lonely.'

'But where was I?'

'Away, but does that matter?'

'I don't know, it could.'

'Come now, what about Madame la Marquise? She's a permanent fixture.'

'She's not my dearest friend.'

'Darlink,' said Lucy, sitting up and looking alarmed. 'Sometimes you sound like a character out of an Angela Brazil book.

Stop being sentimental. You *think* you should feel injured, therefore you will now act out the role of the injured party, and in so doing you may, perhaps, seriously damage our relationship.

'I may seem to you to be out of an Angela Brazil book,' I said, 'but you are a character straight out of *Les Liaisons Dangereuses*.'

'Take that martyred look off your dear little face and come here and give me kiss.'

I uncurled myself from my rug and lay down beside her, burying my face in the ruffle of swansdown round her neck. In the wild attack of sneezing that followed, I temporarily forgot that my best friend had cuckolded me with my husband. When I had wiped my face and composed myself, she said: 'I've thought a great deal about your sex education. I've brought you a copy of the Khama-Sutra and also one of *L'Amant de Lady Chatterley*. In French it is hilarious.'

'But Lucy, we don't have any tame gamekeepers around here.'

'Invent one. What about your friend Etienne, the defrocked monk?'

'He was not defrocked. He simply decided he did not have a true vocation. Much as I like him, he's not exactly Gary Cooper's double. He reminds me of the "Dong with the Luminous Nose".'

Lucy roared with laughter. 'That's the best part of my English education. I know my Lear. If Etienne's nose is any indication of the size of his dong, you'd be far better off than you are now.'

She was joking, but I knew what the real message was. Hurry, before life passes you by. I had never experienced physical passion and I knew that there was a whole gamut of sensations of which I was totally unaware. I realised, too, that there were twists and turns of human behaviour to which I had no clue. I began to look around with a more searching gaze and the moment I probed beneath the surface, I discovered that many of my friends had curious sexual appetites and habits, and that relationships I had imagined to be normal and harmonious, were, in fact, complicated, tortuous and strange.

*

It was Serge Cheremeteff who first opened the cupboard in which dangled his particular skeleton; but, when he discovered that I could never share his passion for the whip and the rod, he banged the door shut again. The impact of this Russian grandee's larger-than-life personality was tremendous and lasting. He adopted me and I became his spiritual child. He was the first of the blessed angels, who at certain flashpoints in my life were sent to direct me. I owe him much.

Serge had spent many holidays in England, staying with various royal relations. He was completely captivated by the British way of life, and used to say, 'The French for *l'amour*, but the British for comfortable sofas.'

He had been bidden to tea at Windsor Castle by Queen Victoria, whose tiny stature and pouched cheeks had astonished him as much as the regal air and dignity which, he said, set her apart from everyone else in the world. 'She was a Queen in the great tradition,' he told me. At a later date he went to luncheon with the Empress Eugénie at Farnborough, and said that though she retained traces of great beauty, '*elle était froide*', and was to him entirely devoid of sexual attraction.

Sergei had certainly knocked around the world. He had travelled widely when he was in the Russian Navy, from which he retired under a slight cloud connected with a 'stupid' little incident, involving a deck-hand who had sustained severe injuries after a prolonged beating with a knout. From his naval days, Sergei had retained the habit of wearing trousers with a buttoned front-flap like those of a child's combinations or of a Regency buck's pantaloons, and a peculiar and not very attractive way of cutting his nails straight across.

The man who was to teach me all I know about pictures, furniture, china, glass and silver was a walking encyclopaedia. He read widely and voraciously and had total recall. He was never at a loss for a date or a provenance, and it was he who taught me to extract the maximum of pleasure from a museum, art-gallery or exhibition. He did not subscribe to the *rubberneck* method of trying to take in everything at once. The only way to enjoy art, he maintained, was to be selfishly selective. 'Go and look at one painting only when you visit an art gallery or museum. Study it well and try to enter into the spirit of the age in which it was painted.' He taught me to associate fine craftsmanship with the social and economic climate of the past. 'A beautiful object,' he said, 'is a message of love and respect from one century to another.'

Sergei made me aware of history. He made me see it as a fast-flowing river that went on into infinity. 'There are no breaks in history,' he would say; 'one century melds smoothly into another. Look at me. My great-great-great grandfather was Ambassador at the Court of the Sun King; but when the Emperor Napoleon foolishly invaded Russia, some of my uncles fought him by the side of the Czar.'

Sergei tutored me. Sometimes we would go to a museum or take a walk through Paris, which he knew as intimately as any French historian. He had a mania for accuracy and insisted I carry a small notebook in which I had to check and re-check my notes to make certain I had taken down the correct information.

We shared a passion for Josephine and Malmaison; for Marie-Antoinette and the Trianon. It was the young Queen's new toy, a gift from her fat, besotted husband. The stolid Louis XVI is reported to have said to his wife, 'You are fond of flowers, Madame, so I have a bouquet to offer you. It is the *Petit Trianon*.'

Sergei was interested in gardens, and in fashions and styles of gardening through the centuries. We did a course together, in which we discovered some fascinating facts. It seemed that a fashion imported from England had seduced the French away from the stylised garden that the genius of the *grand siècle* had brought to perfection. This was the 'return to nature', a protest against stiff formal French gardens. French visitors to Stowe Park sang the praises of an irregular layout, instead of the 'combed and brushed' appearance and laboured designs of the French flower-beds.

The architect of Kew Gardens, Sir William Chambers, added to the general confusion by writing a learned work, *A Dissertation on Oriental Gardening*, in which he summed up his recollections of his voyage to China, and his observations on the superiority of Chinese gardens over those of the Europeans. But nothing equalled the influence of the observations of Walpole and the Prince de Ligne, who, between them, had made a detailed study of every important garden in Europe.

At the time I first met Count Cheremeteff, he was almost penniless. He lived by tutoring the children of the wealthy, by playing bridge, and by escorting the wives and widows of millionaires to theatres and exhibitions.

One day Sergei decided that the story of his life should be

written. He chose me as his biographer and I was puffed up with pride at this honour. The saga began in our Paris flat. At two o'clock sharp, Sergei would arrive and install his great bulk comfortably in a large chair in the library. I would sit opposite, notebook and pencil at the ready.

At first he smoked incessantly and great clouds of cheap 'black' tobacco would float around, irritating my eyes and throat so that I streamed and coughed so much he had to stop dictating. Finally, to give his hands alternative occupation, I offered, rather timidly, to teach him to knit. To my surprise, he accepted with alacrity; and this enormous man, with the face of a Mongolian warrior, would sit happily knitting away like mad.

During our sessions, I learned a great deal about Sergei. A born survivor, he had enough will-power to surmount all obstacles. He summoned up for me a vivid account of life in pre-revolutionary Russia; a nostalgic exercise which sometimes veiled his slant, toffee-coloured eyes with tears. His family used to own so many estates, palaces, town-houses, farms and serfs, that he could not remember how many souls had belonged to them.

His favourite home was the Cheremeteff Palace in St Petersburg. Originally a one-storeyed wooden house, built by his ancestor, Count Boris Petrovitch Cheremeteff who made Russian history by capturing the fortress dominating the junction of the Neva and Lake Ladoga, it became an enchanting baroque palace after the marriage of Count Boris' second son to an immensely wealthy heiress. The talented architect Savva Chevakinsky designed it, with white stucco ornamentation on a yellow ground, and a green roof. The central pediment of the portico displayed the family emblem: a pair of lions holding palm branches in their jaws.

With the help of illustrated books borrowed from private libraries, my tutor took me on a tour of the St Petersburg of his youth, reconstructing on a map the position of many palaces which form the architectural heritage of Leningrad.

Sergei had a special attachment to the Winter Palace; so vivid and explicit were his descriptions of the great rooms there that there were times when I felt I had actually 'seen' the marvels he described, such as the Malachite Room with its most fantastic ornament, a bowl supported by winged figures in gilded bronze.

Sergei was closely related to the Russian Imperial family, and though he had spent much of his youth in various palaces, he was brought up in the same Spartan fashion as his royal cousins, being made to crack the ice in their basins to wash in icy water, and spending much of the winter months lamenting over painfully chilblained fingers and toes.

The State rooms in most palaces were, said Sergei, both draughty and uncomfortable. Meals served in the great dining-halls generally arrived stone-cold after their long journey from the kitchens, situated in the lower regions. In one palace, Sergei said, the dishes travelled *en fourgon*, by miniature railway from one end of the palace to the dining-hall. Once state occasions were over, the family returned thankfully to their over-decorated private rooms, crammed with bibelots, keepsakes and family photographs. The style of interior decoration inaugurated by Queen Victoria was much admired and copied by other reigning monarchs.

Sergei was an authority on the life and times of Catherine the Great. This curious, many-faceted woman fascinated him and he often said he would have given many years of his life to have been a part of the literary and artistic circle she gathered round her at the Hermitage. Another of his passions was centred around the military strategists of the past. He made me read Clausewitz so I could understand the war-games we played on the floor; first with chessmen, later with lead soldiers.

It was a long time before he could bring himself to tell me anything about his escape from Russia. At one point, he had been made Military Governor of Volynia; eventually, having escaped capture at the hands of the Bolsheviks, he had got himself to France, following after his wife and son. The torments and tragedies undergone by Countess Cheremeteff had driven her out of her mind, and some time after she reached Paris she was confined to an asylum. Although she rarely recognised her husband, he visited her every week, returning greatly saddened by these fruitless pilgrimages, particularly on one occasion when he found his wife undergoing treatment during which, he said, she howled like a Siberian wolf in a trap.

My friend was reticent about the state of his finances. I knew he had fled Russia without a rouble; I also knew his family had links, not only with the British Royal Family, but with most

European royalty. However, Sergei did not seem to benefit from any handouts, royal or otherwise. He barely kept himself in pocket money by giving lessons; but he did not lack for princely hospitality and was constantly courted and entertained by the *gratin* of Paris, who considered it an honour and a privilege to have as a permanent dinner guest this cultivated and amusing descendant of the Czars.

Sergei was seldom free at week-ends, many of which he spent at that miracle of sixteenth-century beauty, the Château de Villandry. Whenever he did have time he would come down to me at the *manoir* in Normandy, where he scared my young housemaids out of their wits. Rising early, when they were making up the fires, he would literally catch them bending. He would whisk up their skirts—peasant girls seldom bothered to wear knickers—and in a state of great excitement would slap their pretty, rosy bare bottoms. I ignored all complaints until one day he chased one of my guests round the living-room until her screams brought the whole household rushing to her rescue. I was extremely vexed with my Russian friend, and not only read him the riot act but I had him moved from the guest wing to the little spare room next to my bathroom. The first night he spent there, I was awakened by an almighty bang. Rushing out on to the landing, I found that my burly Boyar had managed to crash right through the delicate little spiral staircase, scheduled in the guidebooks as one of the finest in the province.

Sergei was penitent. His excuse was that having been unable to sleep, he had decided to creep downstairs to the library to look up the etymology of a word we had been discussing. So potent was his charm, and so great his influence over me, that I spent the rest of the night huddled up in a chair, listening to Sergei discoursing on the Encylopédistes.

*

When the Baron was away, my life in Normandy assumed the rhythm and routine that is important to a creative human being. I needed to establish a regular pattern of daily life to give myself the illusion of permanence, but this routine was, in effect, merely a paper hoop through which I crashed whenever the rebellious mechanism inside me called for immediate action and release.

My life with my husband could hardly have been termed

satisfactory. Our relationship had no real roots. He went his way while I remained static, a prisoner of my own inability to come to terms with the situation. So I sought satisfaction in material things. I collected furniture, little boxes, bibelots, books and I grew more and more to rely on my literary expeditions, my 'pilgrimages', as Etienne called them, to fill the void in my heart.

❈

Marcel Proust was quite young when he was first taken to spend his holidays on the sea-coast of Normandy, for which he was to form so deep an attachment. The Proust family generally stayed at the Hotel des Roches Noires at Trouville, overlooking the Chemin des Planches, the famous boardwalk on which Lucy and I had often exercised her 'Frost', while holidaymakers took pleasures in the sight of an eccentric member of the Fitz-James family giving his pet duck an airing. The amiable little creature, on her blue silk lead, seemed quite content to waddle behind her master.

In 1881, in his twentieth year, Proust stayed with Madame Baignières at her villa, Les Frémonts, on the heights above Trouville. This house was eventually transmogrified in his work into La Raspèlière, and was the original of the property let to Madame de Verdurin by Madame de Cambremer.

Les Fréments, which we visited, was famous for its three views: one overlooking the Channel, the second embracing the coastline, while the third commanded a great sweep of woods and orchards. It was during these holidays that Jacques-Emile Blanche sketched the young man for the well-known portrait with the orchid. Blanche completed the painting in a studio in the luxurious asylum which his father ran in the former Paris home of the Princesse de Lamballe. In a wing of this same house Guy de Maupassant was being treated for the syphilitic disorder which was to deprive him of his reason, and finally his life.

One of Etienne's most treasured possessions was an early *Guide Bleu* of Normandy, with maps, one of which showed the environs of Trouville, and marked some of the splendid houses occupied by Proust's grand friends, some of whom were to be melded and metamorphosed into the protagonists in his vast work.

In 1852 Madame Straus, one of Proust's closest friends, rented

Le Manoir de La Cour Brulée, where Proust stayed and met again the girl who was the original of Albertine, Marie Finaly, whose sea-green eyes reminded him of Baudelaire's phrase, 'J'aime de vos long yeux la lumière verdatre.'

But it was in Cabourg, Proust's Balbec, that I came closest to understanding the transformations from reality to the printed page by this strange man whose writing was so powerful and so evocative that it enabled one to relive the sights, sounds and sensations he had experienced in his journey into the past.

Balbec is, in fact, a composite of Trouville, Dieppe, le Tréport and the newly-developed Cabourg—one of the fashionable seaside resorts created by speculators of the Second Empire. Proust's first visit to Balbec was with his grandmother, when he was recovering from his heart-shattering love affair with Gilberte Swann, which, though it had been over for two years, still tortured him.

They left Paris by the train of which Proust wrote:

> And so we were simply to leave Paris by that one twenty-two train which I had too often beguiled myself by looking at in the railway time-table, where its itinerary never failed to give me the emotion, almost the illusion of starting by it, not to feel that I already knew it.[1]

At Mésidon (the Doncières of his book) he would change trains, waving an amused farewell to the Paris express that thundered on its way to Cherbourg and a tender greeting to the little local train that linked Mesidon to Cabourg and Deauville-Trouville. This was the original of the 'little train' taken by the Narrator and Albertine.

The Cabourg of Proust's day was laid out in a semicircular plan, with the Grand Hotel and adjoining Casino as the focus of interest for the guests who enjoyed sitting in the glassed-in dining-room from which Proust saw his frieze of young girls on the beach.

> At night, hidden springs of electricity flooding the great dining-room with light, it became, as it were, an immense and wonderful aquarium against whose wall of glass the working

---

[1] *Within a Budding Grove,* Part I, by Marcel Proust. (Translated by C. K. Scott Moncrieff. Chatto & Windus.)

population of Balbec, the fishermen and also the tradesmen's families, clustering invisibly in the outer darkness, pressed their faces to watch, gently floating upon the golden eddies within, the luxurious life of its occupants, a thing as extraordinary to the poor as the life of strange fishes or molluscs (an important social question this; whether the wall of glass will always protect the wonderful creatures at their feasting, whether the obscure folk who watched them hungrily out of the night will not break in some day to gather them from their aquarium and devour them?).[1]

It was Etienne's and my good fortune to have an introduction to a former chambermaid of the Grand Hotel. This good lady now owned and ran a *bureau de tabac*, given by a grateful government to a war-widow of World War I. Madame Royer vividly remembered Proust's visit to the hotel in early August 1914.

He arrived with the faithful Celeste Albaret, his maid, and a gormless Swedish valet called Ernest. Proust always carried *all* his manuscripts around with him in a battered, but solid, old cardboard suitcase protected by a fawn cover. This valise was never out of his sight.

In his baggage were two alpaca overcoats which had been specially tailored for him to wear at the seaside. The grey-white coat was lightweight and had a violet lining, the other was brown. Each coat had a round, matching hat. Proust was a creature of habit and felt insecure if he could not adhere to every detail of the routine he had laid down for himself. Each summer he booked the same accommodation. This consisted of a three-room suite, No. 137 on the top floor, facing the sea. Above these rooms was a terrace which was declared out-of-bounds to other guests during Proust's stay, as he could not bear the idea of anyone walking about over his head. Each of the three rooms had its own bath. Proust's own room, according to Celeste, was very ordinary and furnished with a bed, a few armchairs, and the tables on which were piled his books and manuscripts. From his windows he had a good view of the sea.

Madame Royer remembered seeing Celeste preparing the great man's special brew of strong coffee each morning in the pantry at the end of the corridor. He spent most of the day in bed and

[1] Ibid.

was seldom seen in the hotel, though he was very popular with the staff, as he tipped generously.

Sometimes he walked slowly along the terrace outside the hotel, weighed down by the lightest of his overcoats. The ravages of his illness and the knowledge that every moment of his life was precious if he were to finish his work had so altered his appearance that his looks shocked the friends who had known him first when Jacques-Emile Blanche painted him in the debonair freshness of early manhood. Colette, meeting him in the Ritz Hotel in Paris (where he lived during the Great War), wrote:

> His agitation and his pallor seemed to be the result of some terrible inner force. . . . Dressed in tails, standing in his timidly lighted hallway, at the heart of a darkened Paris, Marcel Proust greeted me with faltering gaiety. Over his evening dress he was wearing an unfastened cape. The expression of the white, crumpled shirt front, and the convulsions of his tie, terrified me as much as the black marks under his eyes and around his mouth, the sooty, telltale traces that an absent-minded malady had smeared haphazardly across his face. . . .'[1]

[1] *Belles Saisons* by Colette.

8

Sergei and the Babuskas

When Sergei sent me a *pneumatique* cancelling my lesson because he had a cold which he did not want to pass on to me, I did not worry; but when ten days passed without news of him, I realised with dismay that I had never bothered to find out where he lived. Finally, by dint of ringing around I managed to obtain his address. I was not given his phone number. It did not occur to me that he might not have a telephone at his disposal.

I decided to visit my tutor. It was a spring day and I bounded happily down the stairs and into the street, where I sniffed up the smell of Paris, a compound of *tabac noir*, freshly baked bread and expensive perfume. I fairly danced along the pavements, because Paris was so beautiful and I was young, and thought love was around every corner. On my way to the cab rank by the Brasserie Lipp I bought a bunch of freesias, and a box of chocolate caramels which I knew Sergei liked.

By the time I reached his ugly modern suburb, asprawl with bleak grey high-rise matchbox dwellings, I began feeling depressed; and when I walked through a dirty hall, jammed with pushchairs awash with litter, and climbed a bare concrete staircase—the lift was out of order—I began to wish I had never come.

His address was 'third floor, apartment 607'. Beside a flimsy door with a half-panel of cheap frosted glass was a card listing three Russian names. One of them was that of my tutor. I rang the bell and a tinkling chime echoed behind the door.

After much rattling of bolts, it was opened and I found myself eyeball-to-eyeball with a gaunt middle-aged woman with bright cheeks as red as polished apples and coarse black hair pulled back from her low forehead in a bun. She wore a white, peasant-type blouse with a drawstring neck, a long grey skirt of some thick material, and was huddled in a grey shawl. She looked like the biggest of a set of wooden Babuska dolls from Russia which had enchanted me in childhood.

I asked if I might see Colonel Cheremeteff. She looked disapprovingly at my pretty, fashionable clothes, at my flowers, and pink parcel tied with gold string and, stiffly nodding her head, took me into a tiny stuffy room which seemed to be filled entirely by a round table strewn with scissors, sewing-silks, tracing-paper, and pieces of exquisitely embroidered materials. These, I saw, were to cover the plump little cushions piled on the floor. Sitting hunched over her work at the table, was an exact replica of the Russian doll-woman who had admitted me to the flat. Babuska No. 2 wore steel-rimmed spectacles, and when she took them off to stare at me, her eyes, red-rimmed from close work, were as inimical as her sister's.

Once again I asked politely if I might see my ailing friend. This time I was escorted through the flat, and out of the back door, on to another landing and up a narrow flight of dirty stairs to a tiny, top floor boxroom.

There, on a camp bed, covered by a grey army blanket, lay a grandson of a Czar of all the Russias. Sergei had been very ill with double pneumonia. He was still so ill that the two Babuskas had to feed him like a baby.

My visit disturbed him deeply. Not because I was witness to the poverty in which he lived; not because I had stumbled on the ladies whom he euphemistically called his 'bankers'; but because he was unable to receive me upstanding on his home ground. He was far too proud a grand seigneur to try to disguise or apologise for his lifestyle; but I was embarrassed by the curtained orange-box which did duty as a night table, and the thin mattress on which lay the gaunt and wasted body of my old friend. But his cotton nightshirt and thick cotton sheets were immaculate. On the walls were framed, signed photographs of members of the Imperial family, and a tiny golden flame burned steadily before an icon of the Black Virgin of Kazan hanging in a corner.

At a snap of his fingers the ladies sullenly glided away and left us alone. We did not talk much. Sergei held my hand tightly. His spatulate, powerful fingers were now so thin that his signet ring kept slipping off. After a while, Babuska No. 1 came in with my freesias in a vase. She did not look very pleased.

Sergei said, 'Poor Tania, she looks so very unattractive when she is annoyed.'

'Has my visit upset her?'

'Undoubtedly. I told her you were an elderly Englishwoman with pince-nez. A bag of bones, I think I said.'

'You do tell the most terrible lies,' I said severely.

His sad, narrow eyes crinkled as they always did when he was amused. He squeezed my hand so hard that I cried out.

'They are little white lies, Douska, and they alone make my survival possible.'

He was, I am sure, referring to the string of middle-aged and elderly ladies to whom he owed so much. He gave them advice, companionship, and shining nuggets from his conversational treasure, in return for which they fed him, clothed and gave him pocket-money. He never made the mistake of letting any of his 'bankers' meet, and was thus able to give each and every one of his ladies the impression that she, and she alone, was the most brilliant and fascinating creature he had ever encountered.

Very much later I learned that the Babuskas adored him, and were happy to work themselves to the bone to give him some of the comforts he was unable to provide for himself. Secretly, each Babuska thought herself the favourite. Sergei was fond of them and deeply grateful for all they did for him, but, if he was alone with them for too long, they got on his nerves, and he was delighted to get away.

His wife's death, although he had given up all hope of her recovery, devastated him. But after a long period of mourning, some time after he had recovered from his bout of pneumonia, he decided it would be sensible to 'settle' down and bestow the gift of his person and of his ancient name on the wealthiest of his patrons. He and I made out an impressive list together, and quite seriously rehearsed the way in which he would ask for the hand of his future Countess. It was quite an effort for him to kneel down, for he had convalesced and been coddled for so long after his illness that he had become quite portly again, and I feared for his trousers, which were tightly stretched across his stout buttocks.

Having lowered himself on to the carpet, he laid his hand on the region of his heart, and in a voice roughened by emotion, invited me to share his exile, and the great and noble name he had the honour to bear. It was an impressive performance, and I was sure that few women would be able to refuse the advantages which he claimed such a union would bring them. I was wrong. Six out of eight of Sergei's ladies refused him out of hand. Four were grass widows and referred him to their husbands, who enjoyed the joke; of the two who accepted, one had doubts and fled the country immediately in the *Ile de France*, never to return.

Among his other talents, Sergei was a brilliant if eccentric bridge-player. The last candidate, who had long been madly in love with him, had been his most regular partner. She married him instantly, almost before he realised he would have to lose the Babuskas, and that a wife as wealthy as his would claim her pound of flesh, as and when she wanted it. In the event it proved a very happy marriage. His wife took good care of him, and his last years were comfortable and full of interest.

It was Sergei who introduced me to the legendary Moura Budberg. Born Marie Zakrevskaia, daughter of a Russian senator and landowner, she married von Benckendoroff in 1911 when he was at the Russian Embassy in London. He was shot by the Bolsheviks, and later she married Baron Von Budberg, whom she divorced a year later.

Sergei brought Moura to our flat. At that time she must have been in her early fifties, a tall woman with a commanding presence, beautiful slim legs and a smile of extraordinary sweetness. Moura took me under her wing, and sensing I was lonely, introduced me to her coterie of amusing and stimulating friends, among whom were Violet Trefusis and Louis Bromfield, the American author who lived near Paris.

Moura and I became good friends and continued to correspond through the years. Whenever I came to London, my first telephone call would be to Moura. During all the years I knew her, she changed very little. She became a trifle heavier, and her grey hair that she blued took on a deeper cerulean hue. She never wore a hat. Instead, she tied around her head a chic little veil which became her well.

She was always encumbered by an enormous reticule from which she refused to be parted. Once I asked her if I might make an inventory of its contents. We unpacked the bag together and I think she was as surprised as I to find it contained the following items: A bunch of letters, six rather crumpled invitation cards, two manuscripts, a book and its half-finished translation, a large day-to-day diary, a shabby address book bulging with scribbled sheets of names and addresses; a leather photograph frame containing pictures of her children and grandchildren; a leaking fountain-pen, seven coloured pencils, a bunch of holy medals secured by a safety-pin, keys, three boxes of National Health pills, two spectacle cases (one empty), a pair of nail scissors, a powder-compact, comb and lipstick, a box of cough lozenges, a magnifying glass, and, inexplicably, a small carved camel from a child's Noah's Ark.

Moura seldom mentioned her financial problems, though right until the end of her life, she worked very hard indeed. For a long time she was Sir Alexander Korda's chief reader. She was on terms of the warmest friendship with her boss, with his wife and with the stars, producers and directors of his films. She was particularly attached to Laurence Olivier and to Vivien Leigh.

She read voraciously in a number of languages, and kept abreast of all the new works published in France, Italy, Germany and Russia. She translated many works from Russian into English. Her flat was awash with manuscripts, books, papers and letters, and she kept a selection of letters from close friends such as Sir Robert Bruce-Lockhart, Maxim Gorki, H. G. Wells and many others, tied up with pink tape on a shelf above her bed.

She was the soul of discretion, and although she was often hard pressed for money, and had what amounted to a blank cheque from a number of publishers to write her memoirs, she refused to contemplate publishing such a book, which, while it would have alleviated her financial situation, might, she felt, distress the wives and families of some of the men with whom she had been closely associated.

Moura died in 1974 and is still mourned by a remarkably varied cross-section of people, all of whom believed themselves to be her closest friend. In fact, she was an enigmatic personage who very rarely revealed herself to anyone. She never seemed to push her own ideas, but was, somehow, at the centre of a brilliant and interesting circle, intellectual, artistic and diplomatic, a salon over which she presided for many years in a large flat in Ennismore Gardens.

A drink *chez* Moura was an unforgettable experience, partly because she was generally so busy talking long-distance on the telephone that she had no time to introduce her guests to one another. So anyone, not on the international network, might miss the opportunity of exchanging merry badinage with Noël Coward, J. B. Priestley or a visiting Hollywood star.

Moura was not a name-dropper; she simply believed it quite normal to be on terms of affectionate intimacy with many of the famous people of our time. Once when I was visiting her, I sat fiddling with a little pleated paper fan lying on a coffee table by the sofa on which I was sitting. Having waved the fan to and fro several times, I noticed it was decorated in pen and ink with Picasso-type minute sketches.

'It looks as if Picasso had had a hand in this,' I said jokingly.

Moura contemplated me with a tranquil blue-grey gaze.

'Pablo made the fan for me last week-end when I was staying with him. It was terribly hot, you know.'

It is difficult to analyse the secret of Moura's influence on the intellectual life of our time on both sides of the Atlantic. Certainly she had a luminous intelligence and was the ideal catalyst. Her brilliance lay in being a perfect listener, and in gathering together people who used her as a sounding-board and intermediary.

Her only fault, in my experience, was her filing system. This operated on the deep-litter principle, so that any manuscript I sent her, generally at her urgent request, was buried beneath a general avalanche of papers, never more to see the light of day.

I helped Moura move from the spacious flat in Ennismore Gardens to a smaller one in Cromwell Road in the same building that housed her good friends, C. P. Snow and his wife, Pamela Hansford Johnson. Here Moura set up the whole familiar scene again in the same decor; identical furniture, cushions, pictures, tiny silver bibelots on the mantelpiece, down to the small round table on which reposed a bottle of gin and a bottle of orange squash, together with a plate of mummified cheesy biscuits.

However, sadly, some of the sparkle of the old ambience had vanished in transit, and it took Moura and her coterie time to adapt to the new place. Furthermore, Moura was frequently unwell, though she bravely concealed her ill-health and her fatigue. She continued to work as a film adviser and translator until the end of her life. Her going was the end of an era, for with her death the doors of London's last literary salon closed for ever.

9

Ex Africa Semper Aliquid Novi

During the early and most troubled stages of my marriage, I never mentioned my difficulties to Lala, my mother, for fear she should inform that stern grey man, my father, that his unwillingness to let me marry the Baron had been more than justified by his subsequent behaviour.

Lala and I both knew that Papa was seldom right in his hunches about people we liked, for he was not noted for his sensitivity in regard to human relations; relying rather on certain fundamental old-fashioned precepts and guidelines laid down by convention. His reactions to most situations that affected his children were predictably paternalistic and I was well aware of the fact that if Lala, in an effort to rescue me, told him my marriage had foundered, he might well explode into one of the horrific rages we likened to a *bombe Alaska*, because of its boiling exterior and icy centre.

Yet, as always, Lala's maternal antennae sensed that all was not well with her rebellious child, and, without consulting me, she booked my passage home as a surprise for my birthday in April 1936. When told of this splendid treat in store for me, Papa astonished her by piping his eye and saying he had missed me. He added, however, that he did not think it right that a young wife should absent herself from her husband so early in their married life, and there was no knowing what pranks I might get up to without a guiding hand to stay me.

Nor did the Baron take at all kindly to my plans for a long holiday without him. While he never actually translated his fears and doubts about my leaving him into words, he was still sufficiently enamoured of me to be concerned as to how I might react at having my shackles removed even temporarily. To do him justice, I believe he appreciated the frustration, misery and disappointment bubbling within me at the failure of our relationship, without realising the true origins of the cataclysm that had demolished the foundations of our marriage.

With his usual courtesy he accepted my departure and escorted me to the station and saw me comfortably installed in my reserved seat in the *Flêche d'Or*, where I found magazines, chocolates and a bunch of Parma violets which were, he knew, my favourite flower.

*

We sailed into Cape Town harbour on a morning of limpid beauty, and there, snuggled under the great flat mountain, was the tiny settlement Jan van Riebeeck had founded. Not for the first time I wept at the sight of my native land; and my tears flowed even more freely when I discovered that Lala and Papa had come to meet me, not only to welcome me, but to set the seal of respectability on my coming home alone.

Papa looked greyer and older. His great, noble Cyrano-like nose almost devoured the lean sallow face which was akin to the visages of the ancient Hebrew patriarchs I had seen so often in the biblical pictures in some of my children's books. Only the luxuriant beard was missing. Papa was clean-shaven and as immaculate and finicky in his dress as any follower of Beau Brummell.

He wore always, winter and summer alike, silk combinations made specially for him in Paris and shirts of a dazzling whiteness: he had been known to give the rough side of his tongue to our old African laundress if his cuffs and collars were not starched exactly as he ordered. His grey suits—he always wore grey, except in high summer—were of the best material available. His spats matched the pearl grey of his Fedora hat; in summer the only concessions he made to the change in temperature were a straw boater and canvas spats.

Lala was prettier, and more exotic-looking, than ever. Her hair was dyed an improbable shade to match her long nails, she said, rippling with laughter, but the great lustrous eyes she fixed on me were anxious. Immediately I felt secure, safe in the charmed circle of my childhood. With Lala to keep guard, nothing could hurt me. This mood of euphoria lasted for some hours while we sat talking in my parents' suite in the Mount Nelson Hotel, drinking pints of fresh orange juice, and exchanging family news.

The Mount Nelson Hotel in Capetown was a permanent monument to the comfortable, colonial, lavish way of life. As an hotel it was the embodiment of the 'British Raj', designed and built to house visitors to the Cape, and for the descendants of the pioneers and randlords who had struck it rich in the early days. Known affectionately by its patrons and to travellers from all parts of the globe as the 'Mount Nellie', this great rambling caravanserai, redolent of a particular kind of polish used on the stoeps, and set amidst gardens of surpassing beauty, was a landmark and a refuge to those returning to their native land.

After a week of excursions and visits to friends who lived in and around Cape Town, we took the Blue Train back to Johannesburg. Most descriptions of my home town are of a rash, brash, boom town grown too big too fast; a city built on gold, rich in material advantages, yet spiritually bankrupt, a playground for the wealthy and a ghetto for the Africans who live and work there.

I have different memories of the Johannesburg of my youth; of a small town perpetually bathed in sunlight. When I was little I was surrounded with smiling faces, white and dark; each shop was a cavern filled with treasures, with all the tradespeople paying special attention to the needs of the young who come shopping with their parents. There was a sense of community, of cosiness. Everyone knew everyone else.

When I returned, a vast new city had been imposed on my little town which had completely lost its identity. It took me some time to reorientate myself, and to recreate the place as I had first known it when I was small, with its corrugated tin roofs and dusty streets petering out into the veld.

Now, everything was bigger and more imposing. Johannesburg had become Americanised, and life in the upper strata was like that lived in contemporary Los Angeles or Hollywood. Everyone had a swimming-pool, dozens of servants and large, fast cars; the most popular pastimes of the day, apart from money matters, polo, going to the movies, and nude bathing-parties, were weekends in the country.

It had become fashionable to own a week-end estate in which officially exhausted businessmen could relax while their wives enjoyed the beauties of nature. In fact, the majority of these weekend parties were merely an excuse for prolonged drinking-sessions and a good deal of sleeping around. Wife-swopping was the order of the day; but by Monday the couples had sorted themselves out again, and everyone returned home much exhilarated by the 'simple' life and by their change of partner.

Johannesburg had certainly grown and evolved, but my friends were, as always, hospitable, welcoming, kind and generous, like most South Africans. My return to the fold made me realise how much I had missed my family and friends, and what a false, unreal life I had been living with the Baron. Yet, in spite of my joy at being fêted as the prodigal returned, I was always conscious that sooner or later I should have to go back to the ancient parapets of Europe, and that it would be impossible for me to sever my connection with France. I knew that this voyage home was merely an interval, a much-needed breathing space, a holiday in the sun which would have to be accounted for later on.

In the meantime, I slipped back into the life I had led before my marriage, secure, luxurious and pampered. I had tea at the Country Club, with its velvety lawns down which my contemporaries and I had rolled at every children's party given in this enchanted spot.

White-clad Indian waiters served me with China tea, and incomparable fig-preserve, which had the same effect on my memory as the famous madeleine dipped in tea had upon that of Proust. At week-ends, when I was not staying with friends, I went to watch handsome, well-groomed men, many of them employed by Anglo-American, playing polo.

I had left Johannesburg as a plump, bookish young girl, who did not really stir the pulses of any of the eligible bachelors my father would have liked me to marry. I returned, a slim, elegant married woman with a title, a wardrobe of French clothes, and a misleading *oohlala* image which titillated the senses of the men who now saw me as a desirable sex-object, and one, who having lived in France, must know the score.

I tried not to think of what would happen to me when I returned to the Baron. I did not discuss my marriage with Papa. Lala realised I was deeply unhappy, but she also knew that when the time was right, I would come to her for advice. She was infinitely wise in her handling of my bruised ego. Lala was a soft chocolate with a hard centre. She had early tried to inculcate me with her own philosophy that any woman assumed to be tough, efficient and practical would end up by having to look after everyone around her. She, who was both practical and competent, played the 'helpless, clinging' little woman role to perfection, floating about in gossamer negligées, delicately perfumed, exquisitely soignée, smoking endless Craven A cigarettes, and doing only those things she wanted to do and did surpassingly well.

It was healing to slip back into the uncomplicated pattern of life with my parents. Willie the cook still ruled their kitchen with a rod of iron, and the long-standing feud between him and Lizzie, Lala's personal maid, was as active and vitriolic as ever, with the chauffeur, fat Ben, their unwilling go-between.

Lizzie always referred disdainfully to Willie as that 'slim'[1] black Kaffir. Nobody knew just how or when or why the feud had started. Willie and Lizzie came from different tribes: Willie was a Shangaan, and Lizzie a Basuto. Whether they had fallen out over a personal matter, or on some tribal issue, we never discovered. Both served our family faithfully; and Lala reported to me many years later, that, during World War II, when the children of the house, my brother and I, were incommunicado in Europe, caught up in the confusion of the war, mission-trained Willie, who could read, write and cypher, studied maps and communiqués from the theatres of war in the morning papers, giving his opinion as to where he thought Jacques and I might be, while Lizzie practised some particularly virulent form of witchcraft on the photograph of the wife of a former German Consul-General, who had been an intimate friend of my family for many years.

Seemingly, nothing had changed in the family routine, except that Lala, in tune with the habits of her set, had found herself a country cottage which she called 'my Bagatelle'. My mother had a curious, almost ironic sense of humour. She was a true cosmopolite and did not much care about living in South Africa, although it was the place of her birth. I remember one day driving out into the country with her. Suddenly the car came to a halt in the middle of the *bundu*. Lala stepped out. Red dust swirled about us, it was hot, and asvoels circled high above us in a sky that was like burning metal plate. For a moment Lala contemplated the barren landscape. 'What a place,' she murmured; 'nothing but blue gums, and miles and miles of bugger all.'

[1] Slim: Afrikaans term for cunning, devious.

5. *Suzy Solidor, with 'Kaboul'*

6 *Above: My brother Jacques, 1940.* 7 *Facing page: June 1940 – Géa's drawing of myself with Tabou at a roadside café*

Capbreton Villa Alphonse. 19 juin 1940

8   *Home in Johannesburg, 1942*

Lala's new 'property', was some miles out of Johannesburg. She rented it from a friend entirely for her own pleasure, since Papa loathed the countryside unless it was attached to a spa, a race-course or a casino. He was never addicted to fresh air. Although he had lived and worked in Southern Africa most of his adult life, he remained a typical French *boulevardier*, with a keen eye for a pretty woman and an intimate knowledge of the menus and wine-lists of the best Paris restaurants. Papa had always to be cajoled into visiting Lala's country retreat, where she liked to give buffet luncheons consisting of dazzlingly complicated French dishes, most of which she and Willie had concocted together. She was a *cordon bleu* and had imparted much of her knowledge to her African servant, so much so that in time he became venturesome, and I remember they once had an historic row on the right amount of cognac to put into a *coulis de crevettes*.

One Sunday, Papa accompanied me to one of Lala's bashes, dressed in the outfit he considered suitable for such an expedition—a tussore jacket, brown and white co-respondent shoes, and the inevitable straw boater. He carried a cane with a thick gold band.

In his deep, caressing, Maurice Chevalier voice, for he never lost his French accent, or learned to speak English grammatically, he referred to Lala's cottage as 'your dear maman's *petit caprice*'. The moment we arrived, Papa retired to the living-room, drew all the curtains and sat reading a new copy of *La Vie Parisienne*, while I helped Lala and Lizzie get the table ready for luncheon.

It was a scorchingly hot day; one of those typically African days when everything appears to be limned in harsh bright colour, and there seems to be no shade anywhere. I remember that, early on, many of the guests became limp and dishevelled, while Lala remained as crisp as a lettuce. She wore a turquoise green chiffon bandana in her red-gold hair, and over her tailored white dress whe wore an improbable little frilled apron of organdie which looked as if it had been borrowed from the soubrette in a French farce. On anyone else the apron would have looked ridiculous; on Lala it became the epitome of chic, and was eagerly copied by her friends. Lala was a great trend-setter. Some of her more elaborate toilettes set my teeth on edge. There was a certain cape of black monkey-fur with a hat to match which sent me into gales of hysterical laughter. She was not amused, for she was not one to welcome criticism, particularly from a daughter who, until her marriage, she gave me to understand, had dressed mainly in sackcloth and ashes.

She never understood why I rolled about when she appeared before Papa, coiffed by a bonnet à la Mary Stuart, with a floating crepe veil. Startled, Papa asked for whom she was in mourning? 'The fact is,' she said wistfully, 'by the time I have to wear weeds, this particular style which is so becoming now, won't do anything for my wrinkled face.'

At this remove, it may appear that we Johannesburg women were an idle, extravagant bunch of rich bitches. Some women did tend to drink too much and changed partners with monotonous frequency, but there was a kind of innocence about our sexual romps. There was little real vice or perversion. Nobody in my circle took drugs or indulged in the activities which are today features of the permissive society. If young married women were fortunate enough to have servants, cars and no financial problems they were none the worse for these blessings; being for the most part good wives, mothers and, in their own fashion, good citizens. Always they did their best for the underprivileged, the handicapped and the aged, and no cry for help went unheeded.

Certainly there were fewer pressures than there are today. Most white South Africans lived in a honeycomb, far from the sad cold world of poverty and disease. They had their problems, but nearly everyone was secure in the knowledge that not only they but their children and grandchildren could look forward to a golden future.

At this time I am ashamed to say I was not particularly aware of, or interested in, the welfare of the Africans amongst whom I had spent so much of my life. Since my birth, at which I weighed two pounds, I had been loved and made much of by our servants as a specially privileged creature. There was no question of considering them as an inferior race; one did not consider them as anything but as hewers of wood and drawers of water, put there by a benevolent Deity for the express purpose of ministering to the creature comforts of the white bosses and their wives.

With the exception of enlightened souls such as Alan Paton and Nadine Gordimer, the majority of South Africans and particularly the Afrikaaners did not seem to realise that the era of slavery was over. Unless one knew some of the tribal dialects, it was difficult to establish any close communication with one's African servants. The Afrikaans language had been relegated to the kitchen where, in time, it became bastardised, being larded with German, French Swahili and Dutch words, finally turning into 'kitchen kaffir', the lingua-franca of the South African housewife.

Like most of the young women of my generation raised in a city, I was attached to our African servants, just as they seemed to be to the offspring of their European masters. But while I unquestioningly accepted what they did for me, it would never have entered my head to enquire about *their* well-being; like my parents and their friends, I took it for granted that our servants enjoyed the privilege of working all day, and often through the night, to ensure our comfort and happiness, the smooth running of our parties, and the welfare of our babies left at home in their care.

It was not until I returned to South Africa during World War II that I began to grasp the enormity of what our European civilisation had done to the Africans whose country we shared. It had taken the men from their peaceful homes and tribes plunging them into the bowels of the earth, shut away from the sun, in the mines, to find the gold that would jingle in every pocket save those of the mine-workers.

It took some time for the message to be spelled out loud and clear, that we, the Europeans, were responsible for giving the dark children of nature venereal disease and an insatiable craving for material possessions. We had taken from them their ancient gods, replacing them with the image of a jealous and petulant Christ-figure, who was as mealy-mouthed as the missionaries who covered the budding breasts of the young girls under hideous print dresses, and taught them to cook, sew, sing hymns and bed with the white man whose namby-pamby English wives were unable to stand the dreariness of life in a dusty dorp or mining-camp. Eventually I understood that the debt which we Europeans living in Africa, good and bad, pro and anti-Apartheid, owed the blacks was so great that it would one day have to be paid in blood.

But in those peaceful sunlit days, long before Mr Macmillan blew everything away with his 'wind of change' I was preoccupied only with my own small affairs. My horizons were limited because my universe was bounded by my emotional problems. I was unhappy because I felt obscurely that I had failed my husband. I also deeply regretted the loss of my child, and it was in this morbid and negative frame of mind that I met Chris.

*

One of my close friends, Sara de Wet, daughter of a wine farmer at the Cape, had married a Johannesburg stockbroker. She had produced two plain, freckled children, and at the time I returned to South Africa was on the point of taking a lover from sheer boredom. She was an intelligent young woman, depressed by the vacuous existence she was leading. With me she could unburden herself and talk freely about her problems. These consisted in the main of being irritated by her husband's peculiarities. Hugo O'Rourke, Sara's husband, seemed at first sight to be an amiable dolt with an unquenchable thirst for alcohol.

In fact, he was a brilliant, sensitive man suffering from a nervous disease which had made him take to drink, to cushion his nerves and keep him going from day to day. I gathered his performance in bed was fairly erratic, which was, I imagine, the true reason for Sara's frustrations and discontent.

Apart from his vast business interests, Hugo shared a stud-farm in the country with his brother, Niall. Their father, having been one of the chief architects in building up a great and successful mining house, had also been a famous breeder of bloodstock, and Niall, who hated cities, preferred to carry on the family tradition and to live in the country. He was a bachelor.

Sara had always been attracted to her brother-in-law, and was considering him as a temporary replacement for her husband. She liked to believe that Hugo was so drink-sodden that he did not realise what was going on around him.

Nothing could have been further from the truth, for at our very first meal when I was invited to the farm for a weekend, I was aware of Hugo's antagonism towards his brother, caused by the fact that he was deeply in love with his own wife.

When I think of the farm as I have done so often down the

years, I can recapture almost every moment of that week-end which was to be a watershed in my life. Old Okkie, father of Hugo and Niall O'Rourke, had bought his property soon after coming out from Ireland in one of the diamond rushes which had brought so many men to this land.

In the beginning, Okkie had intended his farm to be a retreat for his wife and himself. He was his own architect and had begun building in a modest way. The first dwelling was a rondavel,[1] the nucleus of the homestead I was to know so well.

Okkie was descended from a long line of Irishmen who had always been associated with horseflesh. Down the centuries, his forebears had been grooms, stable-lads and coachmen to British and European royalty. For generations, from the founding of the Royal Stud at Hampton Court, there was always a red-headed O'Rourke in the stables, whistling through the strong, widely-spaced teeth that were part of the family smile. It was rumoured that one of the sad, spinster daughters of George III had had more than a passionate friendship with an O'Rourke, for, skipping the generations, an occasional O'Rourke would be born, bulbous of eye, florid of complexion, and a decidedly Hanoverian cast of countenance.

Through the years Okkie built up one of the finest stud farms in Southern Africa. When Niall took over from his father, he continued in the old man's footsteps. His greatest pride at the time of our meeting was the stallion, Jove, a remarkable animal, a monarch whose dominion over his mares was apparent from the way they craned their necks over the stable-doors, whinnying as their lord was marched past by his adoring groom, a wizened little Hottentot, on his way to pleasure one of his mares.

The farm was a four-hour drive from Johannesburg. Once away from the city, we sped through a lunar landscape scattered with blue gum trees whose bark, peeling away, hung in tatters, reminding me always of the ragged mendicants of Italy. Soon we had left civilisation behind us, and were travelling along a bumpy unmade road that tailed off into narrow rutted tracks inclined to tear the guts out of any but the high chassis of an old Ford.

As the car surged through a sea of rosy dust, my heart lifted. This was my Africa, a country of endless vistas under a sky of

[1] Rondavel: originally a mud hut, thatched with reeds, the home of the African. Adapted and adopted by Europeans to suit their own needs.

aching, burning blue, that seemed to enclose the world under a glass dome.

High above us birds wheeled and turned: asvoels restlessly searching for food. This was the landscape that had so often haunted my dreams, even to the ant-hills, weird, huge and menacing, rearing up into the air like castles and chimneys created by mad dwarfs, and all the time my nostrils were filled by the familiar scent of smoke from the native kraals in which the Africans led their peaceful pastoral lives.

By the time we reached the boundaries of the O'Rourke lands, we were covered by a coating of red dust. Here the road improved; but progress was slowed down as a number of cattle-grids had to be negotiated and cattle-gates carefully opened and then closed again.

Okkie O'Rourke, a dedicated Irish patriot, named his farm Shannon, and to this wild and picturesque place he brought his young bride. Florence was the youngest daughter of an impoverished British peer, and in spite of living in a splendid old manor house filled with treasures, her own taste was for cottage furniture, chintz, and 'sweetly' pretty water-colours painted by her many spinster aunts and cousins.

From photographs taken at the time of her marriage to Okkie, Florence was a plump, pleasant-looking young girl with a square jaw, and a great deal of hair piled high on her head, skewered to her skull by a quantity of amber-coloured combs and hairpins, a coiffure she retained for many years, so that her children, from the time they could toddle, staggered along behind her, gathering up a harvest of combs, pins and slides which she shed like autumn leaves.

In spite of her gentle nature, Flo could be as obstinate as a mule, and though her tall, blond muscular husband was the love of her life, she never hesitated to castigate him if he did anything that ran counter to her principles. Florence O'Rourke was religious, unimaginative, and interested primarily in the welfare of her family, who constantly surprised her by their, to her, unconventional approach to life.

Shannon, when Okkie, fresh from the tranquil English countryside, first saw it, comprised only the rondavel and a lean-to shed for the cart and oxen. By the time I first saw the O'Rourke homestead it had become a sprawling collection of thatched rondavels and cottages linked by a vast living-room. Though Okkie and Florence had simply added to the house whenever a new room became necessary, the proliferation of rondavels and buildings had mellowed over the years, achieving a unity and an individuality which made Shannon a real home.

Florence was an inspired gardener and sublimated her nostalgia for the English gardens of her childhood by creating a small paradise in the midst of the sandy, limitless veld, spiked with thorn bushes.

This garden with its herbaceous borders of exiled flowers was also tricked out with every artifice Okkie could import for her from 'home'. There were benches carved with mottoes imploring the passer-by to 'bide a wee'; and there was, too, 'God wot', a fringed grot, and a pond imported from Japan, on which floated what must have been the most expensive water-lilies in Africa. A platoon of woolly-headed piccanins, under the direction of 'Tickey' the head garden-boy, spent their days carrying buckets around to water the croquet-lawn. I never found out why no taps had been installed in that particular part of the garden.

'Auntie Flo', as she became known in her middle-years, never realised that her 'little English garden' cost her husband as much as the upkeep of a sizeable park would have done in England; and when she was at Shannon she never moved away from the house and garden. The veld frightened her, and she remained always the prototype of the well-born Englishwoman in a baggy, tweedy skirt worn with sensible shoes and stockings. But her blouses of finest lawn, were pin-tucked, and fastened with a brooch set with a blue diamond of great value. As a concession to the ravages of the sun on her sensitive skin, Auntie Flo wore a sunbonnet, a *kappie*, the gift of the wife of one of the neighbouring Afrikaans farmers with whom she had struck up a warm friendship.

Afternoon tea was a ritual at Shannon and, no matter how fine the weather, she insisted on her guests having it in her own sitting-room, which was decorated with portraits of her children at all stages of their development. There were also miniatures of them painted on ivory, pastels and water-colours, as well as bronze casts of the tiny baby shoes of her brood.

Sara O'Rourke did not share the passion of her husband and his family for Shannon. She said that something hideously sterile about the landscape dried up all her juices. I did not share her feelings. From the moment I looked out of the stable door of my rondavel across Auntie Flo's bravely pathetic 'English' garden to the great veld like a blond sea sweeping away to the horizon, I loved Shannon and everything about it. I liked the big shabby sofas in the living-room with their faded Sanderson chintz covers; the moth-eaten lion and impala pelts that did duty as rugs, and the enormous fireplace with two special recesses to house a pair of young Africans, whose only task was to keep the fire going for as long as any member of the family or their guests wished to remain in the living-room.

Everything about the homestead and its surroundings pleased me. At night I lay in my narrow, hard little bed, for the entire O'Rourke clan seemed singularly unaware of what luxury-living meant, listening to the noises of the African night. I had no idea what kind of beasts prowled about in the short dry scrub, but I hoped no predator would leap upon the beautiful little buck I had seen at closing of day dancing down to the river to drink. Sometimes a dog would bark on a neighbouring farm, and far far away would come the shrill whistle of a train as it rushed through the night.

*

Breakfast at Shannon was an informal affair. Family and guests drifted out on to the great paved circular terrace where porridge, a tradition dating from Okkie's early pioneering days, was served with brown sugar and thick cream. This was followed by bacon, eggs, toast, fruit and superlative coffee, brewed by Kikiza the cook, who had been born and raised at Shannon and whose sons, Kambela and Tandi, had grown up with the O'Rourke children, so that there was between the young people of the house, both European and African, a deep and affectionate friendship and understanding, which, if they were not at first apparent to the visitor, were an integral part of the pattern of life at Shannon.

Niall seldom came to Sara and Hugo's large house in Johannesburg which had been decorated to the point of suffocation by a French interior designer, then very much in vogue. Niall was always uneasy away from Shannon; while he made his brother and his brother's guests welcome, he himself could rarely be persuaded to leave the farm, the stud and Kikiza's eldest daughter, M'Bele. Later, I was told that Niall divided his favours between M'Bele, his permanent mistress, and any nubile black girl who took his fancy. His taste for black flesh had ruined his appetite for the paler variety, Sara once told me sobbing bitterly.

It has taken me a long time to bring Chris, the third and youngest brother of the O'Rourke brothers, into this narrative. This is mainly because, for so many years after our parting, I tried to forget his existence. Chris was so important to me that I tried to bury his memory at the bottom of my subconscious, covering it with an avalanche of extraneous emotions unconcerned with what lay frozen beneath the ice. I knew very well that one day the block of ice, with my love frozen inside, would melt and there would be my heart, as raw and bloody as ever. That, I felt, would be the day of reckoning, for then I should somehow have to relive that terrible pain all over again. I should, once more, have to face Chris' rejection and the *dénouement* of a passion which had devoured and dominated me for so long.

Chris strolled into my life one morning at breakfast time. He had been away staying with friends in Natal. I knew of course that Auntie Flo had had a 'change of life' baby, and that the birth of Christian, coinciding as it did with the sudden death of her husband, Okkie, had made the infant a precious legacy to the entire O'Rourke family.

All of them doted on little Chris, and seemingly it was a matter of surprise to those who knew the family well that the child was not completely smothered by the weight of love concentrated upon his small person. But Chris was not spoilt; not then. He was wilful and rebellious, but, as his mother said, he was a child of laughter. She said to me one day, when showing me a golden baby curl of his hair set in a locket, 'Of all my children, Chris is the only truly Irish one, with the gift of the gab, and enough charm to steal the heart from your body.'

At first view the young man—he was now eighteen—looked to me like a sheep-dog puppy. Loose-limbed and floppy, he did not seem to have entire control over his gangling limbs. His head resembled a hastily stacked cornstook with spiky bits standing up at the back. I really did not take much notice of the newcomer until he reached over for the honey, which I handed to him. As he touched my hand, I looked into his eyes, which were as golden as those of a lion; suddenly the icecap that encompassed my heart began to melt, and I sat back in my chair, quivering from the impact of a shock from which I was never to recover completely.

Once breakfast was over, guests at Shannon were free to follow their own occupations until pre-luncheon drinks were served on the terrace. I had no wish to accompany Niall on his round of the stables; nor did I want to ride out with Sara and Hugo, both of whom enjoyed a sadistic amusement called 'shooting for the pot'. I loathed the whole grisly performance of tracking down a beautiful unsuspicious buck, and hunting it down, until with bursting lungs filled with bloody lather, it was finally destroyed. I had only once accompanied the hunters, and was so dismayed at having been a party to what I termed a massacre, that I vowed never again to have the death of any of God's creatures on my conscience. It was this particular episode that triggered off the first of the collection of short stories I wrote later. This story, entitled 'The Meat Eater', was published in a book called *The Slave Bell and Other Stories* by the Unie-Volkspers BPK in Cape Town.

When everyone had gone off to their various ploys, I went to my rondavel to change into a sundress. I loved the sun on my body, and wanted to take a good deep tan back to Europe. Picking up my book and a notepad, I went back to the terrace, where I stretched out on a long rattan chair. I lay supine, letting the hot rays gild my pale flesh, tingling as I thought about the moment when I had looked into the eyes of Christian O'Rourke. At that moment he came out on to the terrace. He had taken off his shirt, and wore tattered old khaki shorts bunched about his narrow loins with a pyjama cord. His body was a deep amber colour. Smiling amiably at me, he stretched himself out on a lilo, and almost immediately fell asleep with his mouth slightly open, and his downy cheeks flushed like those of a child. He looked both childish and vulnerable lying there sprawled out, with his moist fair hair matted on his forehead. I sat quietly on my chair, staring down at his long tanned legs and bare, rather grubby feet, and longed to fling myself down upon him. Something of my urgent desire must have communicated itself to him, for he suddenly sat up, smiled at me with all his big white teeth, and held out his hand to pull me down beside him. Thus did this long-drawn-out affair of the heart that was to end in torrents of tears begin on the terrace of an isolated farmhouse in the middle of the African veld.

I realised immediately that if I was not to become involved in a difficult and demanding relationship, I must exercise great caution and self-discipline. At the same time I knew that already it was too late to retreat, for I was swamped in a great flood-tide of emotional desire; by the time we went down to the dam to swim, I was totally committed, and felt the entire universe was empty of everyone but Chris and myself.

He walked lightly, his face upturned to the sun, happy in a familiar and beloved landscape. He told me how much Shannon meant to him and how much he longed to own it. Attached as he was to his family, he resented the fact that their father had left this particular property, the pride of his life, to his brothers and not to him. There was no way he could buy them out, for though his own inheritance was considerable, he knew Niall would never relinquish Shannon.

At this time, Chris was both unsophisticated and unspoilt. He was, as yet, unaware of the potency of his charm, or of the magnetism he was to use with such deadly effect on his victims. He had just emerged from the mists of adolescence, and neither his heart nor his senses had ever been seriously stirred. Later he told me that I instantly aroused his desire. There was nothing subtle about Chris' approach. As for me, he was, from the beginning, first and foremost my child.

We swam about in the deep rust-coloured water of the sun-warmed dam. I enjoyed swimming, which I did well, and which was my only sporting accomplishment. After a while, I became aware that Chris was circling purposefully around me like a shark. I became terrified of this half-man, half-fish threatening me, so I scrambled out of the water, and lay down on the flat, baking hot stones. I felt cleansed, weightless and happy. I closed my eyes against the glare, and when I opened them, I found Chris leaning over me staring intently down into my face. It was not a superficial survey. He was really looking deep into my heart. His eyes, the fierce, gold-flecked eyes of the predator, were shaded by thick, dark, upcurling lashes which gave his gaze a curious depth of intensity.

I saw that his skin had the colour and texture of a ripe apricot.

On one side of his rather spatulate nose was a tiny beauty spot. The face looking down at me was the living landscape of a soul; a soulscape which would, ultimately, become more familiar and more beloved to me than any other.

Quietly, the tall, angular youth lay down beside me. I took his hand and held it to my cheek. It was a great rough paw with bitten nails, the hand of a schoolboy, and it touched and roused me more than all the splendour of his fine body.

At midday we returned to Shannon to find a message advising us that Sara, Niall and Hugo had gone to luncheon at a neighbouring farm, and that we were expected to follow. Instead, Chris cajoled Kikiza into putting up a picnic and back we went to the dam. There we swam again, ate our lunch, shared a flask full of milky coffee, walked, swam and slept curled up together like puppies in a basket.

We were woken by the loud twittering of the weaver birds. There is no twilight in Africa; but it was evident from the activities of the birds around their home tree that night was at hand. Near where we lay was a big old thorn tree in which, since time immemorial, a colony of weaver birds had built a vast commune of dangling nests. Seen from below, the collection of nests looked like a large untidy parcel of grass cuttings, although, in fact, each parcel was exquisitely designed, woven and lined; and each and every bird in the commune knew the exact position of its lodging, and flying out of the sky dived straight into the narrow entrance of his apartment. Fascinated, we watched the birds return to their nests, and listened to their cries and murmurs, until suddenly, as if a blanket had been flung over the tree, night fell and there was total silence.

By the time we got back to the house, the dressing-bell had long since sounded. My hosts, impeccably dressed—Sara in a pretty housecoat, and her husband and brother-in-law in white dinner-jackets—were drinking martinis in the living-room, where a large fire, enthusiastically maintained by the *fireboys*, was blazing away.

I rushed to my rondavel to find that a hot bath had been prepared for me by Lootie, one of Kikiza's younger daughters who sometimes maided week-end guests. She had put out my white pleated chiffon dinner dress which she had naïvely teamed with a pair of tennis shoes.

I was hot, flurried and dishevelled. In my hurry, I poured half a bottle of Omy bath essence into the rapidly cooling water. As I was about to step into the bath, I saw I was about to share it with a small and very pretty little frog. I scrabbled about in the water, trying to catch it before it was suffocated by the pungent bath-oil. Finally I managed to salvage the tiny creature. It was the colour of jade and could have been carved by Fabergé. I stroked it gently as it sat palpitating on the palm of my hand. I then put it outside and hopped back into the bath, where I sat, flooded with the sheer joy of being alive; grabbing an enormous sponge, I squeezed the scented water over my breasts.

*

We dined formally by candlelight at the long stinkwood table that Okkie O'Rourke had bought at a sale of old Cape-Dutch furniture. Chris looked fresh, scrubbed and glowing in his white dinner-jacket. I thought it strange that we should all be sitting here in the middle of nowhere dressed up like characters in an English drawing-room comedy. I wondered what the African servants made of this charade. The dinner was unimaginative. Sara explained that Kikiza was not well, and that yet another of her daughters, less talented than she, was responsible for the overdone beef, watery vegetables and lamentable tinned fruit salad. Later, Chris told me that Kikiza had been on one of her 'binges', during which she drank so much of the potent *skokiaan*[1] she brewed and sold, that she was incapacitated for several days.

We had coffee on the terrace, and watched the moon rise over the horizon. Throughout the evening Chris and I had hardly exchanged a word. I flirted with Niall, but long afterwards Sara told me that she had from the first been conscious of the attraction between Chris and myself, and was greatly relieved, for she had feared that I might try to take Niall from her.

After a restless night, during which I tossed and turned sleeplessly on my bed, we met again on the terrace for breakfast. Niall had been up most of the night with a mare who had foaled, and was tired, unshaven and grumpy. Hugo had a hangover, having drunk far too much the night before; Sara, pleading a headache, had her breakfast in bed.

It was agreed that we should spend a lazy day lounging around

[1] *Skokiaan*: a potent Kaffir beer made from millet.

the house. Later that evening we were invited to attend a buffet-supper at the house of a neighbour, who was giving a party to celebrate his daughter's twenty-first birthday. The girl was called Marnie, and was obviously one of Chris' special friends, since his brothers teased him about her, asking him whether he had bought her a present. Chris said nothing, but went on consuming slice after slice of toast and marmalade.

The O'Rourke men lingered long over breakfast. They were hearty trenchermen, and even the aesthetic Hugo consumed impressive quantities of kedgeree. During this meal I was made aware that Chris was by far the most important member of his family. His welfare and future were a matter of deep concern to his brothers, who took very seriously their father's last legacy to them.

I soon came to realise that Hugo and Niall and even Sara shared Auntie Flo's obsession with this beautiful adolescent. The course of his life had been carefully planned. Unlike his brothers, and like his father, he was to attend a British university. His mother's wish was that he should go to Oxford, as had most of the men in her family through the centuries. I found it odd that Chris himself did not seem to question any of the plans made for him. I was not then aware of his Houdini-like mentality which made him accept with indifference the challenge of any fetters, only to shrug them off when he had decided on some other course of action.

After breakfast was finally over, Niall went off to the stables, followed by Chris. Hugo stretched out on a long chair, a book in his hand. I was curious to know what he was reading, and was more than a little surprised to find that his book was Palgrave's *Golden Treasury of Verse*, in a limp faded blue suède binding. It was evidently one of the treasures of Auntie Flo's library, but it gave me a different insight into the mind of Sara's supposedly dull and uncultivated husband.

We sat absorbed in our books in an atmosphere of companionable silence. I was re-reading *War and Peace*, as I did each year. Hugo looked at me over his horn-rimmed glasses.

'Doesn't it seem odd to be reading *War and Peace*, here in the middle of the veld?'

'Why should it?'

'I should have thought it a book to be read and enjoyed only in Europe. In my case the African sun comes between me and my book and reduces everything I read to a kind of gibberish.'

'Then you must lack concentration, else you would become totally involved, as I do, in the affairs of the Rostov family, and particularly in the life of Princess Maria Bolkonsky for whom I have the greatest admiration.'

'I prefer Natasha.'

'Most men do.'

'What do most men do?' enquired Chris as he joined us.

'We were talking about Maria Bolkonsky and Natasha in *War and Peace*. Which of the young women appeals to you?'

'I don't know what the hell you're talking about. After all, I'm just an ordinary South African kerel.'[1]

'It's about time you started taking an interest in reading,' said Hugo, unfolding himself from his chair.

'Anyone coming with me?'

'Stay where you are,' his brother cried, 'I'm going to do a sketch of the two of you lolling in the sun being intense about ladies who only existed in the mind of that old satyr Tolstoy. I shall call it "Portrait of Intellectuals in a Vacuum", and maybe, if it is good enough, I'll hang it in my rooms at College.'

'It will have to be a portrait of one intellectual,' said Hugo, 'and I don't for a moment imagine, and nor should you, that she is in a vacuum.'

I still have that painting. It is not a very good picture, nor is it even a good likeness of me, for Chris omitted to give me a face; but the red curls are in evidence, and he captured completely the ambience of this moment when the strong sun struck boldly down on to the thatched roofs of the rondavels, on to the flagged stones of the terrace, on to the great earthenware jar in which bloomed an aloe, tall and fierce as a blood-tipped lance, and on to my bare hands locked in my lap. Early that morning, I had with a sense of finality, mingled with guilt, removed my wedding ring.

*

I had not long returned to Johannesburg after that extended week-end which Chris and I spent walking and talking in a kind of daze, when Papa asked me how soon I intended going back to France. That very morning I had received yet another letter from

[1] Kerel: Afrikaans for chap or fellow.

the Baron telling me, in his usual oblique way, that he missed me and how much my prolonged absence displeased him and his family.

I knew that from now on my position, if I remained in South Africa, would become increasingly difficult. For the sake of my family I had to abandon Chris and return to my husband. Papa was never one to mince matters.

'I have heard rumours' he said, giving me a sardonic look. 'So far I have discounted them, but it is my opinion that rumours, like birds of ill-omen, generally come home to roost. You know how much your mother and I have enjoyed having you with us, but, since we plan to go to France next year, we shall soon all be together again and I hope that this time Renaud will be able to join us.'

The Patriarch had spoken and the dutiful Jewish daughter I should always be took heed of the warning.

I knew that each time I saw Chris would make it harder for me to leave him, and that in the end I should be unable to return to Renaud. So I panicked, and ran away down to the Cape, there to await the arrival of the mailship. I had a week in hand, and decided to revisit one of the favourite haunts of my youth, Plettenberg Bay, a fishing village in the Knysna district, on the Garden Route, where some of the families of my school-friends had homes or farms.

My joyous memories of Plettenberg were of fishing and swimming in an unspoilt paradise, its privacy jealously guarded by the people who lived there and were determined that it should not become a smart summer resort for snobs.

I booked in at the Beacon Island Hotel, a comfortable, old-fashioned hotel situated on a barren rock. It had once been a whaling station, visited mainly by Norwegian whalers. Over the years it had become an inn for travellers, who did not expect too much in the way of comfort and sophistication.

In my day it had become a family hotel, with large, clean, bare bedrooms; with long corridors of polished red concrete, and one bathroom to a floor. The dining-room fronts the rocks, and in rough weather the spray beats against the windows. The menus were British colonial railway, with the emphasis on cold meat, prunes-and-custard, jelly and coffee and tea from the same urn. But the fish was fresh and delicious, and the service prompt.

My friends were hospitable, and the days passed in a succession of picnics, bathing-parties, cocktail parties and other social occasions which usually took place at this time of the year. I plunged into all these activities with a false and hectic gaiety which misled a number of my escorts. Chris dominated my thoughts entirely, and I was tortured by the idea that I might never see him again. I felt it was ironic that we could not be together in so idyllic a setting. Yet the thought of the repercussions of any meeting between us prevented me from using the telephone which stood in a sort of sentry-box just off the dining-room.

One evening my friends gave a *braaivleis*[1] to celebrate their parents' silver wedding anniversary. It was a great occasion, and preparations had been made to entertain friends and relations from all over the country.

As the farm was some distance from my hotel, my friends kindly invited me to spend the night, and installed me in one of the pretty little spider-infested thatched rondavels in their grounds. When I had unpacked my case, I wandered out, enjoying the animation and bustle of the servants with their relations who had come officially to help out, but were also there to see the fun, and later to have their own party.

The house servants ran around, erecting trestle tables to serve as bars. Laughing and chattering, they carried out rugs and cushions, and Japanese lanterns which they strung up in the trees. A local coloured band consisting of a ukelele, guitar and squeezebox arrived early and began practising. Inspired by the sound of the music, some of the younger women broke into a spirited little dance, shaking their breasts and buttocks with naïve and enthusiastic abandon.

When all was ready, members of the house-party came out, freshly bathed and dressed, as our hosts had ordered, in white. White gowns for the women, and white dinner-jackets for the men. We sat around drinking chilled white Constantia wine, and waiting for the party to begin in earnest.

Suddenly people began to arrive in droves. They came in fast cars, on horseback, or in old-fashioned Cape carts. The braziers were lit, and the serious work of cooking the steak, chops and sausages began. The band went into frenetic action, and couples

[1] *Braaivleis*: Afrikaans version of a barbecue.

moved on to the wooden dance floor ringed about with trees abloom with paper lanterns. I was being whirled around in an 'excuse me' dance, when my partner was replaced by Chris, who, taking me in his arms, held me silently close, and finally led me off the dance floor into the night. We did not return to the party. We went to my rondavel and there, in the double bed thoughtfully provided by my hosts, I became a complete human being again.

I have no idea what my friends thought of my subsequent behaviour. We moved to the hotel where we had separate bedrooms, but it was evident we were lovers; we were clamped together as if magnetised, and could not move a step without holding hands, expressing our need and desire for one another by constant contact. Chris had only to touch my arm to make me tremble. This mating game tended to slow up our ordinary daily life, for we were constantly on our way to, and from, bed. We were temporarily oblivious of the world outside our two selves, although the moment when we should have to part was an ever-present shadow which lengthened with the passing of the days.

When the moment came for me to return to Cape Town to catch my ship, we went for a last walk on the beach, and there, naked in a rockpool warmed by the sun, in true romantic tradition we joined hands and swore eternal love. Here in this lovely place between the sea and the sky, the first and most memorable phase of our relationship came to an end. We had been granted a moment of perfection together in the Garden of Eden before being driven out into our separate worlds.

10

Lament for Lucy

On the voyage back to Europe I spent a great deal of time alone. Realising the depth of my feeling for Chris, and knowing that his youth and family ties would be an insuperable barrier to any permanent liaison, I determined to put an end to an affair that threatened not only my peace of mind but my marriage. In spite of Renaud's extraordinary behaviour, I still felt I had a duty to try to build my life with him. I wrote to Chris, telling him that he must not write to me. I posted the letter at Madeira and that evening had a hectic flirtation with a handsome young polo-player who was on the first leg of a journey which would take him and his string of ponies to South America.

The Baron was pleased to have me back, mainly, I believe, to annoy the Vipers, who were hissing with rage at our reunion, for they had hoped and prayed that I would not return. It did not take long to step back into my former activities. I spent much more time with the Baron, determinedly blotting out all thought of Chris from my mind. One day I realised with a pang how far I had drifted from Lucy, and that with her, and her alone, I might discuss my young lover. She had for so long been close to me, so much a part of my life that I was shocked to realise that I had not seen her or heard from her for more than six months.

When I rang her flat, an unfamiliar voice informed me that she had moved, and under pressure grudgingly gave me her new telephone number. I rang it at once. Lucy's heavily accented voice answered. But she was so sleepy that it took her some time to realise who I was; finally she came to completely, and was as warm and loving as ever. I asked her to luncheon, but she said she was on a diet; she would, however, meet me for a drink at *La Coupole* in Montparnasse, which was, I thought, a strange choice of venue for a lady who seldom moved far from the Ritz Bar.

I was, as always, punctual at the rendezvous. I was eager to see my friend, and to pour out all the experiences of the past few months. I wondered what her reaction would be when I told her that I had, at long last, taken her advice and found a lover; and thinking of Chris I drained two glasses of fresh orange juice, emptied a dish of calorie-rich peanuts and amused myself by looking around at the never-failing entertainment offered by the denizens of Montparnasse in general, and of this café in particular.

It had once been the stamping-ground of Ernest Hemingway and of his merry band; it had always had a mixed clientele of expatriate writers, artists and indigenous poets. There were a few regulars, such as the blind singer with his wife, who had once been a famous ballerina, and wore always the thick, grotesque make-up of one of the dolls in *Coppelia*. I recognised the artist who made 'lightning' sketches of the customers, and there too were the *Sidis* from North Africa touting their wares: badly cured goatskins, rugs, brass-ware and other tourist trash. The *Sidis* were as much a part of the landscape as the buildings, and one of them, whose beat was the 'Deux Magots' was later to become a symbol of my 'Bohemian' café life. So long as he was around, in his long djellabah, showing his yellow pointed teeth in a wolf-like grin, I felt secure; when he finally vanished just before the war, I took his disappearance as a sign of impending doom.

Perched, as always, on the ridiculously high heels she affected, Lucy came sailing down the boulevard with her head in the air. As she bore down on my table, I felt a stab of dismay. She was so different from the bonny, wholesome fleshed-out woman I had always admired. Lucy was now emaciated to the point of caricature. When she took off her long tan coloured gloves, I saw that her soft white hands, like the rest of her person, were faintly grubby.

'Have you been ill, darling?'

She shrugged her shoulders. 'Not in the accepted sense of the word.'

'Something terrible has happened, what was it?'

'Frost died. That was the beginning of the trouble.'

It took me some time and a great deal of tactful coaxing to find out what had happened to my friend. It was a banal sequence of events: her beloved dog had died, her current lover, one of those for whom she really cared, had left her. I knew him well. He was a scientist, a distinguished poet and a patriot, and one of the most delightful and cultivated human beings I had ever met. When the Germans entered Paris in 1940, he blew out his brains.

There was no question but that he loved Lucy; but when she told me that as the result of a long and painful illness and a major operation she had become addicted to drugs, I realised what had destroyed my friend. She had become a morphine addict, and was now a grotesque version of the beautiful creature I had known, always so filled with the crackling vitality of the healthy.

After a while it was obvious that our meeting was a dismal failure. Lucy was now a creature of the night; she could not bear the light of day. Her once clear, lambent green eyes were bloodshot, their pupils so enlarged that they almost obscured the whole eye. I was not only saddened, but furiously angry, because I was so immature that I could not recognise the agonised crumblings of a soul and the unspoken cry for help. Lucy lapsed into long silences during which she kept scratching the side of her nose, her neck and arms with her long blood-red nails. Finally she roused herself.

'Stop looking so fucking sanctimonious. You're shocked. Of course you're shocked, because you're a small town puss and I'm beyond your reach. I'm no longer your pal, your dear chum, Lucy. I'm stumbling down a road you've never trodden, and probably never will, because fundamentally you're a bourgeois little creature afraid of getting involved. You'll never have the guts to wade into the shit up to your eyeballs. You've heard of "le gout de la boue", you must have read about it, you intellectual prig; you function only with your mind, never with your cunt. But reading about things and experiencing them are horses of another colour.'

Seeing my flooding tears she tailed off into silence, and taking my hand, held it to her cheek.

'Darling, darling, I'm sorry, so desperately sorry, but don't try to drag me back. It's all over. Let me go now without fuss, there's a good scout.'

She got up and walked slowly and gracefully away down the crowded Boulevard. At the next table sat Foujita, the famous Japanese artist, with one of his models. He too watched Lucy's retreating figure, and when she had vanished, he leant over and handed me a big white handkerchief.

*

Three months later, I was lying in bed reading, in our flat in the rue de Bac, when the telephone rang. It was late. It was the Bursar of the Hôpital Beaujon, calling to tell me that Lucy had been found dying of an over-dose of veronal in an hotel bedroom off the Champs-Elysées. They had found her name on the envelope of a letter from me inviting her to spend some time in the country. The bursar asked me to come at once to confirm the identity of my friend, who he said was *in extremis*.

The Baron was out. I dressed, scribbled a note which I left on his pillow, and rushed out to find a taxi. Once within the massive gates of the hospital, I was handed over at the porter's lodge to the care of a nun who preceded me into the great gaunt building. That walk, through the darkened wards of the old hospital, which had once been a leper house, and whose walls were three feet thick, was like a trip into Dante's inferno. The nun glided along. The shadows cast by her white coif were, alternately, those of a giant cyclamen or of some horned medieval demon. There was the insistent smell of carbolic and sickness, and the whole ancient edifice was filled by the sounds of moans and cries. If there were private rooms for patients, they must have been in some other part of the building.

I traversed endless corridors and over-crowded wards, following my guide up many flights of stairs. Finally she stopped near a small cubicle made up of green screens. Beckoning me closer, she pulled back one of the screens; there, lying on the narrow hospital bed, lay Lucy breathing stertorously, and with great difficulty. Each breath seemed to be torn from her labouring lungs.

'She has pneumonia. She is very ill. Is she a Catholic?'

'Yes.'

'Then we shall send for a priest. Meanwhile, Madame, pray for her soul.'

I sat down on the chair next to the bed and began mechanically to pray. But somehow I did not think I was getting through to God at all. My mind was on my Lucy lying there in a washed-out flannel nightgown which came up to her chin, and was tied behind her back with strings. The nuns had carefully cleansed her face of all make-up, and it looked bare, childish and vulnerable. There was a greenish froth at the corner of her pretty mouth. I felt detached from this grisly scene. I willed Lucy to open her eyes, and assure me that this was a crazy joke, a masquerade arranged to put her creditors off the scent. A jape, as she called it, similar to the one she had once played on a too pressing creditor who had forced her way into Lucy's flat to demand instant payment for three dozen nightgowns, two dozen pairs of French knickers trimmed with Malines lace; four négligées, slips, and goodness knows what else, which Lucy had bought, on tick, to refurbish her bottom drawer. She always bought her underwear, shoes and gloves in dozens.

The lingerie lady was angry and frustrated, and threatened all manner of unpleasant things if her account was not paid. She calmed down, however, when I appeared, dressed up as a nurse, with a seersucker towel doing duty as a veil, and a white apron borrowed from Terka, the maid. I told the infuriated sales woman that Madame de Polnay had brain fever, was unconscious, and incommunicado; but that the moment she recovered, her 'protector' would pay her debts in full. In the meantime, I had had instructions from my patient, during one of her spells of consciousness, to settle part of the account, and to order a dozen embroidered lingerie-covers to help trade along. The poor woman accepted the money I gave her, and scurried away to implement her dazzling and unpredictable client's latest order.

I stared down at Lucy's face, which had now taken on an ashen hue. I talked to her, begging her to regain consciousness, to come back to normal life so we could exchange cracks about yet another of her *suicides manquées*, as her scientist friend had called them. She had tried several times in the past to put an end to what she ruefully called her 'failed life', but someone had always discovered her in time. This time the joke had gone sour. She had covered her tracks too well.

From time to time she moved her head restlessly, her red hair spraying out like flames on the pillows. There were blue shadows under her eyes and her nostrils were pinched. Suddenly I was terrified. I knew that Lucy was dying. I took her hand in mine. It was burning hot. I concentrated all my love, all my willpower on the white, supple hand, with its talon-like nails. Lucy's hands had the texture of the finest kidskin and seemed to be boneless. I gripped the hot hand that seemed to have an independent life of its own; sporadically her fingers jerked and danced in my grasp. There were moments when I thought she was trying to communicate with me through the pressure of her fingers; but she did not open her eyes. From time to time a nun appeared, bent over Lucy, wiped her lips and her forehead, and went away again.

Throughout that endless night nobody offered me so much as a drink of water. This was a charity hospital, with no luxury trimmings. The chair under my bottom was hard as a rock. Yet I continued to cling to Lucy's hand until the doctor came in and brusquely sent me to wait in the main ward. When he came out I asked him how Lucy was. He shrugged his shoulders and moved on down the ward. I went back to my vigil. At one point, I saw a priest standing at the foot of the bed. Once again, I was consigned to the ward outside.

When I returned, Lucy's breathing had become louder. I had never heard the death rattle, but I recognised it instantly, and began to tremble with the blind panic that animals have in the presence of death. At five o'clock in the morning, as the first light pressed against the window above Lucy's bed, I suddenly felt the hand under mine grow cool. I thought that perhaps the fever had abated; but the chill hand became icy. My Lucy was dead.

11

These Foolish Things

Lucy's death brought my first adult sorrow. Until the moment when I had had her body laid in 'waiting' in the church of 'Les Quinze Vingt', I did not really comprehend that she had left my life for good. Death to the young is as unimaginable as old age, infirmity and wanting to stay at home at night. I had always promised my friend that, should she die before me, I would do everything in my power to return her remains to her native land. Unfortunately, there were, at that time, all manner of official difficulties which I was unable to overcome. I tried several times to enlist the assistance of her brother, Peter de Polnay the writer, who was in Paris at the time of her death; but he was no more successful than I at overcoming French bureaucratic resistance, and to my shame, I must admit that, so far as I know, Lucy's body never made that last journey home.

After her death I went very often to the Manoir de Rollo, back to my superficially peaceful life in the depths of the Normandy countryside; but, if I appeared outwardly tranquil, inwardly I was in a turmoil. The loss of Lucy, allied to my desperate need for Chris, together with the knowledge that there was not, and could never be, any future in his and my relationship, which I had in any case broken off, made it difficult for me to pretend I was enjoying the futile and frivolous kind of existence on which the Baron thrived. My visit to South Africa had produced in me the equivalent of a violent seismic shock which had so shaken me, so fragmented my personality, that, when I returned to France, I *was* a different person. The Baron felt vaguely that I had 'changed', but his image of me remained intact. So far as he was concerned, I would always be the young savage he had rescued from the bush, jungle, veld or whatever; he alone had civilised me, tamed my mane of hair, taught me to wear the right clothes, to choose the right dishes, and, above all to grace the social circles to which I could never have aspired, had he not bestowed the honour of his name upon me.

Renaud had no idea what went on in my mind or of my painful spiritual development. My body still excited him. Intent only on his own satisfaction, he would bed me as often as he could, and since I was still a prisoner of the myth of the submissive wife, I gave in as gracefully as possible, while abstracting my mind from the gyrations performed by my physical self.

Fortunately, as I have said, the Baron was a rapid mover. Sometimes, when all was over, he would lie beside me, his eyes closed, looking like a cross between an ageing *Chéri* and the portrait of a Florentine nobleman on his deathbed. Sadly, his dark, chiselled good looks left me totally unmoved, and I became ever more irritated by his fussiness which expressed itself in details such as his preparations for love-making, which were attended by great splashings with Fougère-Royale; the removal of a Holy medal (blessed by the Pope) which he wore always on a slender platinum chain around his neck, and arranging his slippers neatly together by the nuptial couch. He invariably kept his black silk socks on, and was, I believe, slightly shocked because I always slept in the raw.

*

I was growing more and more attached to the Manoir de Rollo, and to my little world, in and about Honfleur. Few of my Parisian friends could understand why I chose to spend so much time away from the capital, in a dilapidated old property in the heart of the country. I should have been hard put to it to explain my reasons. I know now that my life of solitude was an apprenticeship of the soul, for a time later, much later, when I should begin to try to slip the bonds of material things, emptying myself of vanities, in order to come to terms with the human condition. At that time, however, my approach to the spiritual life was entirely superficial. Although I read omnivorously and eclectically, I responded only to emotional literature with which I could identify. The more arduous and stony paths of religious philosophy, even of philosophy itself, were closed to my understanding.

I had made few close friends. The families who lived in the neighbouring properties were wary of me and of our way of life. They were both attracted and repelled by what they heard and saw of our week-end parties: the carloads of young women with long painted finger-nails and hair coiffed *à la gamin*[1] by Antoine. With this hair style went the breastless boyish figure dressed by Chanel, Lanvin and Schiaparelli.

When I looked at photographs of the fashionable beauties taken at this time, I marvel at the ingenuity of women in the grip of fashion-fever. Most women of my mother's generation had been born with the fuller breasts, sloping shoulders and tiny waists, which were the correct shape for the ladies of the nineteenth and early twentieth centuries.

Plastic surgery was still in its infancy, and only the most daring of females would have contemplated a plastic operation. Binding was the most satisfactory method of flattening the breasts, and of course, dieting or banting, as it was called, to melt unwanted poundage. Strangely, the females of the following generation were, in the main, born with small high breasts, and the long legs considered so desirable by their mothers.

Although I was slim-hipped, my curves were unfashionable; and on the only occasion I allowed Antoine to cut my hair, he cropped it so short that I looked like a hedgehog, which set the Vipers buzzing with malicious excitement for weeks.

Our neighbours confined themselves to asking us to dine occasionally, as a gesture of goodwill, not to me, but to the Vipers. It was obvious that they thought I did not conform to the exigent standards laid down for a young matron of good family. I had no children, I smoked, I was reputed to be following the example of the scarlet woman of Nohant, Madame George Sand, by writing books. This automatically made me a *Bohemian*. Furthermore, my father was Jewish, and in trade, two of the most heinous offences in the social calendar of the country squires around us. I did not fit into any slot. I was not an American or a Brazilian heiress; so why, clucked the dowagers and their daughters, had that eligible Baron chosen to marry me?

I was well aware of what the cabala thought of me and there were times when I was hurt at not being admitted to the charmed circle of young mothers who took their children to the beaches of Trouville and Cabourg. There, as in delicious paintings by Boudin, the young women in their thin summery gowns sat sewing, chatting, reading and laughing, while their children,

[1] Urchin cut.

attended by nurses or governesses, made sand-castles or paddled in the freezing sea. Often the little family groups were swelled by the arrival of a mother, or mother-in-law, elderly matriarchs garbed in dark rustling silk, whose only concession to the fine weather was a straw hat and a parasol.

I came to know the beach of Trouville well, for the Vipers owned a vast family villa there, which was opened at Easter and was filled always with younger members of the clan recovering from divers childish ailments. 'Les Pins' was typical of the seaside villas of the nineteenth century, being over-gabled, turreted and balconied, with a conservatory, and many dark rooms carelessly furnished with bits and pieces that nobody wanted. I never stayed in the house, but was bidden to occasional Sunday luncheons which bored me extremely. Since the family adhered rigidly to a seasonal migration, they never knew that by leaving on the last day of August they missed some of the finest and most spectacular days of autumn, when the sea was emerald green and the empty beaches sparkled in the sun under the opalescent light so dear to the hearts of the Normandy painters.

While the Baron was in Paris I went on with my cooking lessons. Madame Hauchecorne was a great teller of tales. She was also the repository of many terrible local secrets. One family particularly amused her perverse nature. They were known as the 'Black Blanchards'—a Gallic play on words—in the community. Blanchard, a farmer, was married to a woman whose successive pregnancies had turned her into a limp rag, so that she was known as 'Chiffe' Blanchard.

Halfway through one of her pregnancies, her young unmarried sister, Bernadette, came to lend a hand in the house and around the farm. She never went home, replacing her sister in Blanchard's bed. By the time I arrived at Honfleur, Bernadette had, in her turn, been supplanted in the farmer's couch by her youngest sister, Lisette.

The Blanchards had no friends; strangers were not encouraged to take an interest in their affairs. Their farm was guarded by large and vicious mastiffs, and Blanchard never moved anywhere without a gun under his arm. Madame Hauchecorne, seemingly, was their one link with the outside world.

Late one afternoon, when I was drinking my usual cup of coffee with the Widow, who had broken her ankle and was confined to her house, there was a timorous knocking at the door. Adeline, Madame Hauchecorne's niece, who was caring for her aunt during her indisposition, had gone shopping. I opened the door to a pale little boy with a long nose, and a mop of tow-coloured hair. I took him into the kitchen where Madame Hauchecorne interrogated him.

'So her time has come, has it?'

The child nodded.

'It's his aunt,' said the Widow, 'she's one of Blanchard's women, the youngest sister. This will be her first. I helped bring most of the others into the world. This one will have to arrive without me. How far gone is she?'

The boy, who could not have been more than six or seven, stood there picking his nose.

'Well, speak up, boy,' snapped the Widow.

I bent over the child, and recoiled from the stench of stale urine emanating from his body.

'She's screeching,' he said, 'screeching fit to bust a gut,' he added.

'That's it then,' said Madame Hauchecorne. 'Crippled or not, I must get to her. Where is that blessed niece of mine? She's another of the ones who are never around when you need her; but if that dratted baby is to live, there's no time to hang about.'

I looked into her soapy, kitten-blue eyes and knew what she expected me to do. She nodded her head as if she had read my mind. Turning to the child, she ordered him to see to it that her trap was harnessed immediately. Old 'Gorille' brought it round and helped us in. Madame Hauchecorne had some difficulty in getting comfortable. She was wearing a mantle like one of my Grandmamma's. Under it was the spotless coarse linen apron she wore for cutting up the dog's offal she fetched once a week from the abattoir.

'Gorille', the taciturn old farmhand who was reputed to relieve Madame Hauchecorne's urges whenever she felt the need of male company, drove us at a fast clip through the darkening, scented green countryside. The horses' hooves made a pleasant clip-clop on the dusty road; and I thought again of Emma Bovary, slight, dishevelled and crazed with desire, running across the marguerite-spangled fields to the arms of her lover.

The Blanchard farmhouse was dark and untidy. The boy took

us into the kitchen, which, at first, seemed to be empty, until we made out the shape of an old crone asleep by the embers of a dying fire. The silence was punctuated by a series of sharp tortured screams.

'Who is up there with her?' asked Madame Hauchecorne.
'She's alone.'
'Where are her sisters?'
'Away.'
'Fetch your father,' snapped the Widow, slipping off her mantle. 'As for you, pretty Madame, go up and see how the poor stupid creature is going along. I'd come with you, but I'd never make those steep stairs. Take a lamp and be careful you don't trip and set fire to the whole stinking barracks.'

The lamp held high showed me a small room almost entirely filled by a large bed. Huddled under the faded quilt was a very young girl. She was fifteen. She stared at me with the dilated eyes of a frightened hare. Her hair was stuck to her damp forehead. A chamberpot next to the bed was filled with excreta. The stench was foul. The windows were hermetically shut.

I went over to the bed and took her limp, sweaty little paw. I had absolutely no idea what I was supposed to do to relieve her pain. She clutched at me, and then began to pant and scream again.

'Where is Madame Hauchecorne, why doesn't she come up to me?'
'She's hurt her ankle.'
'My time is very near. I need help. I'm frightened. I know I am going to die. Help me, please help me.'

Feeling totally inadequate I stumbled down the stairs, just as Blanchard came through the door. He was a massive, shaggy man with the beaked nose and blond hair of a Viking.

'Who the hell is *she*?'
'A little respect if you please, Blanchard, Madame la Baronne has come to lend a hand. Where are your women?'
'Pushed off, the fucking bitches.'
'Now, at this particular moment?'
'Yes.'
'But why, in the name of the Madonna?'
'Because they're a bunch of idle, jealous cunts. They want her upstairs to suffer alone.'
'Because she's having your baby?'

'Yes.'

'Well, I wouldn't exactly give you the Légion d'Honneur for your services to France,' said Madame Hauchecorne, 'but something has to be done to help her, and fast too. I can't get up there, so you'd best bring her down, and we can do the necessary down here.'

This conversation was punctuated by screams and moans from upstairs, and wild cackles from the ancient beldame crouching by the fire.

'What on earth can she find to laugh at?' I exploded, 'particularly at a time like this.'

'She lives in a world of her own. She's pleased her eggs are hatching. See how crouched up she is, she's sitting on a clutch of eggs, and she gets a few sous for every live chick she produces. Now get that fire going properly, and make sure there's plenty of hot water.'

Lisette's bastard was born on a mattress on the floor, after a difficult and bloody labour which, several times, sent me out into the courtyard to vomit. It was a superb, healthy boy weighing nine pounds. When it was all over, Lisette lay white and still on the mattress, clutching the swaddled babe to her breast. Blanchard sat opposite his mother, watching the girl. Several times I caught his fierce, cruel eyes fixed on me, and in spite of myself, I felt a great stab of desire for this dirty, muscular man.

Finally the farmer went off to the cow-byre to see to an ailing beast, and Madame Hauchecorne and I kept vigil. The boy had long since gone to bed in the loft which he usually shared with his cousins and brothers. Towards dawn, Lisette suddenly got off her mattress, and lighting a candle, stood there in her blood-stained shift, building up a roaring fire. She then made coffee, and when she had swallowed a great bowl of it, picked up her son, and went upstairs.

'She'll be all right now,' said Madame Hauchecorne, collecting her possessions. The old woman in the corner laughed shrilly, and lifting up her skirts, showed us with pride that during the long night, she had successfully hatched her brood of chicks.

*

One Thursday I decided to drive up to Notre Dame de Grace. It was a fine sunny day but my heart was heavy. I was sad and troubled. The Baron never ceased to complain that, since my return from Africa, I carried out my conjugal duties with a marked lack of enthusiasm. He also pointed out that there was no need for me to resort to play-acting, but if I felt impelled to emulate Bernhardt, I should improve my performance, which he said, was lamentable.

I was shaken and annoyed, for I knew he was right, but I refused to allow myself to examine the real reasons for my total lack of response to my spouse's sexual prowess.

The little chapel was cool and dark. The thanks and hopes of the faithful flickered in a myriad of candles. I was conscious of a great loneliness. I knelt in front of Our Lady, a penitent, for I knew I had been at fault in marrying the Baron for his title and worldly goods. In becoming his wife, I had promised to take him to my heart, to integrate my feelings for him into the wellsprings of my being. Feeling that I had successfully hoodwinked the Mother of God by concealing from her and from myself the true reason for my state of emotional bankruptcy, I drove home resolved to make a true and lasting peace with my husband.

Chris was lying asleep on the lawn in front of my tower. A golden cocker spaniel puppy was curled up in the crook of his arm. The sight of Chris sprawled there, gangling, dishevelled and dusty—he had walked from Honfleur to the Manoir—made me realise immediately, and with a profound sense of foreboding, that I loved this man passionately, and that I should love his golden sunflower face and bright, sweat-matted hair for the rest of my life.

When he woke, he presented me with Simba, the puppy. I thanked him formally, thus raising a barrier between us. Although his arrival filled me with joy, I made it clear to him that as he was a guest in my husband's house, I was not prepared to treat him differently from any other honoured visitor.

The puppy immediately became the centre of attraction for the whole household. It was a most engaging small creature. Chris himself was obviously exhausted. He said little about how he had occupied his time during the ten days he had spent in Paris before coming to find me. Because I loved him, I knew instinctively that he had spent that time in the pursuit of pleasure in stews and brothels. There was in his hair the scent of stale perfume, and the dark stains under his eyes bore testimony to his obsession with the pleasures of the body, an obsession which was to grow until it occupied him to the exclusion of all else. At that moment, however, Chris reminded me only of a young dog returning, lame, thin and weary after an extensive foray amongst the neighbourhood bitches.

My role was clear. I must be there only to soothe and comfort. Mine must be the cool hand upon the fevered brow; so milord was put to bed and the shutters were closed, but the windows remained open so that the scent of the stocks and roses beneath them could waft through his dark dreams and purify them.

Chris slept for thirty-six hours at a stretch, waking only to sip an egg-flip laced with brandy which I fed him. I told the servants he was suffering from a tropical fever contacted in Africa, and they believed me. The Baron, tiptoeing in to look at his uninvited guest, did not. His deep love for me warned him that here, stretched out like a panther asleep, was a dangerous beast who would threaten his marriage.

In the tower he handed me a glass of porto which he knew I did not care for.

'I hope you don't mind Chris being here? The poor child is quite worn out,' and I dithered on about his being a friend of the family and being in need of care and protection.

He listened to me in silence for some time, then, lifting my hand to his lips, he said, 'Ma mie, it is you who are in need of care and protection, and that child, as you call him, will skin you alive, and eat your heart.'

After this outburst the Baron never again mentioned Chris. As soon as he had recovered from his 'fever', Chris took a room at the nearby Ferme de St Siméon, and having recovered the use of his sports-car which had broken down near Le Havre on his way to see me, flung himself enthusiastically into visiting Normandy, with myself as his guide.

My great enjoyment was visiting churches, castles, cemeteries, museums and art-galleries, and 'antiquing' in the little junk shops which, at that time, were of little interest to any but real collectors. Chris, on the other hand, preferred more active pursuits such as sailing and racing. He liked eating massive meals in the best restaurants in the region. He enjoyed sitting on the terraces of cafés, ogling pretty girls, and had a positive passion for picnics, at which he ate heartily, and then, stretching himself out on the grass, with my hand in his, would stare solemnly and silently up at the sky, as do babies in their prams, until he fell asleep, relaxed and happy with Simba close to him.

At this point in our relationship, my feelings were confused. Chris attracted me as violently as before and I longed only to be in his arms again; at the same time, what he had admitted about his debauchery in Paris had shocked and revolted me; I began to look upon him as a kind of Rimbaud, divining that he, like the young poet, would not lightly be turned from experiencing every sensation life could offer. Furthermore, I had sternly resolved not to complicate my life with the Baron by being again unfaithful to him with a young man at the very beginning of his adult existence.

At the same time, Chris was a unique and enthralling companion. He was endearing and funny; since nobody had ever denied him anything, he carried himself like a young god, walking into the lives of those about him with complete assurance that he would always be welcomed and loved. His ruthlessness and selfishness were already, at this stage, quietly developing, but since in minor matters he was outgoing and generous, one did not sense that still sheathed in its scabbard was the steel blade that he would later wield with such expertise.

Chris, unlike myself, enjoyed our week-end parties, which he attended together with other guests, most of whom liked going over to the Casino at Deauville then presided over by the urbane Monsieur André. Deauville was then one of the favourite watering-holes of international society. The Duke of Westminster berthed his yacht here and gave splendid parties aboard. His special guest was always Mademoiselle Coco Chanel, the couturière, who revolutionised women's fashions, creating for them the comfortable, well-cut little tailored suit which is as popular today as when it first liberated the female body from its constricting corsets.

The old, immensely fat, wise, brilliant, and charming Aga Khan, a friend of Lala, was also a frequent visitor to the Casino, and never failed to stake me at the tables. When I used his *jetons*, I invariably won. I treated these winnings as 'fairy gold', and spent my francs on gifts for my household and friends. I once put all my booty into buying a little gouache by Dufy, and for ever afterwards when I looked at it was reminded of that summer, which was as gay and magical as his representation of yachts bobbing about in the harbour at Deauville.

Once the guests had gone back to Paris, Chris and I would go off on our voyages of discovery. That we were 'discovering' each other did not strike me. Once we found the inn of Guillaume-le-Conquérant at Dives-sur-Mer, and my writer's heart was rejoiced by the long and complicated life story of its *patronne*, as she poured it out to us one rainy afternoon, while she and Chris downed more than one bottle of her best Calvados between them.

The famous hostelry got its name because it was from Dives that William the Conqueror set out for England. The port now serves as an anchorage for yachts. On a tablet over the door of Our Lady of Dives is a list of the names of William's chief companions.

The origins of the inn were lost in the mists of legend, but by the time Madame de Sévigné passed through Dives on her long journey south to Grignan, the inn was well established, and in honour of this most brilliant and maternal of literary ladies, one of the best bedrooms in the hotel bore her name.

'By the time I came to work here,' said Madame Bonnet, pouring Chris yet another glass of 'calva', 'the building looked much as it does now, but then it was a poor and shabby place, badly furnished and uncomfortable. I was taken on as kitchen-maid by the *patron*'s mother, who was a thorough old Attila. The other staff consisting of a couple of young wenches like myself, together with a half-witted fellow who acted as potman and general handy man, were up at dawn, and she worked us like horses right through the day, and well into the night.

'The *patron*, Monsieur Pierre, was the chef, but he hadn't much interest in cooking. It used to make me mad to watch him ruining good victuals. I longed to be able to try my hand at cooking, but nobody would give me a chance. At the time I came, he was a moony, weedy-looking fellow, always whittling bits of wood, which infuriated his mother. Then suddenly, one day she died. She was a massive woman—she must have weighed all of twenty or so stones—and just collapsed in the kitchen like a burst paper bag. Her son took over.

'It did not take him long to reorganise the running of the inn. One of the serving-wenches was sacked, and I took over her duties, as well as those of head cook. I seemed to be on my feet twenty-four hours a day, but I couldn't leave, because by then I'd got involved with the patron, and I was a poor girl with my future to think of. So I stayed on, and Monsieur Pierre started doing what he'd always wanted to do. He had a passion for old things, furniture, pictures and suchlike bits and pieces. He was a collector, and as he was one of the first people in this part of the world to be interested in antiques, he was able to buy up at bargain prices the superb collection he finally amassed, and which turned this place into a real museum. Pierre made it his business to be around when most folk, even the gentry, were interested in replacing their dilapidated old bits of family furniture with fashionable modern stuff. The *patron* never had any qualms about going to the châteaux to ask whether they had any junk in their attics. That "junk" was what you see around here today. Like those candlesticks over there. Worth a fortune they are.'

Parrot-fashion, the good lady recited, 'That *guéridon* was made at the workshop at Maincy, and was designed by Le Brun. It is similar to that made for the Château of Vaux-le-Vicomte. As for those charming little Louis XVI chairs, they were in a shocking state when the *patron* brought them home. But he had taught himself how to repair antiques and worked long and lovingly to restore his "cripples".

'When the patron had satisfied himself that I was a good cook and thrifty manager, he married me. I've always been grateful to him for that, although I soon discovered that he had only taken me to wife to ensure that his inn and his possessions were safely guarded in his absences. Normandy had become too small for him, so he began to rove further afield. He travelled hard-arse, I grant you that. He was never one for indulging himself, and he was something of a miser if truth be known.

'Italy fascinated him, he bought that cupboard with *intarsia* decorations in Verona. As for the marble table in the Voltaire room, I remember him bringing it home on his back. Slipped a disc that trip he did. Italy yielded him a rich harvest. Then he went off to Spain, and the first thing he brought home was that great big ugly Crucifix with the Christ carved in ivory. It came from a Cathedral, and goodness only knows how the *patron* persuaded the priests to part with it.

'By that time Guillaume-le-Conquérant had become a famous inn. The *patron* had a flair for showing off his pieces, and in the end the place was stuffed as full of antique treasures as a museum. People were tickled to death to spend the night in the bed they thought had once belonged to Madame de Pompadour. It became fashionable to dine and to spend the week-end here, and all sorts of grand people used to come from Paris and all over the place: kings and queens, and even actors from the Comédie Française. Our cider was as good as champagne, or that's what that writer, Monsieur Marcel Proust, used to say when he stopped by for a meal with us. He used to stay at the Grand Hotel, not ten minutes from here.

'Quite honestly, my cooking had a great deal to do with our reputation. It attracted clients just as much as the *patron*'s museum pieces. Yet I longed to get shot of the kitchen duties. I was sick to death of slaving all day and night to feed those greedy bellies. But *le patron* was adamant. He wouldn't hear of my giving up. I was young and wanted a bit of fun, you understand. I'd never had anything in my life.... There was nothing doing. We had endless rows until one day the *patron*, just like his mother, collapsed and died, and I became *la patronne*.

'I kept everything just as he had left it. But I took on a chef, and a couple of waitresses. I've kept the traditions of the restaurant going just as he would have wished; but I've not allowed it to swallow me and chew me to bits as it did to his mother and to him. I go away every year to Monte Carlo. I quite enjoy a flutter at the tables, and I have a special friend who takes care of me.'

*

Chris and I lived only for the moment, secure in our own climate. We did not discuss our feelings. I did not want to give voice to my love, believing that in remaining silent I should be less guilty.

Superficially, all was normal. To all intents and purposes, Chris was a young English student, a friend of my family, who had come to France to learn the language. But the Baron was well aware of what was happening to me, for it was at this juncture that he bought two copies of Colette's book, *Chéri*, which he had expensively gift-wrapped, and presented one to me, and the other to Chris one morning.

Chris' family had arranged for him to begin his university life at the end of the summer. Knowing this, I felt acutely that we were living on borrowed time and I totally ignored the Baron's unspoken plea for me to abandon Chris. At that time, everything about him was marvellous in my eyes and all my thoughts were for him only. Even the most trivial events of the days we shared became startling and memorable. I was happy ordering his favourite dishes and buying him surprises. Like a child he loved receiving gifts: like a child he enjoyed them briefly and then forgot all about them. All his young life people had tried to amuse and please him, and a cheap fountain-pen with views of Honfleur on its stem pleased him as much as his mother's gift of a sports car.

Chris had elected to stay on at the expensive and fashionable Ferme de St Siméon at Vasouy, on the Trouville road. In his letters home he described it as a simple, rustic farmhouse, which is what it had been in the 1850s when the corpulent and hospitable Mère Toutain had provided board and lodging for the painters who loved Normandy. One of the faithful, Courbet, painted his famous *Jardin de la Mère Toutain* in 1859, and it was there that Eugène Boudin, master of the St Siméon Group, worked on those admirable paintings, at first recognised only by connoisseurs such as Corot and Baudelaire. Boudin was obsessed by the changing colour of sea and sky on the Norman coast. In 1854, he wrote:

> I still feel this abundance, this delicacy, a shining light which transforms everything before my eyes ... and I simply cannot put that across with my grubby palette. It must be twenty times now that I have started all over again to try and recapture that delightful quality of light which plays on everything around. What freshness there is about it, at once soft, fugitive, a shade pink. Objects become dissolved, so that there are only variations in density everywhere. The sea was marvellous, the sky mellow, velvety; whereupon it changed to yellow, became warm, then, as the sun began to set, the loveliest shade of violet crept over everything; the shore, as well as the dykes took on the same shade.[1]

*

I became very attached to Simba, the little golden puppy Chris had given me. In spite of the Baron's remonstrances—he did not much care for animals, and certainly did not want them in *his*

[1] Eugène-Louis Boudin: *Saint Siméon Notebooks*, 1854.

bedroom—the dog slept in my room in an eighteenth-century basket, shaped like a pagoda and lined with coral velvet. It was a copy of that owned by the 'old, blind debauchee of wit', Madame du Deffand.

Chris loved animals, and cared particularly for Simba. He was a link between us, and when the little creature refused his food, I began to worry. I tried tempting his appetite with every delicacy, from *croissants* to buttered eggs, which he usually devoured with zest. But now he turned his head away, his nose was hot, his coat lifeless and staring.

We summoned the local vet, a tough country realist, more at home with cattle and horses than with a lapdog. He held out little hope of recovery. Chris and I refused to believe him and nursed Simba with almost fanatical dedication. I wanted, more than anything in the world, to save the puppy's life. On the third day, I saw he was weakening. The vet called again, shook his head and went away.

Chris and I sat on the floor looking into the ridiculously ornate basket in which the dog lay, staring at us with loving, fast-glazing eyes. We kept vigil all one night, and then, towards dawn, overcome with fatigue, I went off to lie down for a while. I fell into a heavy slumber from which I was woken by Chris stroking my cheek. I switched on the light. 'I've buried him under an apple tree,' he said. Then he knelt down beside me, and we both cried, because the death of the puppy he had given me was an omen and we both knew it.

*

I cannot remember the exact moment when I decided to leave the Baron. Certainly I was influenced by my love for Chris, but the most important factor was my total inability to submit any longer to the conjugal embraces of my husband. After my return from Africa and my meeting with Chris, I felt both hypocritical and diminished. I also realised that I could no longer endure the rigid and conventional framework of my life. But in those days one did not lightly step out of marriage. Now that Lucy was dead, there was nobody in whom I could confide.

I finally left the Baron's family home after a minor dispute with his mother. It was an insignificant quarrel as quarrels go, but the principles involved were important to me. We did not raise our voices, but four years of mutual secret loathing frothed silently on our lips.

It was the custom of the family to recruit their female domestic labour from the peasant families who had been established on the estate for generations. These shy, raw little country girls started work when they were fourteen and were treated with less consideration than our African servants. They worked for a year in the kitchens, before being allowed into the reception rooms. By the time they had graduated to the bedrooms, they generally went off to marry, so that in the château, apart from a few old retainers like Madame Mère's formidable personal maid, there was a floating population of young female domestics, all apparently terrified out of their wits.

Perrine, the little maid who attended me on the occasion of the quarrel with Madame Mère, was the indirect cause of my departure. I found this child sobbing in our bedroom. When I questioned her, she bellowed ever more desperately into her apron. Finally, having calmed her with *fleur d'orange* and lumps of sugar, I got the truth out of her. Madame Mère had been holding one of her famous 'interrogations' of the staff, during which she grilled her victims in a manner directly inspired by her Borgia ancestors.

A box of crystallised plums had vanished, and the finger of suspicion pointed to Perrine, who was known to have a fondness for sweetmeats. How Madame Mère had discovered this weakness was a tribute to the OGPU regime which operated in the château. Divide and rule was Madame Mère's theory, and most of her servants informed not only upon one another, but on members of the family, and guests at the château.

I knew Perrine had not touched the box of crystallised plums, since the Baron had taken it to Paris in his suitcase to crunch during the night. He was a poor sleeper, and spent many wakeful hours propped up in bed, nibbling bonbons while he read devotional literature and pornographic magazines. Even when I told Madame Mère that her son was the culprit, she refused either to believe me or to apologise to Perrine, let alone reinstate her.

'It is not my habit to apologise to my staff,' she said dryly, and her creamy, cameo-like face, was mottled with angry pink patches.

'If Perrine goes, I go,' I cried dramatically. 'I mean it.' She smiled, a smile of pure triumph. She knew I would carry out my threat and that the family would at last be rid of me. It had never really entered her head that her son cared deeply for the young stranger he had married and brought into the nest of vipers. She wanted only to be quit of my influence and of my undisciplined ways. I was the only daughter-in-law in the whole history of the family to have used a typewriter in the Blue Salon and to have asked for a key to the locked bookcases in the library so that I could read the books that had been put on the Index by the Church.

I was the heretic who had advised the youngest of my six sisters-in-law to run away with the man she loved, although he was only a penniless clerk in the office of the solicitors who took care of the family's affairs. Poor Minette; my advice was her undoing, for she confessed her plans to the fat, sly old village curé, who managed, without contravening his vows, to alert Madame Mère; in no time the romance was nipped in the bud, the young man was sent packing, and Minette whipped away to the Convent which housed her sisters. The Baron told me later that she had been taken, in a strait-jacket, to the mental asylum, where she spent the rest of her brief life, sitting rocking a 'baby' made of sheets ripped off her bed.

I left the château without any drama, and returned to our apartment in the rue du Bac, where I was instructed by the Baron to go to our Father Confessor. He reasoned with me, pleaded with me, prayed with me and for me, but I was adamant. I said I would never, in any circumstances whatsoever, have anything more to do with the Baron's mother.

There was a brief and lunatic moment when I saw a strange gleam in the priest's eye, and realised that he thoroughly agreed with me and understood my motives. I also sensed that he knew about Chris. When I left him, he blessed me and took both my hands in his. I saw then that his eyes were filmed with tears.

When I told the Baron that I wanted to leave immediately, there was such pain in his face that I almost relented. Then, remembering he and his mistress had between them wrecked all chance of our happiness together, I said, 'If I asked you to give me your word never to see the Marquise again, what would you say?'

'If I asked you never to see that terrible boy, that fallen angel, with his flaming sword again, what would *you* say?'

*

I soon found a pleasant and comfortable apartment in the rue de Beaune. It belonged to a French diplomat who was *'en poste'* in Washington and let me have it, complete with staff, for a year. Leaving the Manoir de Rollo was a traumatic moment, but I realised I must cut all the links that bound me to my husband and to my former life. I knew he hoped that what he thought was my 'caprice' for Chris would prove less overwhelming than my nostalgia for the manoir.

Though Chris, during this trying transitional period, remained very much in the background, the fact of his being at hand gave me the impetus and the courage to pursue what seemed to my family and friends a crazy course of conduct.

Surprisingly, only the Baron gave me real support. He was so helpful and understanding that there were moments when I wondered whether he had really understood that I was trying to escape him and all he stood for, or whether he thought I was preparing a love-nest in which we could finally be reunited. Even at this stage it was evident that this very strange and complicated man was going to remain in my life, at whatever cost to his pride and dignity as a *machismo*.

While all this turmoil was going on, I was outwardly leading a normal Parisian life. I went to first nights with Cousin Laurent, exhibitions, and cocktail parties, although I avoided dinner-parties and social gatherings to which the Baron and I had been invited as a married couple. I breathed no word of my plans, even to Lala. I was frightened that she might inadvertently let something slip to Papa, who would immediately have alerted Chris' family. As always, I wrote long letters home, some of which Lala kept, so that reading them some years later I was astonished at the breathless, boundless exuberance and vitality which crackled on those pages.

My literary interests were widening as I met more writers, artists and poets. Most of these, like Cocteau, Louise de Vilmorin, Marie-Laure de Noailles and Serge Lifar were the birds of paradise of the literary and artistic world; I was dazzled by the richness and variety of the lives which they seemed to lead at so many different levels. I was still far too captivated by the outward symbols of success as expressed in amusing parties and social entertainments, masked balls and the like, to understand or appreciate the dark turmoils to which many of the élite were subject, even though they seemed to be sitting securely on the pinnacles of success. In fact, at this time I was much given to hero-worshipping at the shrines of the great or near-great. Since my values were thoroughly confused, I was unable to differentiate between gold and dross.

I moved into the new flat with a sense of delighted anticipation, with little Perrine, whom I had annexed from the château, a Siamese kitten from Chris, and a box of red roses from the Baron. Now, I thought, my life as a writer and as a woman will really begin. I likened myself to George Sand, quite forgetting that she happened to be a genius, well able to survive financially on her own earnings, besides having a private income from her grandmother. I was still using the Baron's money which, as Géa later pointed out, made me just as much of a pimp as he was. This, however, was the dark side of the moon: I preferred to keep my thoughts on sunnier matters.

I was working on a novel, written in French, which had borrowed so much from Alain-Fournier's *Grand Meaulnes*, and, in turn, from *La Grange aux Trois Belles* by Robert Francis, that it became a carbon-copy of a carbon-copy idea. It was, incidentally, at that time, that reading through one of Rimbaud's poems I became convinced that I had discovered the genesis of the idea that had triggered off the *Grand Meaulnes*. Never one to hang back when making what I hoped was a literary discovery of the first magnitude, I wrote a piece elaborating my thesis in a literary journal. A smart letter from Alain-Fournier's executors (inspired perhaps by his sister, who jealously guarded the mystique that had grown up around the book) gave me to understand that I was treading on dangerous ground, and that if I did not want to find myself seriously involved in a dispute which could end in the courts, I must at once write a letter of apology, admitting that my theory was wild, woolly, and totally without substance. This I utterly refused to do, and I still believe that Alain-Fournier was inspired by the prose poem 'Enfance' in *Les Illuminations* by Arthur Rimbaud.

'Dames qui tournoient sur les terrasses voisines de la mer; enfantes et géantes, superbes noires dans la mousse vert-di-gris, bijoux debout sur le sol gras des bosquets et des jardinets dégélés—jeunes mères et grandes sœurs aux regards pleins de pélerinages, sultanes, princesses de démarche et de costume tyranniques, petites étrangères et personnes doucement malheureuses. . . .'[1]

*

I had my scruples about letting Chris move into the flat with me. This excess of conscience annoyed him and was the reason for our first quarrel. He pointed out, correctly, that my main reason for leaving my husband had, in fact, been to live with him, so that by obliging him to continue living in the Hotel Jacob—in the rue Jacob, the street that would mean so much to me in the future—I was 'shutting him out of my life', and must accept whatever consequences this ban might have upon him and his actions.

History and fiction teem with heroines who leap cheerfully from their husband's bed into the arms of a lover, seemingly without torment.[2] I was certain that had my child lived, I should never have gone away, although I blamed the Baron for the fatal crack in our marriage. It was not so much his having a mistress that had shattered my confidence; it was because, deep down, I was certain that the ageing Marquise meant more to him than I did. This wounded my pride both as a woman and as a young bride. Yet today, I know that the Baron *was* in love with me and that my defection destroyed him. In the final analysis, he behaved better than I, by being patient and loving towards me always, even when he knew for certain that I should never return to him.

When I married, I took my conversion to Catholicism very seriously. Born into a family to whom religion was important only when it provoked conventional lip-service at christenings, weddings, and funerals, I was early beguiled by the religious practices of the nuns in the Convent des Parcs where as a child I spent some time before being whisked off dramatically in the middle of the night with a septic appendix.

I was taken to the hospital in the rue Oudinot, where the gentle nuns cared for me for many long weeks. During this period I was

[1] *Oeuvres d'Arthur Rimbaud, vers et prose.* Paris. Mercure de France.
[2] Tolstoy's Anna Karenina was certainly a great exception.

exposed to a shower of devotional and religious literature about little girls of my age departing this earth to the sound of celestial music from crystal trumpets blown by heavenly hosts. Also, I fell in love with Ste Thérèse de Lisieux. This admirable young woman represented to me all that was noble and admirable in the human race and during all these long years she and I have gone on very comfortably together. Due to her loving intercessions many of my prayers have been answered.

But my initial obsession with the Saint was dangerous, for during the time it was at fever-pitch I lived in a rose-coloured, saccharine universe of fantasy, in which I moved gently among the sick, laying my healing paws on the damp foreheads of astonished patients, who were convinced I was sleep-walking.

My deep concern with Ste Thérèse and the Catholic faith soon exasperated my nearest and dearest, for no provision had been made by my family for an eleven-year old candidate for martyrdom. Lala, for one, was having no part of a daughter who refused all nourishment but dry bread, turned her room into a chapel, with wax tapers placed dangerously near the curtains, and sent the cook into near hysterics by trying to wash his feet when he was cooking the Sunday joint.

Fortunately for the peace of the household, I soon lost interest in becoming a saint, mainly because of my inability to prove myself by performing even the tiniest miracle. In no time at all I had convinced myself that my talents lay in the theatre, and that I was a budding Sarah Bernhardt or Duse.

This was an easier fantasy for Lala to handle, but even her patience was sorely tried when I spent my days lying on the chaise-longue in her bedroom, draped in one of her cast-off négligées, a lace handkerchief clasped to my mouth, and my chest torn by a rasping cough. My *Dame aux Camélias* act ended suddenly when I spilt a bottle of red ink on Lala's new carpet. It was the first and only time Papa attempted to chastise me with a hairbrush. He never tried it again, because when he finally caught up with me, after a mad chase round the house, I bit his ankle to the bone.

*

In times of stress and turmoil I have turned always to the sea for comfort and healing. At no time have I been entirely happy away from the ocean; in its vastness and eternal movement I return to my primeval beginnings. There are folk whose affinity with nature—the sea and the earth—is such that their physical well-being can be affected by climatic disturbances. Such a one was my old friend, Charles Marais, who was so closely attuned to the South African land he loved that in periods of drought, he, like the parched vegetation about him, withered and shrivelled without water.

Now I felt the need of the sea, so I travelled down to the South of France, to St Tropez, where I had friends. In those days it was still a typical little port of the Midi, dedicated to fishing and bathed in the luminous sunshine which intensified the hues of the small colour-washed houses and the sails of the fishing smacks moored alongside the quays.

Madame Colette and many of her friends had long since 'discovered' the joys of St Tropez, but unlike their successors, they had no mind to change its simple ways; they went happily along with its ancient customs, shopping in the market with the other housewives, drinking their apéritif on the terraces of the little cafés, and dancing with the fishermen and their girls in the café on the port.

My friends owned an old farm atop a hill. It was a plain, stone-built house in a large unkempt garden tangled with vines, and planted with cork and olive trees. The air was sweet with the scent of thyme and broom which grew in profusion on the mountain slopes. From my bedroom window I had a panoramic view of the great curve of the Golfe de St Tropez, and of the stretch of beach which would, one day, be the playground of the 'topless' brigade.

It was then that I made my first visit to Colette's house at Les Salins, on the outskirts of St Tropez. I was taken there by my friends, one of whom, a young artist, was a protégé of Madame Colette. I remember her warm welcome, and the laughter and gaiety of her guests, most of whom were writers, actors and painters. The atmosphere was one of relaxed *camaraderie*, for all those present were part of the St Tropez group of which Colette was the heart.

We sat in a sort of patio, drinking wine and eating fruit from a great platter heaped with peaches, figs and grapes. Colette's sturdy frame was enveloped in a loose-fitting white garment, rather like a kaftan. She wore sandals on her bare feet, a daring innovation in those days for a middle-aged woman, and there emanated from her wholesome, sun-tanned person an aroma of perfume, honey and garlic, of which she was extremely fond.

There was nothing startlingly unusual about the house. It was an ordinary little Provençal house, painted contadini pink, with green shutters. But Colette was a magician, with the gift of transferring the ordinary into the exceptional. She loved the little property she had bought in 1925, at the time she was entering into the last and greatest attachment of her life; for it was here that Maurice Goudeket, aged thirty-five, wooed and won the woman and writer he had admired since his early boyhood.

In August 1925, Colette wrote to her closest friend, the actress, Marguerite Moréno:

> To find it [the house], I had to tear myself away from the little Mediterranean port, from the tunny boats, from the flat-roofed houses with their washes of faded candy-pink and lavender blue and pale green, away from the streets with their hovering scent of sea-urchins, or nougat, of disembowelled melons.... I found it by the side of a road that automobiles avoid, and behind the most ordinary-looking of iron gates—but a gate that was being choked by oleander shrubs behind it, anxiously reaching out behind the bars to offer the passer-by their posies sprinkled with the true dust of Provence, as white as flour, and finer even than pollen.... Four acres, a vine, orange trees, fig trees with black fruit—and when I have said that the furrows of the vine, between the shoots, were brimming with garlic, pimentoes, with aubergines, have I not said everything?[1]

The house itself was small, and low of ceiling, and behind it were more vines and a palisade of false bamboo, supposed to act as a windbreak, and to protect the house from the wild mistral. A rickety gate led directly on to a crescent of shining beach.

By the time I was invited to *La Treille Muscate* Colette, aided and abetted by Maurice, had worked her usual little miracles. She added on a room which provided a terrace for the first floor, 'a patio pierced with arcades which claimed to provide shade, but

[1] From *Prisons et Paradis (Earthly Paradise), op. cit.*

was chiefly an excuse for climbing plants', wrote Maurice, ruefully, in *Close to Colette*.[1]

The garden was jaunty with flowers, and tiny crystal drinking troughs attached to the branches of the trees slaked the thirst of the songbirds who chirped away the lazy sun-drenched hours. Colette wrote many memorable pages in her study, the tiny room she had chosen as a workroom. Of all her books, *La Naissance du Jour*,[2] written here, is the greatest expression of her craft, both as a writer and as a mature woman. Here the joys of the spirit and the joys of the flesh became one and indivisible:

> I hear the bottles clinking, as they are carried towards the well whence they will emerge, chilled and refreshing, and ready for tonight's dinner. The one that contains wine as rosy as red currants will flank the green melons; the other belongs as of right to the salad made of tomatoes, pimentoes and onions drowned in oil and to the ripe fruits of the earth.[2]

During dinner someone extolled the joys of Porquerolles as one of the most romantic and unspoilt of the islands off this coast. I had, of course, heard of the 'Golden Isles'—the islands of Hyères, and particularly of the Island of the Levant, home of the nudists, and of its sister island, Port-Cros, a natural bird sanctuary. Suddenly I decided that it was at Porquerolles that the lump of ice around my heart might well be dissolved in this magical unknown island. I have always been attracted to islands and by the notion of living on one. In the fantasy world in which I so often took refuge, I saw myself living in peaceful exile on some coral isle; a female Crusoe, spending my days in the water or on the lint-coloured beaches, gathering tropical shells. Yet I was well aware that I was, in truth, far too gregarious and dependent upon my fellow-man to be able to live alone. Even so, all my life, whenever possible, I have pursued this particular mirage by visiting islands all over the globe.

In the Seychelles I came as close to the Garden of Eden before the Fall as was permitted a poor sinner; at St Helena I looked out over the great bastions of heaving water that had kept

[1] *Close to Colette* by Maurice Goudeket (Secker and Warburg, London, 1957).
[2] *La Naissance du Jour* (*Break of Day*), (Secker and Warburg, London, 1961).

Napoleon trapped in the house at Longwood, against whose walls he finally bashed out what remained of his life.

So I telephoned Chris, and he met me at Hyères. We embarked from la Tour-Fondue on a sea so blue that it looked as if it had been woven from bits of the Madonna's mantle. We were both well aware that this brief crossing from one shore to another was of great importance to us. It was a symbolic step in our relationship; the crossing of the final bridge, into the uncharted country of love.

In those days, Porquerolles had not yet become a tourist trap. Real people lived out their lives on the island that was their home. The little boat was filled with provisions; apart from ourselves, there were only two other passengers, a large white woolly dog and a housewife with as pure and classical a profile as the statue of a Roman Empress. She was obviously returning from her weekly trip to market, for her baskets were brimming over with provisions. She and the boatman were old friends, and were on excellent terms, laughing and joking in the throaty, garlic-scented accent of the Midi which is as special to this part of the world as its honey-sweet figs and great sun-warmed tomatoes.

We sat, Chris and I, speechless with pleasure, encapsulated in a bubble of gold, crystal and blue formed by the sea, sun and sky. Although we sat apart, I was as conscious of his body as if we had been lying naked in bed. I looked at his brown hand lying on the wooden slatted seat, and was astonished at the surge of love it provoked in me.

I had been advised to book in at the Mas du Langoustier, originally built as a sea-house for the Fournier family who, then as now, owned the island. It was a pleasantly proportioned old house, filled with fine pieces of Provençal furniture. The hotel was three kilometres from the village in a setting of umbrella pines and other trees. It had its own jetty and private beach. Many writers and painters came there to work and to enjoy the charm of the clean, airy rooms and excellent *cuisine*.

We feasted on grilled lobster and on *loup* grilled and *flambéed* on branches of fennel. For the first time I tasted *tian*[1] and mussels with spinach stuffing.

I had booked two single rooms with windows opening on to a communal balcony. Before I had finished unpacking, Chris

[1] Tian: a cod-and-spinach pizza-type dish.

bounded in through the open window, and flung me on my bed. Brilliant sunshine poured into the room, flooded through me and bearing me away on a tide of suffocating pleasure. Chris was then neither an experienced nor a gentle lover. He was an eager, clumsy, selfish young male, anxious to assuage the pent-up desire that made me momentarily in his eyes the most desirable sex-object in the world.

We fell asleep snuggled up together in the narrow bed, with its now stained and rumpled white coverlet wrapped round our ears. I woke first and gently disentangled myself from my companion, whose long limbs were sprawled across me, and who murmured sleepily when I tried to slide from under his legs. I was hot and tousled and longed for a bathe. I had just succeeded in wriggling free, when an arm pulled me back and held me close. I looked into the beloved face, and deep into his eyes. I became absorbed in their pattern.

'They are like paperweights,' I murmured, 'like one of Colette's paperweights.'

'Time for a bathe,' cried Chris, jumping up and rolling me off the bed, and in an instant, the naked, apricot-tinted savage was off. Love-making was over for the time being.

*

Our short stay on the island was memorable for many reasons, not the least of them being that our relationship reached a peak of perfection never again to be equalled. Chris, when he concentrated on the object of his affections, was the ideal companion. He was thoughtful, tender, loving and merry. For the first and only time in my life, I was so completely absorbed in another human being, that my critical faculties were completely lulled and dulled. I read into Chris' behaviour-patterns all manner of attributes, which, with hindsight, I realise he did not possess. Had he done so, he would have been a demi-god, not simply a virile young male with an urgent sex-urge and great potency. But to do him justice, there was more to Chris in his salad days than to most youths; he seemed to spread a golden radiance that emmeshed all who had contact with him, regardless of age and sex, in a web of enchantment.

Each night in his arms, I surrendered more and more of my secret self; by morning the fusion of our two selves became a torch that ignited the rest of the day with splendour. We soon developed a routine, a pattern which was invariable, and was the frame of our days of love.

We woke early, made love and went down to the beach to bathe. Chris was an excellent swimmer, and sometimes I became exhausted following him out into the blue depths where he dived and curveted round me like a dolphin. Often we floated lazily on our backs, hand-in-hand, exchanging salty kisses and identifying completely with the ocean and the sun. We breakfasted late on our balcony, and then bathed and sunbathed until it was time for luncheon and the siesta on my bed, behind closed shutters, while the cicadas in the pinewoods made scratchy music.

In the late afternoons we went fishing with an old sailor who had become our friend. Sometimes we sailed or walked or just lay under the umbrella pines reading poetry aloud or just talking. Although the flora on Porquerolles was not as abundant as on Port-Cros, which is covered with rosemary and lavender bushes, the air was honey-scented with sun-warmed genista, and everywhere there was myrtle and yellow jasmine. We were told that in the eighteenth century date palms and pistachio trees had been grown on the island. We were so completely at one that we hardly noticed any of the other visitors in the hotel. The nearest we got to a quarrel was when we sailed over to the Island of the Levant, a nudist colony. We had to get special permission to land. I was not anxious to see anyone but Chris, but he wanted to know how the nudists lived.

The Isle du Levant is a rocky crest, girdled with inhospitable cliffs, and I was immediately dismayed by the sight of a bunch of nudists of assorted sexes sitting on the rocks and looking, for all the world, like a baboon family.

We had been invited to take tea with one of the doctors who lived in Heliopolis, capital of the island. It was suffocatingly hot, and we trailed limply along to the doctor's bungalow. The front door was opened by a little maid in a black dress with a white frilly apron and beribboned cap. She showed us into a waiting-room, as dreary as nearly all such places. We sat thumbing through ancient periodicals until a well-groomed, middle-aged secretary or assistant, in a crisp white coat, came to fetch us.

She guided us through the house, into a drawing-room stuffed with ugly modern furniture. Here, the doctor and his family awaited us, all stark naked. It took great self-control not to explode into hysterical giggles. I was pleased my dear Lala was not with us, for had she been, she would already have been lying helpless on the floor, a prey to gales of mirth. Chris was admirable. He bowed over Madame's hand, shuddering slightly as her large breasts bounced perilously near to his nose. She was surrounded by young ladies, one of whom was exquisitely beautiful. She was sixteen or seventeen at most, and well aware of her youthful charms. Chris could hardly tear his gaze from her small, enchanting breasts with their virginal pale rose nipples.

Indeed, he was singularly silent as we sat there drinking cups of very weak tea, and crunching little biscuits that tasted of sawdust. Neither the doctor nor his wife had been to England; but their eldest daughter, who looked like a bad carbon copy of her beautiful sister, had spent some months with an English family at Folkestone. Her ideas about British habits were mimsey, to say the least.

The doctor sported a small black goatee beard and looked like a satyr. He was the first health freak I had met. He poured out a stream of facts and figures relating to the value of ultra-violet rays on naked flesh; on how to become a centenarian by eating *koumiss*, which I gathered was fermented mare's milk, obtainable mainly in parts of Russia and much esteemed by Tolstoy. While I was wondering with one part of my mind how *koumiss* was exported, I was observing, with considerable annoyance, the pantomime going on between Chris and the ravishing Armène. When she took him on to the terrace to look at the view, I could willingly have stuck a knife between his shoulder-blades.

After offering us a glass of sticky Porto, accompanied by soggy sponge fingers, the doctor invited us to visit the beach, and to meet some of his patients and friends. Before Chris could answer, I said I had a headache and wished to go back to Porquerolles. The doctor accompanied us back to our craft. He wore a panama hat and carried a cane, and his genitalia—he was particularly well endowed—swung up and down as we walked down the dusty path from the villa *Mon Plaisir* to the quay.

On the way home Chris started to laugh, and he laughed and bellowed until he fell, as helpless as a mating tortoise, to the bottom of the boat. Every time he thought of the doctor, he burst into a fresh guffaw, and ended by laughing so hard that he choked, and had to be banged on the back.

Late that evening, while we were taking our usual after-dinner stroll, he said, 'Let's go and have coffee and a cognac at Marius' place.' This was the little café on the port to which we went when we wanted local colour.

It was a very hot night, and the air was thick with insects, which flew into our eyes and mouths whenever we opened them. At the café Chris ordered coffee for two, a *cerise à l'eau de vie* for me, and a *fine* for himself. I was wearing a white, deceptively simple linen dress which had cost a fortune, with white and gold Pinet sandals. Chris said, 'You look so sophisticated, so very Parisian.'

'You're making fun of me?'

He gave me a strange, glinting look, 'Not really.'

At that instant, I heard the phut-phut of an engine. One of the *belote* players at the next table, lifted his head, and listened attentively. 'That's Gros Loulou's boat from *Le Levant*.' I knew immediately that Loulou would be carrying a passenger, and was therefore not at all surprised to see Mademoiselle Armène, now clothed in an ordinary and rather unbecoming little dress, walking towards us. She seemed rather crestfallen at seeing me with Chris. I wondered whether he had told her he would manage to sneak out to a rendezvous. She ordered a sticky syrup drink. I realised that Chris had lost his grip on the situation and relied on me to help him out by making Armène welcome. I made her so welcome, that her pretty mouth drooped at the thought of her duplicity. She looked at her watch and then in the direction of Gros Loulou, who was chatting with his friends.

'I mustn't be too late. Maman may be waiting up for me,' she said.

Chris spoke sharply: 'I don't want her to go.'

'Where will she sleep?'

'We'll work that out later.'

'But, Chris, what about her parents?'

'Ring them and tell them she's not feeling well, or better still, tell her to send a note by the boatman.'

I knew, of course, what the outcome of Armène's visit was likely to be. But, when we got back to the Mas du Langoustier, she clung to my arm and refused to leave me. She accompanied me to my room. My bed was slightly larger than Chris'. I lent Armène one of my nightgowns, and she flopped in beside me, looking beguiling and childish, with her corn-gold hair in two plaits, and toothpaste at the corner of her lips. I had just turned out the light when Chris, with a Nijinsky-like leap, landed from the window on to the bed between us. He's learning too fast, I thought cynically, as he snuggled in between us, but Armène was terrified, and wound her arms round my neck, begging me to protect her.

After that I remember only a tangle of bodies. Armène's hair smelled of almond soap. When she began to whimper, I took her in my arms. Her body was pliant and melted into mine. Gently, I kissed her soft mouth. In the end, Chris took what he wanted from her, and when she cried out, I hated him and hit out at him with my fists. But when he took me into his arms I forgot Armène. I forgot I had just shared my lover with another female, and loving him, I floated away into another dimension.

An Unofficial English Rose

Chris and I set up house together in the flat in the rue de Beaune. It did not take me long to realise I should have to be both tolerant and patient with him—two qualities most alien to my nature—for Chris was unpunctual and untidy. He had no thought of time, and only the vaguest idea of how to look after his own creature comforts. Always there had been a posse of African servants to minister to his slightest whim. Fortunately my staff became as magnetised by Chris' charm as I was, so they served him willingly. He rewarded them with largesse, for he was generous; but they treasured even more his swift and flashing smile which never failed to melt me, even when he was behaving like the spoilt child that he was.

In the early days of our liaison we had little use for the world outside our flat. I did not think the Baron's circle would take too good a view of my 'scandalous' behaviour, so I avoided seeing anyone even remotely connected with my marriage. We lived happily from day to day, insulated from all mundane cares and material considerations. Chris did not have to rely on his allowance from his family. He had inherited a large fortune from a paternal uncle who had amassed his wealth in South America. Uncle Penrose had never married, and had seen his nephew Chris only once, when he visited his brother in South Africa. But something about the radiant little boy had enchanted him, and he had left him a considerable sum, together with an estate called 'La Stella'.

This estancia exercised Chris' imagination, and he often said that instead of going to university, he was tempted to go and live on his ranch. He described the ideal existence we could lead there, away from all authority. Evidently 'authority' had curious connotations for him, for although he was the spoilt and beloved child of his mother, he resented her constant efforts to tie him to her apron strings. Yet, there was always something of Peter Pan in Chris. He did not really want to face up to the responsibilities of being an adult.

I soon gave up trying to write, and concentrated instead on keeping Chris happy and amused. This was not easy, as our views on what constituted amusement were widely divergent. In all the years I had lived in Paris, I had never really sampled its tourist attractions; but now, with Chris who was determined to 'go on the town', I found myself spending every night at one or the other of the popular spectacles devised to attract foreigners.

Fortunately this was the era of stars of the calibre of Maurice Chevalier, Mistinguett, and Josephine Baker, so it was no hardship to be Chris' companion at the Lido, the Folies-Bergère, and even the Grand Guignol Theatre, where every act was drenched in torrents of stage blood.

It was more difficult for me to follow my young man in the perigrinations that took place after the leg shows were over. I was almost a teetotaller, but Chris soon developed a taste for Scotch-on-the-rocks. He was also addicted to small, smoky bars and nightspots of every kind. Both of us were naïve enough to be impressed by what seemed to us to be haunts of vice, but which were, in fact, carefully baited tourist-traps to lure visitors to spend time and money, either as voyeurs, or taking part in dubious masquerades.

There were *boîtes* in which men dressed as women, and others in which women dressed up as men in boiled shirts, trousers and dinner-jackets, danced solemnly with their excited clients, or with one another when trade was slow. Few of these ladies were truly dedicated to Sappho. Most of them were originally poor girls from the country, struggling to bring up illegitimate children, or to provide a living for ailing husbands or lovers. Some of the clubs offered extraordinary 'attractions'. One was concerned with a girl and a donkey; another went in for a very sophisticated kind of strip-tease act. The cabaret I liked best specialised in witty and polished songs and poems that lampooned the government and current events. But *Le Lapin Agile* in Montmartre was not to Chris' taste. He preferred taking me to a particularly plushy brothel, where we could watch the sex act being performed by clients, through a two-way window.

Gradually our lives began to take on a pattern. We slept late into the morning, which was hardly surprising, seeing we seldom got home before 4 or 5 a.m. Most days Serge and I tried to educate Chris by taking him to exhibitions, museums and art-galleries. But he soon grew sick of artistic manifestations and went off to play golf, to ride, or to play tennis or squash.

We dined late, sometimes with acquaintances we had picked up in the course of our wanderings around the nightclubs, and we always paid a visit to the *Dingo* in Montparnasse, where a consumptive Negro pianist, a disciple of Fats Waller, a lovely man and our dear friend, kept an audience of admirers enthralled.

After the Dingo it was time to look in at Bricktop's or for a drink at either the Dome or the Select, at Montparnasse. The Boulevard St Germain was not then as popular as it is today, and most of the action took place in Montmartre or in Montparnasse.

There was always a party in progress, in a studio or in someone's flat. If there were poverty-stricken geniuses like Modigliani wandering around, Chris and I did not meet them. We tagged around with a band of playboys and girls, sons and daughters of foreign diplomats *en poste* in Paris or wealthy businessmen who were managing the French off-shoots of great international consortiums.

I had little in common with the majority of these young people, many of whom resented my influence over Chris; but, because he was determined to ride this merry-go-round of idleness and pleasure, and I could deny him nothing, I went with him. He was drinking far more than was good for him, and most of our squabbles were brought about by my badgering him to curtail his intake of 'hooch', as he called it.

Inevitably when one moves about in a group of this kind, there is a slick kind of in-patter, and a number of signs and symbols, like the wearing of a particular Hermès scarf and a gold charm bracelet for the girls. The young men sported a gold Dunhill lighter. These were the *beautiful* people of the time, and they did not differ much from those of today. There would be embarrassing incidents when one of the group had too much to drink and, after a furious row, he or she would stalk out into the night. I did not then realise that Chris was drinking heavily to paper over the cracks in our relationship; he was subconsciously aware of these cracks long before it dawned on me that the love of my life was no longer happy.

We had problems. Chris' family were becoming increasingly

curious and suspicious about his way of life, particularly since our encounter with a couple, friends of his eldest brother, with whom we teamed up in a nightclub. They reported back that Chris was well on his way to becoming an alcoholic, and that I, his mistress, would not allow him out of my sight.

The arrival of his brother Niall did little to improve the situation. Niall was appalled at what he called Chris' 'rake's progress', and blamed me severely for setting an innocent young man on the road to ruin. The situation was not improved by Chris' violent denunciation of his family who were, he told Niall in one of his tempests of rage, trying to sabotage the only significant relationship he had ever had. I admit to being slightly surprised at Chris' passionate defence of our love. At the same time I was greatly reassured and comforted. After appealing dramatically to me to allow his little brother to return to his former 'pure, clean and blameless life', Niall left Paris, having spent his last two nights there in a brothel to which Chris introduced him. Niall, like Chris, was partial to captive tarts. Chris once told me it was something to do with the 'harem instinct'. After that I teased him by calling him Pasha.

Rumours of our liaison were by now flooding Johannesburg, and I knew that sooner or later Lala or Papa would take me to task over my dissolute existence with Chris. Papa had not taken at all kindly to my break with the Baron, even though I had never given my family my real reasons for this extreme step.

Whenever airmail letters from South Africa invaded our breakfast-tray, Chris and I simply took to the road. We packed our cases, had them loaded into his car, and off we went with the sunroof down, and our noses to the wind. Chris was a brilliant, if eccentric, driver and drove much too fast for my peace of mind.

In those days the pound sterling was master and was in our favour. We had no problems about money. The sun-circuit took us to Cannes for a brief fling at the Casino. We then drove up to see friends at St Paul de Vence, at that time filled with an uneasy mix of nymphos and homos. From England there was quite a colony of 'emancipated' couples, both of whom were women. One wore the soft corduroy culottes of the peasant; while her friend, in chintzy smocks, wove or 'potted' in studios in the damp, picturesque houses they leased in the enchanting old town which curled like a snail about itself, confined by its great bastion of a wall.

The hotel, the Colombe d'Or, was already acquiring an international reputation, as much for its superlative cooking as for the pictures the *patron* was collecting. Many of these by famous artists were given to him in lieu of payment for his hospitality.

I preferred comfort to roughing it. Chris did not care whether we had a bathroom or not; he preferred sea-bathing to lying in a tub, and there were times when I had to go to work with cotton wool soaked in Cologne on his grimy neck and ears.

Our absences from Paris became longer, our travels more feverish. We were beginning to pursue a fugitive Eros. In a tiny, mosquito-haunted room Chris loved me fiercely and frenziedly. When he was asleep, I stood at the window and looked out at the wild horses of the Camargue as they galloped along the shore, manes and tails flying in the wind; and I covered my young lover tenderly with the sheet, and went out into the dawn, where I walked by the sea, and all the time tears were sliding down my face and lips that were cut and bruised by the violent pressure of Chris' mouth.

In Venice there was a truce, and we knew such perfect ecstasy and harmony that I knew I should never again go there without him. There was a film festival in progress at the Lido, and somehow we got sucked into the razzmatazz of the celebrations. In Harry's Bar, we met and were adopted by a famous Hollywood magnate who wanted to make Chris into a star. For a moment he was beguiled, and then, having spent three days shut up in a movie-theatre, watching endless films, he got bored, and we ran away to Capri.

I had first visited Capri with Lala on one of those astonishing and rewarding 'tours' to which she treated me whenever she thought I needed educating. After a week in Rome, during which she shamed me by setting fire to an old lady's tippet in the catacombs, we went to Amalfi and then to Capri where she had a date with Axel Munthe, an old flame of hers.

He wanted to show her round his beloved San Michele, so he called for us at the hotel and took us to see the lovely place he had created. I thought his home the most original and beautiful I had ever seen, for though it was small and sparsely furnished, the pieces in it were perfection. But most of all was I impressed with his library. This he had assembled in the ancient chapel, once known as *La Polverière*, the powder-magazine. In this white-washed room, with its old cloister-stalls, was a splendid refectory table on which stood books and fragments of terra-cotta figurines. Here, Dr Munthe had assembled his most precious possessions. I remember vividly the marble head of Medusa which he said he had found in the sea; and a stained-glass window of great beauty, the gift of Eleonora Duse.

I had great hopes of Capri as a place of healing for myself and my young man, whose inner tensions were revealed by the way he tossed, and turned, and mumbled in his sleep. But Chris was not interested in Capri or in San Michele, with its terraces, loggias and cypresses. Ancient monuments had lost their lure for him. He was on the hunt, a male animal a-quiver with lust. It was here in Capri that Chris first espied Miss June-Mary Driver, an English rosebud, aged seventeen, who was touring the Continent with her parents, Colonel and Mrs Driver, of Paradine Manor, near Cheltenham.

It was I who first drew Chris' attention to this non-pareil of feminine perfection. I was fascinated by the sight of this demure young girl, in her childish blue and white striped cotton dress, wolfing down an endless succession of ices and sticky cakes. I itemised her charms aloud to Chris who was languidly leafing through a newspaper. I praised her flawless complexion, delicate features, silver-gilt hair, and slim bronzed legs. Chris did not once look over the top of the paper at this paragon. He seemed totally unaware of the existence of Miss June-Mary Driver.

Soon afterwards I was laid low with some kind of virus, and had to retire to my bed. Chris popped in and out with fruit and armfuls of flowers which gave me a headache. I knew that like all healthy young animals he disliked the aura of illness, and did not therefore think it strange that he spent so little time in my bedroom.

It was my sloe-eyed chambermaid who told me that I must not worry about Chris pining for me. He was being taken care of by the beautiful young English girl and her parents. Miss June-Mary, unlike myself, to whom exercise meant breakfast-in-bed, was an open-air girl who played hockey for her county, and in spite of her seeming fragility, was as tough as an ox, and liked nothing better than a long hike before breakfast. Her rose and silver beauty enchanted Chris. Furthermore, she played him like a fish tantalising him with her pretty little ways. She was a virgin, and had every intention of retaining her maidenhood until her wedding night. Chris had never met anyone so beguiling, pure, and as blissfully stupid as the rosebud from Gloucestershire. Unlike myself she could teach him nothing, but he could mould her as he wished, and this was a blessed relief from a mistress who not only knew most of the answers, but insisted on imparting them to him.

Yet, all the time this charming little romance was shaping up, it never once entered my head that Chris had fallen out of love with me, and violently in love with someone else. He made love to me as often and as vigorously as ever; and my much-vaunted feminine intuition was sadly at fault, for it was not until the final débâcle that I discovered that while he was spending passionate hours in my arms, he was also paying assiduous, if discreet, court to Miss June-Mary.

*

Our favourite restaurant in Paris was 'La Petite Chaise', a small, intimate place close to our flat. It was very old. 'Le Cabaret de la Petite Chaise' had first opened its doors to travellers on the stage coaches from Le Havre in 1681; and one of its earliest patrons was Philippe d'Orléans.

The archives of the restaurant record that in the eighteenth century it was patronised by Bourrienne, Napoleon's private secretary, and his aide-de-camp, Junot. Later it became a popular meeting-place for writers and poets such as Huysmans and François Coppée.

Chris and I felt comfortably at home in this little room with its Louis XIV grille, old beams, rafters and shabby velveteen seats. It had an ambience attractive to lovers, many of whom, like ourselves, were greeted warmly by the head waiter and always given the same table.

The management of the time, besides employing a good chef whose execution of the *specialité de la maison*, an *omelette à la Brillat-Savarin*, was nothing short of extraordinary, was anxious to attract the wealthy foreigners who thronged Paris in the season, and so they provided a cabaret composed of an indifferent pianist and of an exciting young singer called Roberta. She had a small, throaty, throbbing voice which she used with great effect to croon the song hits of the day. These included 'Miss Otis Regrets', 'Music Maestro, Please', 'La Vie en Rose', and 'These Foolish Things', which, more than any other, can be said to have been 'our' song, for its bitter-sweet lyrics could have been written specially for us, and even today when the tunes of the thirties are played in the style of the moment, I tremble, and block my ears to the siren song of the past.

*

This was the apogée of the reign of Charles and Marie-Laure de Noailles and her coterie, which included 'beautiful and brilliant people' of that era. Periphery figures were Salvador Dali, with long antennae moustachios and his lovely and beloved wife, Gala.

The tout-Paris who numbered Cousin Laurent as one of its members talked of little else but the forthcoming visit of George VI and Queen Elizabeth. This turned out to be the biggest and most popular event since the state visit of Queen Victoria and her consort to Paris as the guests of Napoleon III and of the Empress Eugénie. The French, having effectively disposed of their monarchy by cutting off their heads, have always had a nostalgic respect and affection for the British Royal Family.

People were staggered at the popularity and high prices asked for and *obtained* for Cézanne's paintings. 'Des Stacks', a study of chimneys, for which the Master's son was asking one million old francs, made headlines in the newspapers. Cousin Laurent took me along to look at this painting, which was on view in the flat of the painter's heir known simply as Cézanne fils.

He lived in an unpretentious apartment in Montparnasse. It was difficult to get a good view of 'Les Stacks', as Cézanne's grandchildren were swarming around a toy train which seemed to take up most of the available floor space. Once one had straddled a few tiny tots and pushed others out of the way, for Cézanne fils was every bit as prolific as his sire although in a different way, there was a powerful display of some of the old man's works, notably some early panels, 'a picture of a mountain', and a dazzling portrait of the artist's wife by Renoir, whom I infinitely prefer as a painter to the gaunter and greater Cézanne.

Another event in the world of art was Gertrude Stein's move

from her house in the rue de Fleurus to a flat once occupied by the enigmatic Queen Christine of Sweden. Here, Miss Stein rehoused her famous collection of paintings. Laurent, invited to a private view in the new setting, reported the existence of one hundred and thirty-one canvases, all of them masterpieces. The writer meticulously supervised hanging the major canvases in her salon. Among these, said Laurent, were her portrait by Picasso, a full length nude (rose period) and the 'Girl with the Basket of Flowers' by the same artist.

Chris did not choose to accompany me to parties or to art exhibitions. He was frankly bored by the array of fashionably garbed and bejewelled women and their escorts, most of them elderly, discreetly sporting the narrow red ribbon of the Légion d'Honneur in their buttonholes. Since most of the people I met at these parties and receptions were friends or acquaintances of the Baron, I soon realised from the stiff bows and cool nods of salutation that greeted my arrival that I was persona non grata, and an embarrassment to a society not prepared to accept me on my own terms. So I decided to concentrate entirely on Chris, his education and general welfare. It was soon evident, however, that his life was taking a totally different direction from mine, a path which caused me deep concern, since he was spending more and more time carousing the night through in nightclubs and bars with a group of parasites, attracted as much by his personality as by his generosity.

Chris sowed his wild oats in spectacular fashion. He drove a Bugatti or rode a bicycle; one night he brought home some of the members of an American jazz band, whose playing he had enjoyed in some night club. In company with the other occupants of the flats in our building, I was woken to the strains of Alexander's Ragtime Band. I was not amused, nor was our concierge, who arrived at our door to threaten me with police proceedings.

Chris was drunk, wild-eyed and unrepentant. With exaggerated courtesy he introduced the concierge and myself to a yellow-skinned, slit-eyed drummer, who was, he said, the only representative in Europe of a sect of Chinese Jews.

*

Chris slept away most mornings, rolled up like a hedgehog in my bed. In the afternoon, he rode in the Bois, played tennis, golf or squash, or went swimming or racing with friends of his own age, and all the time, unbeknown to me of course, he visited Miss June-Mary Driver, whenever possible, at the expensive school in Passy in which she was being 'finished'. Chris passed himself off as her South African cousin, and was allowed to take her out, provided she was accompanied by the dim elderly arts mistress, who quite enjoyed these outings.

Thanks to her, Chris was taken to all the more respectable and old-fashioned *salons de thé* in Paris. Among these were Rumpelmayer, and the Marquise de Sévigné, whose décor, all gilt and velvet, had not altered since 1908. The Marquise de Sévigné was particularly popular with old ladies, since it was an absolute rule of the house that anyone entering these premises must wear a hat.

Although I knew nothing of Chris' growing passion for Miss June-Mary, I was well aware of the rapid disintegration of our relationship. I was equally aware that there was nothing I could do to stop the rot. If I wished to keep him, it would have to be on his terms, and I would have to accept unquestioningly the life he offered me. There were times, particularly when I had waited in all evening for him to take me to a dinner-party, when I rebelled, and swore that I would stand no more of his high-handed nonsense, and threatened to throw him out.

Inevitably, when he finally came home, pale and dishevelled, with glittering snake eyes, stinking of drink, stale cigarette smoke and scent, I allowed him into my bed, where he curled up contentedly against me, and, murmuring tender endearments, dropped off to sleep. Many were the dawns that saw me, wide-eyed and desperate, with the bedside light on, leaning over Chris, committing to memory the curve of his cheek, the faint blue smudges of dissipation under his closed lids, and the still childish mouth that touched my heart. I never loved him as much as during those early morning vigils, when the scurrying creatures of the night had, at last, gone to rest, and Paris was beginning to wake to a new day with a symphony of familiar sounds.

There were the hiss and spray of the watercarts, the noisy engines of delivery vans on their matutinal errands, and the pealing of church bells. My bathroom window opened on to one of the narrow little streets behind the rue de Beaune. It was, as are many Parisian streets, a complete entity. It had the air of a tranquil provincial town, and I looked down with interest, as, one by one, the shutters of the shops were rolled up. The windows of the charcuterie were dressed with art: with shining galantines, succulent pâtés and sausages, of every shape and size, artfully arranged to tempt the palate, and to act as foils to the truffled aspics and rosy *jambonneaux*, looking like choirboys in their neat white frills.

The *laiterie*, though impeccably clean, still made use of the large, old-fashioned churns into which the milkwoman dipped a ladle in order to fill up pots and jugs brought her for this purpose by the housewives of the *quartier*. I grew to recognise some of these ladies, many of whom seemed to be prematurely aged. Most of them wore flowered wrapover pinnies, with a black shawl draped across their shoulders to keep out draughts. Their hair was screwed in a scrawny bun atop their heads, their only ornaments were a worn gold wedding-ring and tiny gold rings in their ears. Most of them wore black felt slippers, which used to be the hallmark of the French working-class woman, who took infinite pains not to mark her waxed and highly polished flooring.

Equipped with the capacious and ubiquitous *filet*, they trotted from shop to shop, as if on a crusade, which is what their shopping was. No French housewife ever bought more than was necessary for her daily needs; few homes possessed a refrigerator, and as everything had to be fresh, it was simpler and more economical to go food-shopping each day. The shopkeepers were used to their clients delicately handling their wares; it was quite in order to press a melon, sniff a cheese, pinch a chicken, prod a fish; only the touching of soft fruits was taboo, as they bruise so easily.

Sometimes Chris would wake up, and seeing me at the window would ask what was going on in the street; I would embroider the scene below, making up fantastic incidents which amused him. Once I told him that I was watching a nanny-goat being milked on the pavement; he roared with laughter and accused me of having gone too far. Then he leaped out of bed and stood staring down transfixed at the little Savoyard shepherd who, like many of his kind, came down from the mountains to earn a few francs by selling goat's milk and cheeses, wrapped in leaves, to the Parisians.

More and more I was losing touch with Chris. At first, like a sheepdog trying to bring in a lost lamb, I used to dash off to find him, losing all dignity in a bar and nightclub crawl. As he was lavish with his tips, I never did catch up with him, since the patrons of the establishments he frequented covered up for him, either disclaiming all knowledge of his existence or actually hiding him, when, in the plushier night joints, my arrival was signalled by the commissionaire to the maître d'hôtel. Naturally the habituées everywhere followed the course of our disintegrating love-affair with breathless interest and curiosity.

Everyone was very polite to me. Polite, kind and slightly mocking. It is always amusing to see a woman making a spectacle of herself over a young, a too young man. I was well aware of the irony in the eyes and voices of those I interrogated; but my pride was submerged in the panic I felt whenever I thought of life without Chris.

We did not have many scenes. Chris did not like confrontations. He preferred simply to drift out of a situation that had become too involved, too claustrophobic. Also, and most important of all, there was his secret involvement with his English rosebud, and the fact that he still cared enough for me not to want to hurt me.

He took to disappearing silently and without fuss, leaving me to fill the empty hours as best I could. His drinking began to affect his health; the doctor we consulted told him bluntly that unless he moderated his drinking he would become an alcoholic. This diagnosis scared Chris, and for a time he reduced his intake of spirits, and cut down on cigarettes. But he continued his nocturnal maraudings, and I would lie awake, waiting for the telephone to ring, or for the handle of my bedroom door to turn.

He seldom told me where he had been, or with whom, although it sometimes amused him to torture me by describing an encounter he had had with a prostitute, or with a foreign girl picked up in a bar. He was always scrupulous in imparting any scraps of information appertaining to new sexual deviations or perversions, and he always insisted on my trying out with him any new tricks that pleased him. I said it salved his conscience to have me share his degradation.

There were times when, sickened by the aimless and destructive existence he was leading, Chris would promise to abandon his bad habits and to reform. At such moments, wallowing in an excess of self-pity, he would cling to me, imploring me not to abandon him, and I would cradle him in my arms. He knew exactly how to play on my emotions; how, with his little-boy-lost technique, to make me melt with tenderness. After one of these 'cleansing sessions', we would get into the car, hoping to escape from ourselves; sometimes, in the pleasant old-fashioned country inns and hotels in which we stayed, the peaceful and lovely countryside acted as a sedative; Chris would relax and we found again something of the harmony that had governed our early days.

During this traumatic and transitional period in our affair, Chris never once mentioned the name of June-Mary Driver, and I had no idea of the hold she was gaining; he was, as I later discovered, by now deeply in love with the beautiful, boring virgin, and hoped to marry her. Their relationship was innocent and charming. She was bowled over by his good looks, virility and charm, and he felt towards her as a *preux chevalier* was supposed to feel towards the damozel of his choice.

Like his parents, Chris had a conventional and formal side to his nature, and I believe he had formulated a design for his future. Once he had sown his wild oats—of which I was the wildest and most indigestible of all—he would go to university, return home and settle down to farming with his stupid, simpering little bride.

The end came suddenly and with a bang. Chris stood staring down at me as I lay in bed with a chill. He said.

'There is another person in my life. I love her and I want to be with her always.'

I sat bolt upright.

'You look like a carp,' Chris said pleasantly, 'opening and shutting your mouth like that. Please', he pleaded, and I saw that his hands were locked tight together to prevent them from shaking, 'please, no fuss, no tears. I want us to part as friends, *comme de bons copains.*'

'But I've never been your pal. Your nannie often, your mistress yes, but your chum never.'

'I just don't want a fuss.'

'What about me?'

'Older women,' he said, planting the banderilla straight between my eyes, 'are supposed to be, well... wiser... more mature ... more understanding. I just want to go to her with a clean slate that's all.'

'Who is *her*? For Christ's sake, Chris, stop mumbling and speak up.'

He looked at me sadly. 'That's what it's all about, I suppose, your being so bossy and governessy. You always forget I'm not a boy, but a man.'

My heart was beginning to flutter about in my chest like a mad parakeet. I said, 'I'm sorry you think me bossy and governessy, and I am well aware of the fact that you are a man, but you still haven't answered my question.'

'About my girl? Her name is June-Mary Driver. She's eighteen years old.'

'You met her in Capri, a dazzling porcelain dolly.'

'Right.'

'You never mentioned her again.'

'No.'

'So, all this time, behind my back . . .'

'I just didn't know how to tell you.'

'Why not?'

'Because I loved you. I didn't want to hurt you.'

'Now you do?'

'You know that's not true. But it had to end some time. You used to say so, remember?'

'I didn't believe it.'

'It was true. It is true. I've got to go now. My bags are in the car.'

'Your bags are packed?'

'Yes, early this morning.'

'But you can't just move out of my life like this, as if you were just a transient in an hotel.'

'That's just what I am in your life. A transient. Now I must get cracking. We're driving to Calais. I have to take June-Mary home to Cheltenham. Her parents are expecting us.'

'What is going to become of me?'

He came and knelt beside the bed, and took me in his arms.

'I know,' he said, 'I do know. I did love you so very much, but I just can't help myself.'

I held him tight against me, and for an instant he succumbed to the old spell, but only for a moment. Then, disentangling himself from my arms, he rushed out of my room. By the time I reached the front door he had gone down the stairs. I stood there, barefoot, and shivering, in my long chiffon nightdress, staring out at the empty landing. I could not believe that Chris had gone from my life for ever.

Numbed, I stumbled back to bed, gave orders that I was not to be disturbed, had a long hot bath, put on my prettiest nightgown, sprayed myself lavishly with scent, and then got into bed where I swallowed a quantity of veronal tablets.

I remember very little of the days and nights that followed Chris' departure. The Baron appeared by my bedside, his head seemingly floating about like the Cheshire cat's grin. My friend Jodie, hearing from Perrine of my plight, flew over from London to be with me. She and I drank half a bottle of brandy together. It made me extremely sick. While her back was turned, I took another massive dose of veronal, and was taken to hospital, where I had my stomach pumped out.

The Baron, who seemed to have taken charge of me, drove me back to my flat and put me to bed. He then ordered my servants to hang a variety of pots and pans on to the door-handles throughout the flat, in case I should try to escape. I was weak and confused, but I managed to give everyone the slip, and was picked up by the police, just as I was trying to find a convenient jumping-off point on the banks of the Seine. Unless one jumps off a bridge, it is quite difficult to get into the river, and there didn't seem to be a bridge nearby. One of the *gendarmes*, covering me with his big warm cape, stroked my hair and remarked that I was too tasty a bit of flesh to be offered to the greedy river Seine.

Jodie returned to London and was replaced by another close friend. It was like a bereavement, only I was the corpse. The Baron was in his element, entertaining my friends and keeping a close watch on me. He was convinced that, once I had recovered from the first impact of despair at Chris' defection, I would return to him and that we should resume our life as before.

Nothing was further from my thoughts. I could not visualise any kind of existence without Chris, and I said so, loud and long, all day and all night, keening and wailing like a banshee, so that the Baron or whichever of my friends was in charge of me at the time kept sending for the doctor to give me yet another *piqure* to quieten me. The French are great believers in *piqures*, and they

give courses of them for almost every complaint. But even the
French do not have an injection to heal a broken heart. And
broken mine was, spiritually speaking, although the physical
organ went pumping along in its accustomed splendid rhythm.
Only I knew that the delicate and intricate mechanism that had
loved so passionately and to such little avail was fractured into a
myriad of tiny pointed splinters. With Chris' going, a dark cloud
enveloped me completely. My grief was ridiculous and overwhelming, and I wallowed in it.

I clung to the Baron even though I knew that every evening
he went off to regale his Father Confessor and the Marquise with
the latest development in what he called 'The drama of the rue
de Beaune'.

As soon as I was strong enough I went every night to 'La
Petite Chaise', where I sat bowed down in an orgy of sentimental
nostalgia. The pianist, who had also had his share of life's little
miseries, always gave me a fraternal nod before playing 'our
tune', 'These Foolish Things'. I began writing poetry again, each
sonnet a lament for my lost love, who, from all accounts was
greatly enjoying the genteel delights of Cheltenham in company
with Miss June-Mary Driver and her parents. My spies, who were
numerous, gleefully reported that Chris had never looked more
bronzed and carefree; he seemed, they said, to be enjoying an
endless round of parties and to be rapidly becoming the darling
of the county.

I wrote him endless letters, sending them care of his London
bank. He did not answer. I sat alone in the 'Petite Chaise',
writing poetry and crying like a fool. I published a slim volume of
execrable verse, which I dedicated to my young lion. I dragged
myself through the endless days, waiting for the moment when
the dismal pianist should play the music which, for an instant,
bandaged my wounds.

I had no thought for the future until Elodie van Hoorn came
back into my life. She was working on a new book on the life of
the salonnière, Madame du Deffand, and asked me to help her
again with the research. This was a magnanimous offer, for my
marriage to the Baron, lover of one of her closest friends, had
caused a serious and lasting rift in their relationship, and I knew
from many sources that Mrs van Hoorn had not approved of my
liaison with Chris.

It was a relief to get back to my former routine in the Bibliothèque Nationale. I found solace in the long quiet hours spent reading and note-taking in the company of other scribblers and readers. It was high summer and Paris was empty. I ate my fruit and biscottes in the gardens of the Palais-Royal, almost opposite the windows of Colette's flat.

One morning, the telephone next to my bed woke me at six o'clock. It was a long-distance call from London.

'I wanted to be the first to tell you,' Chris said. 'Last night we got unofficially engaged, June-Mary and I. Everyone is very pleased.' His voice was pleading, and he was willing me to congratulate him. I said nothing.

He said, 'Are you all right.'

'No', I said, and hung up.

That same day, the afternoon post brought me a little flat parcel posted in Cheltenham, Gloucestershire, England. It was from Chris and contained the copy of *Chéri* that Renaud had given him.

13

Nat-Nat, Bright Angel, and other Sacred Monsters

Mrs van Hoorn's book was not progressing. This made her nervous, so she decided to go off to Switzerland for one of her cures. She left me with plenty of work to do. Gradually I forced myself to go out more, although I avoided anyone whom I had met with Chris. I gravitated towards sophisticated and off-beat friends. I did not want to be with normal happy couples.

Once, with Serge, I had met a strange pair. They had been together for many years. Tamar was French, Margaret hailed from Shipley in Yorkshire, and her vowels were as broad as her comfortable bosom. I often thought of them, and one day I phoned them. Their response to my Mayday call was immediate. Without asking any questions, they took me in, cared for me and comforted me.

Tamar's wealth and beauty had made her the prey of men and women alike, who yearned to possess the exquisite creature who resembled a Tanagra statuette. Tamar spent most of her life trying to extricate herself from the clutches of predators and parasites and, until Maggy appeared in her life, she was as a tower besieged. Plump, cosy Maggy loved all that was weak and helpless. She was also impervious to financial considerations, being herself the daughter of a textile magnate. She instantly realised that Tamar, so beautiful and so aloof was, in reality, a terrified child living in the body of an adult. Immediately, Maggy became her champion and her protector, and so strong was her personality, so unselfish her love, that, within a short time, Tamar was rid of her tormentors; and for the remainder of her brief life, she led a coddled, peaceful and protected existence in Maggy's shadow.

At the age of sixteen, Tamar had been married off by her scheming and worldly mother to her ex-lover, an aged French duke, who, on his wedding night, all but terrified the life out of his young bride. Donning a jewelled dog-collar, he capered up to Tamar on all fours, with a silken lead in his mouth. He then asked her to call him *Toutou* and to chastise him because he had been a naughty doggie. To make his point he lifted a leg and copiously watered a priceless Louis XVI bergère. Tamar fled the nuptial chamber in hysterics, but the Duke, who had old-fashioned notions about the duties and responsibilities of a wife, had her fetched back by force, and finally she had to submit to his fantasies.

To her relief, Duke *Toutou* dropped dead a year later, and she inherited his fortune, his estates, and some magnificent emeralds, the gift of Catherine the Great of Russia to one of the Duke's ancestors, who also happened to be a relation of Serge. Tamar never really recovered from the horror of life with her husband and she suffered from fits of nervous prostration, during which she lay shaking and feverish in bed, with Maggy sitting beside her reading her fairy stories for hours at a time.

Staying with Tamar and Maggy was a soothing experience. Their house was as silent as a tomb. Tamar disliked noise of any kind, and her Annamite servants walked soft-footed on a priceless collection of silk carpets. The whole house was stuffed with splendid loot acquired through the centuries by hard-headed members of the Duke's bewitching family who capitalised on their great name and influence with the reigning monarch of the time to obtain favours for *parvenu* friends who never failed to reward them.

Against the background of this antique dealer's paradise, were played out a variety of major, and minor, feminine dramas which never involved Tamar or Maggy. They introduced me to the legendary circle of the (by then) aged ladies who had once provided so much titillating gossip. Undisputed queen of the sapphic coterie was the still-vital, endearing Natalie Clifford Barney, a wealthy American expatriate, whose salon, opened in 1908 in Neuilly, was later transferred to the rue Jacob, where it was still in active being in 1968.

Born in Dayton, Ohio, in 1876, Natalie died in Paris in 1972. She was the daughter of a millionaire father and of a gifted mother who was both a distinguished musician and painter. From her cradle, Natalie was spoilt and loved, and from her adolescent years her one dream was to become a female Don

Juan. Equipped with charm, beauty, intelligence, and unlimited money, she was indisputably successful in all her undertakings, and until her extreme old age, could not resist seducing any attractive woman who took her fancy.

Yet she also had the gift of friendship, and amongst her friends were Lucie Delarue-Mardrus, like herself a poet and writer; Lily de Clermont-Tonnerre, Gertrude Stein, Colette and the enigmatic painter, Romaine Brooks, who was the enduring love of her life until the end.

Early in her life, Natalie fell in love with Paris, and made her home there. The Parisians took her to their hearts. They were enthusiastic about her wealth, good looks, intellect and superb horsemanship. Natalie rode each day in the Bois, which was why Rémy de Gourmont, the writer, christened her *l'Amazone*. Her chief claim to fame was not that she was the most famous and uninhibited Lesbian of her time, but that she lighted such a torch of passion in the heart of the ugly little man whose splendid letters were addressed to *l'Amazone*, whom he worshipped.

Natalie and Romaine Brooks met in 1915 and from that moment *Nat-Nat* and her *Bright Angel* became inseparable. Romaine Brooks' background was as turgid and complicated as a Greek tragedy. Born in Rome in 1874 of an unstable and peripatetic mother who was on the move almost until the hour of her daughter's birth, Romaine's early life was shadowed by the fact that her neurotic mother cared only for her son, St Mar, who was mentally afflicted.

Having early discovered that only Romaine could handle this terrifying crazed boy, Mrs Brooks insisted that she dedicate herself entirely to the care of her brother. As St Mar refused to wash, and was obsessed by sex, his behaviour was both obscene and menacing, and Romaine, whose only wish was to become a painter, was subjected to unendurable pressures by her mother.

In spite of all these obstacles, she finally managed to escape from her family and to become a famous and distinguished painter. Amongst her sitters were most of the celebrities of her time. These included Gabriele d'Annunzio, Jean Cocteau, Una, Lady Troubridge (companion of Radclyffe Hall, author of the *Well of Loneliness*), the dancer Ida Rubinstein, and of course, *l'Amazone*.

During the time of her liaison with Missy, ex-Marquise de Belboeuf, daughter of the Duc de Morny, Colette and her friend, 'resplendent in starched shirt and emerald cufflinks', were part of Natalie's coterie. Colette appeared to be fascinated by Natalie Clifford Barney and her circle, but most of all was she fascinated, intrigued and saddened by one of Natalie's little friends, the poet Renée Vivian who died of drink, drugs and too much lovemaking at the age of thirty-two.

Renée was born Pauline Tarn in London in 1877 of a British father and an American mother. Of her, Colette wrote:

> I still have in my possession some thirty letters Pauline Tarn (Renée Vivian) wrote to me.... If I were to publish the correspondence of this poet who never ceased claiming kinship with Lesbos, it would astound only by its childishness.... Blonde, her soft cheek dimpled, with a tender laughing mouth and great soft eyes, she was, even so, drawn down beneath the earth towards everything that is no concern of the living....[1]

Renée Vivian was Natalie's first real love with whom she lived on terms of constant intimacy. She lost her to a wealthy Dutch baroness, whose constant and extraordinary sexual demands finally exhausted Renée. Her remains lie in an ornate mausoleum in the Passy cemetery where strange happenings were rumoured to take place on the anniversary of her death.

I myself was a frequent visitor to this most fascinating of burial places when I was interested in writing a book about Marie Bashkirtseff, a young Russian diarist and painter of genius who died of consumption at the age of twenty-four. Marie reposed in a Byzantine edifice, erected by her sorrowing family, which housed some of her paintings, her palette and paint-brushes. I used to wonder whether the same faithful disciple who put lilies-of-the-valley in Marie's mausoleum was also the donor of the magnificent bunches of Parma violets which were placed on Renée Vivian's tomb.

An invitation to one of Natalie Clifford Barney's Friday afternoon receptions was the entrée to one of the last of the great Parisian literary salons. I was taken there by Tamar and Maggy. Miss Barney had lived at 20 rue Jacob since October 1909 when she moved into the pavilion at the end of the cobbled courtyard. The main delight of this home was the charming, overgrown garden the chief ornament of which was a tiny Doric temple,

---

[1] *Le Pur et L'Impur* (*Earthly Paradise*), op. cit.

dedicated to friendship and to goodness knows what strange rites through the years, when Natalie and her friends gathered there to honour the shades of Sappho, Bilitis and their contemporaries.

By the time I saw the house it resembled a rather dusty provincial museum. It was as if the whole pavilion, together with its legendary hostess and some of her guests, were fixed like flies in amber in the sub-aqueous gloom of an aquarium.

We were met at the door by the amiable Madame Berthe Cleyrergue, who for many years had been Natalie Barney's housekeeper, cook, and confidante. The salon was smothered in tapestries, portraits, bibelots and day-beds covered with rather mangy furs.

Old friends made straight for the dining-room where, on a large table with an old-fashioned lace cloth on it, a magnificent spread was set out. There was something for all tastes, for Natalie was generous and Berthe a superb cook. Her specialities were chocolate cake and Chicken Maryland.

Miss Barney was smaller than I had imagined, and plumper. Age had softened the planes of her aquiline, blade-like nose, but her eyes were ice-blue, with a brilliant diamond-like quality. She wore a grey satin gown with a twist of matching grey satin in her abundant hair. She was an attentive hostess, moving from one group to the other, making sure that everyone had what they wanted.

While generous and friendly, Miss Barney did not encourage familiarity. One of her friends, the writer Bryher, said, 'Natalie was always rather grand, whereas my group were rather more lax and easy-going. Natalie had exquisite manners.'

When I later moved to the rue Jacob, I was often invited to the Friday receptions where I was always fascinated by the diversity of the guests, old and young, who came to worship at the Temple of Friendship. Often I used to see Miss Barney going out to take the air in her beautiful grey chauffeur-driven limousine. Berthe always solemnly accompanied her mistress to the door, and saw her safely into the car. When Natalie Barney died she was buried near Renée Vivian's grave in the Passy cemetery.

Grief develops its own rhythms and every night I was to be found at La Petite Chaise. The moment the clock struck eleven I went to Suzy's *boîte* in the rue Ste Anne where I spent the rest of the evening lulled by the routine of a familiar programme. There was something unique about my friend Suzy and her nightclub. Tiny, dimly-lit, it was decorated by framed canvas upon framed canvas of one of the finest collections of modern paintings in France.

Suzy's magnificent body, and Red Indian features, topped by a head of white-gold hair, cut à la Jeanne d'Arc, had stimulated the imagination and talents of an extraordinary variety of famous artists who had painted her, mainly in the nude, and nearly always against a background of sea and sky and boats, all of which symbolised her obsession with the ocean.

Suzy, who was always amused at the mysterious legends surrounding the circumstances of her birth, was reputed to be the daughter of a peasant woman and of a nobleman. Certainly she spent the early part of her childhood running wild on the beaches of her native and beloved Brittany and it was from the famous and ancient Tour Solidor that she took the name by which she became known.

She was still very young when she began working as a maid for a woman whose chief interest was collecting antiques and selling them in her fashionable shop in Paris. She realised that her wild little protégée was no ordinary girl, and soon made Suzy her pupil. Before long, Suzy was driving around the countryside, astutely picking up bargains for her patron, who told her that one day she might hope for a partnership in the shop. Suzy was young, fiery and impatient; the idea of waiting for years to become independent did not appeal to her, so she decided to make her own way. When we first met, she had just established herself as an antique dealer on the Quai des Grands Augustins. The ground floor was dedicated to stock, while the minstrels' gallery, reached by a small winding stair, served as Suzy's bedroom.

As soon as trade was over for the day, Suzy would entertain her friends in the 'shop', which then became a drawing-room. There were never less than twelve to fifteen people clustered round the piano, listening to Suzy singing sea-shanties and the lovely songs that well-known poets were already writing for her. As one critic put it: 'Suzy Solidor has a very special voice; it is like honey running over stones; it is like the sound of the surf breaking upon the rocks of her native land.' Fanciful, but certainly Suzy's voice, which was not that of a diva, had a haunting quality. Always she sang of the sea and of ships and of the sailors who sailed in them, and did not return to their women. When Suzy sang, one was rocked in the great swells of the

Atlantic, drenched with spray, shaken by thunder and pierced by the lightning of storms in which all hands went down into the deep.

So many people came to drink Suzy's porto and listen to her songs, that what had been a friendly, intimate little entertainment became a great expense. There were many gatecrashers, and not even Armandine, Suzy's admirable and faithful maid, could separate the sheep from the goats.

At this crucial moment she decided to become a *chanteuse*. A backer came forward, and in a short time Suzy's friends were happily paying for the privilege of sitting, packed like sardines, in her night-club. Almost immediately, Suzy's *boîte* became the rendezvous of elegant Parisian society. The correct ending to a grand dinner party was a visit to Suzy, who proved to be not only a great *artiste*, but also a superb hostess. She never forgot a face, and it was her habit, after her act was over, to move from table to table, talking to clients and friends.

Suzy was clever enough to back up her own act with a brilliant accompanist, and with a number of other sophisticated and talented cabaret artists. She used her night club as a platform from which to try out the songs of unknown young composers and poets of promise, and nobody who ever heard her sing 'Les Filles de St Malo' has ever forgotten the poignancy and nostalgia of her delivery.

Mrs van Hoorn returned from her cure and I tried to throw myself heart and soul into the life and times of Madame du Deffand. But the worthy lady bored me, and I made the mistake of letting Mrs van Hoorn see this. She very rightly told me I was wasting my time devilling for her, and that I should go away and write my own books. We parted on excellent terms, but I took her advice seriously, shut myself up and scribbled all day and most of the night.

This mood of dedication pleased my literary agent, Denise Clairouin. She was a most remarkable young woman. She too came of a distinguished old Breton family. She had a madonna-like face, illuminated by wide cornflower-blue eyes. She was small, chubby and extremely intelligent. She lived and worked in a comfortable old-fashioned flat, filled with books, papers, family portraits, well-polished silver and antique furniture. Few of the writers from her 'stable' will ever forget Denise's tea-parties held in front of a blazing wood fire.

Denise was one of the first to join the French Resistance. She was caught by the Gestapo and tortured to death. She has never been forgotten by her friends, who perpetuated her name, her courage and services to literature by setting up the Denise Clairouin Foundation.

Denise was not certain that my works would achieve immortality. She liked my short stories, particularly those about South Africa. She did not care for my French *pastiche* of Alain-Fournier's work. But she was good enough to encourage me to persevere in my chosen craft, saying that I had the heart and mind of a writer, and that perhaps one day, when I had ceased to take myself too seriously, my muse might take fire and soar with me into those rarefied regions where classics, major and minor, are created.

Denise had no doubts about the future of one of her other clients. She told me often that one day Anais Nin's diaries would bring her international acclaim. At that time, although I had never had a sight of the famous diaries, I did not think that Anais would make any contribution to world literature. Denise was right. Anais Nin's Journals have been internationally acclaimed, not only for their literary merit, but also for her subtle and delicate prose style. My judgement was entirely at fault, and I have now come to admire her work greatly.

I did not find Anais *simpatica*. She was not my kind of woman. I met her through Serge Cheremeteff who thought her brilliant and unique. Although her husband was an American banker, the coterie in which she moved seemed to me to be composed of somewhat fevered intellectuals, all scratching their 'isms'. Amongst them were Henry Miller, his wife June, and the surrealist poet Antonin Arnaud.

Anais used to wear snakeskin gloves, fishnet stockings, a hat with a veil and was drenched in a particularly pungent scent which made me sneeze dreadfully. I was somewhat shaken by her 'black' bedroom and by her utter absorption in and dedication to psychoanalysis, of which I knew nothing. I thought at that time that Anais was very similar in temperament, character and outlook to Marie Bashkirtseff.

Besides being my agent, Denise was my friend, and knowing of my distress at Chris' defection, she did all she could to keep me busy. She introduced me to the editor of *Les Nouvelles Littéraires*, then France's most important literary journal. He was a passionate admirer of the works of Charles Morgan and asked me whether I knew the great man well enough to ask him for an interview. I dared not admit that I had never seen Morgan in the flesh, and that in fact I had never met a single important English writer.

Over a delicious luncheon with this editor, I let it be understood that I should have no difficulty in producing a series of interviews with great English literary personalities. Denise seemed amazed at the way I tossed famous names around, but said nothing, and when I next visited the offices of Les Nouvelles Littéraires, I was the proud bearer of an official letter commissioning me to write a series of 'Profils Anglais'.

I had another reason for wanting to get to England. Deep down I still clung to the hope that Chris might, by now, have become bored with June-Mary Driver, and might welcome my arrival. I had by then lost all pride and dignity, and this was to be the first, and only, time in my life as a writer when I used my work as an excuse to promote a private relationship.

I had few friends in London. My brief and stormy *passaggiato* as a pupil at the Royal Academy of Dramatic Art under the aegis of Kenneth Barnes had brought me into contact with a few young Thespians far more talented than I. One of them, Beatrice Dutton, had, like myself, been told in no uncertain terms by Mr Barnes that she had absolutely no talent for the stage. Instead of repining as I did, she turned her charm and good looks to making a brilliant marriage, and having landed a noble earl, she improved the shining hour by breeding beautiful blond babies and by making her husband comfortable and happy.

In her house in the country, I met again an old friend of my mother, Marjorie McCall. She was then secretary to Fryn Tennyson Jesse, writer and criminologist of international repute. Fryn was married to a well-known playwright, Tottie Harwood, and their pretty house, Pear Tree Cottage, in Melina Place, St John's Wood, London, was a meeting-place for writers, dramatists and cricket fans from all over the world. Tottie was mad about cricket and about his wife. Fryn and Tottie were an adorable and devoted couple. Sadly, they were childless and Fryn, divining that I was bereft, took me to her heart, looking upon me always as an adopted child to be consoled, cherished and scolded. Fryniwyd was a grand-niece of Alfred, Lord Tennyson. She hailed from Cornwall and loved the sea with passion. She was tall and blonde, and wore a black patch over one eye which gave her a slightly rakish and piratical air. She was also one of the few great women criminologists this country has ever produced. She evolved the theory that there were 'born murderees', i.e. people destined to be murdered. Among her contributions to the Notable British Trial Series were the volumes on Madeleine Smith, Samuel Herbert Dougal and Rattenbury-Stoner. Fryn's book, *A Pin to see the Peepshow*, published in 1934, is a classic. It was based on the Thompson-Bywaters case, and Fryn told me she would always be haunted by the memory of her last visit to Edith Thompson, on the day before her execution. She found the poor creature screaming like an animal in a trap, as she clawed and scrabbled with bloody hands at the walls of the condemned cell.

I have heard that experts consider Fryn's Preface to *Murder and Its Motives* to be one of the great achievements of its kind. There was nothing sloppy or mawkish about Fryn's writing. Her style was clear, brilliant and incisive. Later, when we worked together on one of what she called her 'cases', I was astonished at her single-minded dedication to the work at hand. When she was gathering material on a murder case there was no stopping her, and I remember silently cursing her passion for absorbing atmosphere, as I crawled along behind her in a muddy, isolated grotto in the Forest of Fontainebleau where the German murderer, Eugene Weidmann, had killed and buried Madame Keller, one of his six victims.

The last time I dined with Fryn, when she was already very ill, she was busily writing up the trial of Neville Heath, whom she called her prize monster. She was interested to hear that I had often met this man, and had danced with him on a number of occasions at parties at the Country Club in Johannesburg.

As an R.A.F. pupil pilot, he had wooed and married one of my contemporaries. Heath was tall and well built, with a fresh complexion, charming blue eyes and fair wavy hair. He was fastidiously well groomed, and was proud of his slender, well-tended hands. He was a plausible individual with great sex appeal of which I was well aware when we danced cheek-to-cheek in the fragrant African night.

After dinner, during which Fryn hardly touched her food, she took me to her study to show me some very 'special' photographs of Heath's victims. I could hardly bear to look at them, and was amazed and repelled at her almost ghoulish glee as she pointed out the details of the atrocities committed upon the bodies of the victims. One of them had had her nipples torn off, or bitten off, while another had been left with a poker or some kind of metal rod rammed up her vagina.

*

But this episode was many years later. At this time I discussed my mission for *Les Nouvelles Littéraires* with Fryn and Tottie, and with their co-operation their famous friends were blackmailed into letting me interview them.

I imagined that famous English writers, like their French counterparts, were a close-knit group who met often to discuss views and ideas. I was surprised to discover that, in the main, the English *literati* studiously avoided meeting one another, although many of them were very Francophile, and maintained a respectful relationship with French poets, playwrights and authors.

The golden age of the Bloomsbury group had faded away, and while a number of its distinguished members were still very much alive and writing, they were, in the main, destined to languish in limbo, until they were again 'discovered' with passion in the late sixties.

Cyril Connolly with his magazine *Horizon* was, it seemed, the standard-bearer of the new young writers, while Evelyn Waugh was their spokesman. I asked Tottie if he could arrange an interview for me with Mr Waugh for whose books I had a profound admiration.

'Certainly *not*,' said Tottie, unusually testily: 'fellow's a perfect bounder.' So that was that. The nearest I ever got to meeting my idol was many years later at a P.E.N. gathering, when Mr Waugh trod heavily on my toe and apologised, profusely and politely.

The first of the famous writers I interviewed for my series was Charles Morgan. He was, at this time, considered by the French critics to be the greatest British writer since Thomas Hardy, an assessment which the British literary world found hard to swallow. Charles Morgan agreed wholeheartedly with the French, for he took himself and his *œuvre* very seriously indeed.

I was immediately attracted by his lean, athletic good looks. He looked like every romantic novelist's hero. He received me in a chintzy room, liberally besplashed with roses, comfortable armchairs, and a surprising number of portraits, busts and statuettes of the Emperor Napoleon, for whom Morgan had so passionate a regard that when he showed me a contemporary print of Napoleon bidding farewell to his *grognards*, from the steps of the Palace of Fontainbleau, he became so emotional that he dissolved into a flood of tears. I was transfixed with horror, never before having seen a grown male blubbing. I sat on the sofa, clutching my notebook and wondering whether I should leap up and offer Mr Morgan my handkerchief.

Fortunately the appearance of tea created a diversion. Morgan recovered himself, and was soon smiling brightly at me as he sketched out his future work, which included the writing of books and plays, prolonged lecture tours and finally a tomb in Westminster Abbey, or St Paul's Cathedral, I forget which, but I knew it was the ultimate in grand burial places, and I was deeply impressed.

Charles Morgan enjoyed talking about himself and his books, and I was a good listener. Dear Lewis Rose-Macleod, my first editor, to whom I am deeply indebted for teaching me the rules of my trade, told me once that the function of the true journalist was a sponge-like ability to absorb conversation, in order to expunge it as succinctly as possible.

Morgan told me that already at the age of seven he had determined to have his books published in dark green covers with gold titles. It became a sort of obsession, and he was greatly miffed when the first edition of *The Fountain* was published between blue covers.

Charles Morgan began his career in the Navy, and having campaigned in China, decided to resign his commission and go to Oxford. Before he could put this plan into operation, he was scooped up by the war of 1914, and returned to the Navy. He was with the Naval Brigade defending Antwerp, and when the troops were forced to fall back into neutral territory, he was interned in Holland. After several months spent imprisoned in a fortress, he was paroled.

He was hospitably received by a number of aristocratic Dutch families, among them an old Countess who had, in her youth, been a pupil of Chopin, and later became lady-in-waiting to Empress Eugénie. The old lady taught Morgan to read and write French by making him read the works of Chateaubriand, and extracts from the *Revue des Deux Mondes*.

Morgan wrote his first novel, *The Gunroom*, while he was in Holland. He brought the manuscript home in his suitcase; but, within sight of the white cliffs of Dover, a mine blew the ship in which he was returning sky high. Morgan's life was saved but his papers were lost. Gritting his teeth, he sat down and rewrote his book. It was published in 1919 and sank without trace, as did his second work. His next book, *Portrait in a Mirror*, met with great acclaim. *The Fountain*, which followed, was a runaway best-seller, and with *The Flashing Stream* and *The Voyage* his reputation as a writer was firmly established, particularly in France, where the cult for the works of Charles Morgan reached its apogee.

The Voyage was set in the district of the Charente, and in 1936 the English author was awarded the Legion of Honour. It was an honour he deserved, for he was a loyal friend to France, and understood the more disconcerting aspects of the country and her people.

None of us who love France ever forgot his *Ode to France*, written during her darkest years; the effect of this poem was like a light shining at the end of a long tunnel, both to those in exile and to those working towards the Liberation.

> Thou art the wisdom, O France, within all knowledge
> The salt of all delight. Who dies for thee
> Dies for mankind's perpetual redemption; and none can live
>   in thee
> That has not died the death of saints and lovers
> That has been raised up, in hate and holiness
> To beat down Satan under thy feet.[1]

*

I do not remember what pressure Fryn exerted upon Vita Sackville-West to allow me to interview her. I knew from mutual friends that she hated publicity, and that press interviews were anathema to her. However, like Charles Morgan, she loved France, and the paper I represented was as good a passport to her good graces as any credentials I could have presented to the Lady of the Tower.

[1] Reproduced by permission of Macmillan Publishers Ltd., London and Basingstoke.

I journeyed down to Kent in a ferment. I knew that Miss Sackville-West was a fine writer and a great poet. I had also been told that Sissinghurst, one of the show-places of the central Weald, had been jointly created by the writer and her husband, Harold Nicolson.

In view of the late Violet Trefusis' persistent claims to be Vita's one and only love, I found it difficult to understand how it was that the Nicolsons were known all over Europe to be completely devoted to one another. I had been asked to luncheon. As ever, I was too early, and was greeted by Harold Nicolson, who told me that Vita was shut away working in her tower, but that she was looking forward to seeing me later.

We sat in an immense and pleasant room drinking excellent sherry, while Harold, who was charm incarnate, told me something of the genesis and development of Sissinghurst, which they had bought only a few years before, in 1930, when it was, in the words of Nigel Nicolson, 'the battered relic of an Elizabethan house in which not a single room was habitable.'[1]

The house touched me because it reminded me of the Manoir de Rollo. Although infinitely grander in concept, this house, like mine, was dedicated to matters of the mind and spirit. At the same time it was also a comfortable, ordered English home, and I remember the sweet and pervasive fragrance which rose from the great bowls of pot-pourri that were everywhere, and the lovely shapes and colours of objects collected by Vita and Harold during their many voyages abroad.

Harold was the perfect host, for he made me feel both intelligent and welcome. I discovered that he, like Gide, kept a journal, and we talked at some length of the diary habit and of the importance of keeping a record of one's daily life. I had to admit that, like most people, I always began a new diary on New Year's day; but, before Easter it was put away, together with the dozens of unused notebooks I collected and hoarded.

At one point Harold fetched a book of English diarists, and read me extracts from the journal of Kilvert, of whom I had never heard. I thought I was making a dazzling and lasting impression on my host. I was mistaken, for I later discovered that he thought I was someone quite else, and always, at our future meetings, had great difficulty in remembering which of

[1] *Portrait of a Marriage* by Nigel Nicolson (Weidenfeld and Nicolson, 1973).

Vita's motley collection of foreign friends I was. But he was a diplomat, and had all the urbane courtesies of an embassy man.

Vita Sackville-West (she disliked being called Mrs Nicolson), joined us just before luncheon was announced. She was tall and slim, and wore with great distinction and elegance riding-breeches and a tailored jacket over a floral and feminine blouse, tied at the throat with a bow. Her brown hair was badly bobbed. She wore no make-up and her large, luminous deep eyes searched mine. She was accompanied by her shadow, a beautiful Alsatian.

She was silent, shy and aloof. She seemed to be in some kind of trance, which I imagined resulted from having been so totally immersed in her work. At first she reminded me of what I had read about George Sand, of whom it was said she had gobbled up the most eminent men (and women) of her day, by staring at them silently with 'fathomless brooding eyes'. I was slightly unnerved by my hostess' silence, and wondered how I should manage to break the ice when the time came for me to interview her.

I need not have worried. Vita the writer, in her turret room, on her own ground, was an entirely different person from Harold Nicolson's wife. She was relaxed and amusing, with a penetrating charm that had turned wiser heads than mine. She was a secretive, complex creature whose motivations were as mysterious as some of her relationships. She could be endlessly warm and loving; but she could also be cruel and relentless, and when she judged, and it was always she who made the decision, that an affair of the heart was over, she had no hesitation in discarding a lover who had, in her eyes, become importunate.

She was dazzling. Virginia Woolf, one of her close friends, wrote of Vita at the beginning of their friendship: '... I like her and being with her and the splendour—she shines in the grocer's shop in Sevenoaks with a candle lit radiance, stalking on legs like beech trees, pink glowing, grape clustered, pearl hung.'[1]

Vita was a loyal friend and a bad enemy. She knew this, ascribing the violence of her reactions to her foreign blood, to the Spanish background she described so well in *Pepita*, the story of the romantic love affair between Pepita, a Spanish dancer, and the British diplomat, Lionel Sackville-West, to whom she gave seven children, one of whom, Victoria, was Vita's ravishing and unpredictable mother.

[1] *Virginia Woolf*. Quentin Bell. Vol. II, pp. 117–18 (Hogarth Press, 1972).

Vita cared passionately for her husband, her sons, her home, and the splendid garden she and Harold were creating. She loved the earth and the fruits thereof and was a fine poet. When we first met she was in the throes of a new affair which was to last many years. I was greatly impressed by Vita's library and by the turret room, which was her exclusive domain. Indeed, she told me that even her husband and children did not invade her privacy and never visited her uninvited. On her writing table was a portrait of the three Brontë sisters which I greatly admired. Some months later, Vita sent me a copy of this painting by Branwell, which I still possess. It was a typically kind gesture.

She knew immediately that I was not happy. She asked no questions, but she knew, and she shared my pain, and comforted me with the tender and restrained solicitude that marked our long friendship. While my peripatetic life made it difficult for me to see as much of Vita as I should have liked, we kept up a correspondence which ended only with her death in 1962.

*

The first time I saw Rosamond Lehmann was in the street, outside her house. She was on her way to a luncheon party at the French Embassy. I had made a muddle of our date. Rosamond was the prettiest author I had ever seen. She was vivid and sparkling, and pinned to the lapel of her elegantly tailored suit was a Cattalaya orchid.

As in the case of Charles Morgan, the works of Miss Lehmann were, at that time, more highly esteemed in France than in England. Her first book, *Dusty Answer*, was published in 1927, and met with great acclaim. But when it was translated into French, the critics were hysterical in their praise. She too, perhaps unconsciously, had been touched by the magic of *Le Grand Meaulnes* and had evoked poignant memories of her own childhood and adolescence. In all her books, the children about whom she wrote were lapped about with mystery, and with a kind of unease; an ambience reminiscent of *The Turn of the Screw* and Kipling's *They*.

*

Thanks to Fryn and Tottie's open sesame, I was whirled from one interview to the other. I lunched with H. G. Wells, who had a high, reedy voice and tiny hands. Bernard Shaw addressed me as if I were a public meeting, and I had the privilege of meeting a daunting salmagundi of lady novelists, among whom were Margaret Kennedy and G. B. Stern, who lived in Albany with a pretty secretary and a collection of antique walking-sticks.

I had tea with Enid Bagnold, who was the prototype of the handsome Englishwoman. All her children had pretty and unusual names and she expressed great admiration for the German way of life. I interviewed March Cost in her flat which was hidden away in the top of a building. I seem to remember that I could not find the staircase, and that Miss Cost's flat was served by her very own lift. I had drinks with Cecily Isabel Fairfield, who wrote under the pseudonym of Rebecca West, and she impressed me more than any of the others, with the exception of Vita, by her erudition and flashing intelligence.

I had a crazy bus ride with Rose Macaulay, and a brief encounter with Edith Sitwell at the Sesame Club. Sergei was in London at the same time as myself. He promised to introduce me to Lady Ottoline Morrell to whom he was devoted. Unfortunately, she was away, and I never had the good fortune to meet this remarkable hostess, although years later Sergei arranged a meeting with her daughter, Julian, and we had tea in the garden of her house in Gower Street.

Moura Budberg arranged for me to meet Lytton Strachey's sister, Dorothy Bussy. She was a wiry, energetic little person, with black hair. She reminded me of a Japanese dolly. She and her painter husband lived mostly in France, and while she refused to discuss her book, *Olivia*, a minor classic, which she had published anonymously about her experiences in a girl's school, she had much to say that was new and interesting about the widely divergent attitudes of French and English writers to their contemporaries and to each other.

'In France,' said Dorothy, 'writers who share a café life with other writers are in tune with one another. They make the same music. They meet daily, and the cross-pollination of their ideas is evident in some of their works. The French are passionate about leading what they call "a literary life", whereas English writers have no need to communicate with one another, to form a group, and vastly prefer to fraternise with foreign visitors rather than with their own British peers. In Lytton's day things were rather different. He had such sweetness and charm that he became the centre of a group of English writers.' She spoke at length about his amusing, ironic and disrespectful style of writing about Sacred Cows, a style which had a great influence on biographical writing.

All in all, my visit to London was highly productive, and I was piling up enough copy to satisfy the most exigent of editors. I had made many interesting contacts and had found a new friend in Vita. And at all times I still ached for Chris. I had not tried to see him or to contact him; but I had heard that his family had come over from South Africa to meet the young lady from Cheltenham. She was a great success and it was thought that an official engagement would soon be announced.

The very first morning I returned to Paris, I was woken at dawn by a call from Jodi, the friend who had seen me through the early stages of my despair over Chris' departure. Chris, she said, had been killed in a car accident. June-Mary Driver was on the critical list. Jodi said she would fly over to see me that day. When she arrived, she found me dead drunk in bed nursing an empty Cognac bottle.

I have no real recollection of the days that followed. I walked about in a state bordering on catalepsy; talking hardly at all, and spending each night at 'La Petite Chaise', where the pianist rubbed salt into my soul, by playing the mawkish, brittle, lovely, cheap tunes that had tied my poor little love affair together with the coloured ribbons of sentimentality.

Eventually, even the patient, sympathetic Jodi rebelled at what she termed my lack of gumption, and once again, as before, the Baron reappeared, rubbing his hands with covert glee at the way the Fates had sorted out my affairs.

During this time of mourning, I lived on the dark side of the moon, in a bleached inhospitable landscape where the simplest actions caused me pain. It is difficult to breathe with a dagger in one's heart, and it seemed to me that my life blood, like sawdust, was flowing away. Jodi and the Baron both tried to go to bed with me, hoping to obtain some kind of normal reaction but reported to one another that my sex urge was non-existent, while my extremities were icy.

While I was tortured by the thought that I should never, ever again in this life, see Chris again, there was, at the same time, a strange and terrible feeling of relief in me that he was dead, and that nobody now could ever possess him. From now on, for the rest of my life, he would live on in my heart and memory.

It took a long time to return to a semblance of normality. Jodi, her mission accomplished, went back to London, while the Baron went off to North Africa with the Marquise on their annual visit to her estates. Before he left, we dined together. The Marquise, he said sadly, was becoming a little erratic with age, and insisted on going to bed hatted and wearing her famous ruby and diamond necklace. 'Diamonds,' he said, 'are not the cosiest of things to snuggle with.' This made me laugh. It was a long time since I had laughed, and I was grateful to Renaud. At long last there were days when I did not think only of Chris, though often I dreamed about him and woke with tears streaming down my face.

I had one last curiosity, one last abscess to burst. I wanted to see June-Mary Driver again. Jodi kept me informed of her progress, and as soon as she was off the danger list, I returned to London to stay with friends who lived in Portman Square.

It was again the invaluable Jodi who arranged for me to have a glimpse of June-Mary. Auntie Flo had shown little visible emotion at the death of her favourite son; but she clung to his fiancée and would not be parted from the girl, and June-Mary, now convalescent, was her guest in the hotel in which the O'Keefe family had taken an apartment overlooking Hyde Park.

I saw June-Mary when Jodi and I lunched in the hotel restaurant where the indefatigable Auntie Flo was giving one of the large parties that were her forte both at home and abroad. Among the middle-aged guests was a young man, a friend of Chris, obviously invited to squire June-Mary.

I could see her plainly from where I sat, an emaciated child, with a great scar tearing across her face and lifting her lip in a permanent and derisive grimace. When she bent her head over her plate, the bell of silver-gilt hair I remembered so well from Capri, hid her damaged face. Owing to her injuries, she was obliged to incline her head to one side, which made it appear she was perpetually on the alert for the sound of a call summoning her away. My rival, I saw, was now an empty shell, a zombie from whom all hope, zest and gaiety had departed; I longed to take her in my arms and comfort and warm her back to life, for Chris' sake and because of the pity I felt for her shattered life.

14

Murder was His Business

No sooner had I written my articles for *Les Nouvelles Littéraires* and settled back into my Parisian life, than I met Paul Churchod, a descendant of Madame de Stael's mother's family. Paul was a handsome, rubicund millionaire in his early fifties. He had made a large fortune in manufacturing pharmaceutical products, and visited his Paris office once a month. He was happily married to a sinewy wife who spent half her life waiting for winter snow to fall, so that she could go skiing, a sport at which she excelled. They had three children.

Paul fell violently in love with me. He was a family man constantly provoked by lusts of one kind or another and always enmeshed in the reactions set up by guilt when he indulged his passions. His immediate reaction to me was a bid to take me over, as if I were a company he wanted to add to his flourishing group.

At first I was flattered by the stream of gifts and flowers that poured into my flat in a steady flow. Paul loved gladioli, a flower which makes me grit my teeth with irritation at the stiff banality of their ramrod stalks and regimented blooms.

Even when I protested, baskets of gladioli and carnations, another flower I do not care for, continued to arrive by the shoal, and were rapidly sent to various hospitals in the district. The baskets of flowers were followed by crates of marrons-glacées and glacée-fruits. They took the same path as the flowers. Next came bottles of perfume. Having a passion for scent, I could not wait to open one elegant package after the other. I then mixed all the scents together in a cocktail-shaker and christened the result *Hara-Kiri*. Paul was not amused, but a sense of humour was not his strong point.

Paul had an account at a famous jeweller's in the rue de la Paix where he selected whatever might be the latest whimsey in vogue. It was the time of lapel pins made up in the shape of insects. I did not much like lapel pins and returned them to Paul. Nothing daunted, he bought me a diamond watch, and a pretty platinum bracelet studded with impressively large square-cut emeralds.

By this time, though we had not yet gone to bed together, he had established a branch office in my flat which became littered with files and papers, and from which he telephoned constantly, and at length, to all parts of the world. I found this international telephoning habit pleasing and catching, for soon I too began to phone long distance as a matter of course; a luxury in which private individuals indulged less freely than today.

This was not the only bad habit I caught from Paul Churchod. During our brief and sterile liaison, I learned some of the arts of subterfuge, of evasion, of the half-lie and of silence. He was a jealous and possessive lover, and during his régime I was forbidden to ask any of my friends, male *or* female, to the flat. My constant companion was his secretary, a flat-chested jailer who followed me around like a robot. Paul had his own network of spies, both in the flat and outside. His creatures reported all my movements to him. But he baited the trap. For the first time in my life I had *carte-blanche* to buy anything I pleased.

At first, in order to test the validity of the magic pass, I went on a wild shopping spree which flung me panting into the salons of Mesdames Schiaparelli, Lanvin and Chanel. There were hats from Reboux, furs from Reveillon, and bags, belts and scarves from Hermès.

By the time I had filled several cupboards with new clothes, I could hardly bear the sight of a fashion-magazine. So I went to the sales at the Hotel Drouot, or to exhibitions or museums, always with the robot in attendance. I generally finished up by taking tea at the Ritz or at Rumpelmayer's. I was always astonished at the way in which chic Parisiennes wolfed down quantities of éclairs and cakes bursting with cream, the whole washed down with cups of hot chocolate or creamy coffee. The French do not really care for tea, but are partial to tisanes and infusions made from a decoction of leaves, petals, herbs and simples.

Paul never drank tea or coffee and always embarrassed me when we dined out together by asking, at the end of a meal, for a *tisane à la menthe*, explaining to the waiter in great detail that he suffered from a sour stomach. He was what is today known as a health freak; nothing gave him greater pleasure than long discussions on the ailments which seemed to keep his children perpetually away from school. He himself had all kinds of minor, but unattractive, weaknesses, such as bad breath, moist palms, and a maddening habit of wanting to treat me as if I were a doll. He got his main kicks by undressing his women. At first, when he began expertly fingering my zips and buttons, I thought he had taken leave of his senses; but I soon understood that the unbuttoning sessions were his form of love-play, that undressing his partner stimulated his desire, and gave him the necessary impetus to carry out his manly duties. He was an ineffectual and selfish lover. Lucy would have said that he employed the postman's knock method, three sharp rat-a-tats, put it in the letter box, and away.

Invariably, after making love, Paul used to talk about his family, and try to get me to reassure him that what we had just done was entirely unimportant in the context of both our lives; so we lay in bed together, spiritually miles apart, smoking endless cigarettes, and discussing little Bernard's grades, and his wife's chances of winning a ski championship.

When he was not being tiresome, Paul was a pleasant and intelligent companion. My real reason for sending him packing was that he really did fall in love with me and therefore no longer enjoyed being with me. He wanted to divorce his wife and legitimise our dreary relationship. I did not want him to leave his wife and family, and I could no longer endure the tedium of the ritual unbuttoning and love-making. So I gave him his congé and returned all his gifts. To this day I wonder what he did with that collection of charming baubles. There were some fine ruby and diamond earrings, which I deeply regret. I kept only one object, a small strawberry made of rubies with emerald leaves, which I wore constantly until it was stolen.

My liaison with Paul was my only experience of being kept in a gilded cage. In a way it was a salutary lesson, for it taught me that all the clothes, furs, jewels and cars in the world mean nothing unless one can share the pleasure of one's possessions with a companion for whom one cares.

*

I did not have much time to regret Paul, for within a week of his departure from my life, I had a telephone call from Fryn

Tennyson Jesse in London, asking whether I would like to be her assistant at a trial she had been asked to cover for a famous English newspaper.

This trial was to take place in Versailles and Fryn decided to make her headquarters at the Trianon Palace Hotel in which I had spent my brief honeymoon. I joined her there for my first briefing. The trial was that of a criminal from Frankfurt-am-Main. His name was Eugene Weidmann, and he was no ordinary petty criminal, having committed six murders. This trial was to be the most important French murder trial since that of Landru.[1]

It was the disappearance of a pretty little American tourist in July 1937 that finally flushed the monster out into the open. Jean de Koven, a dancer, had come to Paris from the States as a tourist, and like most tourists she spent the first few days of her tour sightseeing. On the fifth day, Jean and her aunt, Miss Ida Sackheim, nicknamed Sacky, met an athletic young 'Swiss', who happened to be standing by when they ran into difficulties with the French language. He was charming, helpful and friendly. He said his name was Siegfried. Jean and her aunt were greatly impressed by his respectful and courteous manners. He told Jean he would feel privileged if he might show her the Paris that tourists never saw, and ended by inviting her to visit his villa, which was just a step away from Malmaison.

Jean had no reason to distrust the young man who talked so warmly of his parents and home. The young couple exchanged confidences, and presently, the gentle, well-brought-up little dancer, wearing a becoming blue dress with a red plaid top, carrying a camera and swinging a white handbag which contained some four hundred dollars in travellers' cheques, accompanied the handsome Siegfried to his villa at St Cloud.

Back at the hotel, Sacky waited for her niece to return. On Saturday, 23 July, 1937, the concierge, knowing how worried the American lady was, hurried to her room with a telegram from Jean, telling her not to worry as everything was fine. A little later came a letter stating that, while Jean was safe, she had been

[1] Ever since 1792, when Doctor Joseph Guillotin's machine began its work in France, it had been the privilege of the public to attend a *décollation*. Weidmann was the last murderer to lose his head in the presence of a gawping crowd who brought their children along to see the sight.

kidnapped, and was being held to ransom. The sum demanded by *les gangsters* was five hundred dollars.

Almost out of her mind with distress, Sacky hurried to the American consulate and to the police. Poor Sacky got little help from the constabulary, who were inclined to be blasé about pretty young ladies who vanished on the arm of virile young gentlemen.

Obeying orders from the kidnappers, Jean's aunt used the Agony column in the Paris edition of the *New York Herald Tribune* to insert desperate messages asking for news of her niece. But in spite of threatening notes from the kidnappers, one of which said, 'Remind, the least sign we have of the police and we don't send nobody to get the money', the girl did not reappear.

There was no sign of Jean, but her travellers' cheques began to surface. Some of them, bearing forged signatures, were accepted by a number of luxury shops. This was something the police could not ignore, and a fortnight after the girl had left her aunt for her outing with Siegfried, police and press alike went after him.

In mid-August, Jean's brother, Henry de Koven, arrived in Paris and in his father's name offered a ten thousand dollar reward for news of his sister. Nobody came forward to claim the reward and no more of the dancer's cheques were cashed. She, poor child, was silent, which was not surprising since Jean de Koven, strangled by her pleasant new friend, was lying buried in his front garden. None of his victims was ever sexually assaulted. Weidmann was a businessman, and murder was his business. He killed for gain.

Jean de Koven's aunt and her brother returned shattered to the States, convinced that the girl was dead and that nothing more would ever be heard of her. In September, Jean's long-limbed Siegfried, finding himself once more short of ready cash, looked around for means of re-inflating his wallet. He hired a car, and told M. Couffy, its owner-driver, that he wanted to be driven to Cannes. In a forest near Tours, M. Couffy was shot through the nape of the neck, and relieved of the money in his wallet.

In October funds were again low, and Siegfried took his new cook-housekeeper, Madame Jeanine Keller, for a joy ride in the forest of Fontainebleau. She too was sent to her Maker with a bullet through the neck. Siegfried rifled her purse and wrenched a frippery little ring from her finger.

In mid-October, a blood-stained body, wrapped in a green and brown curtain, was found in a parked car, appropriately enough, near a cemetery. The victim was one Roger Leblond, said to be a press agent. His mistress said he had gone to keep an appointment with a man called Pradier about an agency for a cinema.

In November Siegfried, finding his coffers empty, struck again. This time his victim was a German-Jewish youth called Frommer. Siegfried killed Frommer and having taken the three hundred francs the youth had on him, buried his body in the basement of his villa. The owner of this desirable residence must, at this point, have thought of moving to larger premises, for the garden of his home was becoming uncomfortably overcrowded with decaying corpses.

However, Siegfried was not one to repine for long, and a few days after Frommer had vanished for ever, Siegfried shot and killed an estate agent who was escorting a client around a property. He then calmly took five thousand francs from the victim's wallet.

From that moment, however, Siegfried's luck deserted him. The death of M. Lesobre, the estate-agent, was investigated by Commissaire Primborgne, an unusually active and intelligent detective, who was *Sous-Chef* of the State Police at Versailles, county seat of the St Cloud district.

A blood-stained visiting card found by the body of Lesobre gave the detective his first real clue, which, after many dramatic twists and turns led him finally to a villa at St Cloud. Siegfried was apprehended by two of Commissaire Primborgne's men as he returned to his house. He was armed, and shot at them. They were unarmed, but they flung themselves upon him and finally managed to knock him unconscious. Siegfried-Bobby-Sauerbrai-Karrier-Pradier's horrible game was up.

*

'Never since the trial of Landru,' wrote Fryn, 'has there been such a glittering turn-out of press and judicial talent.' Weidmann's chief defence lawyers were Maîtres Henri Geraud and Moro-Giafferi, who had not managed to save Landru's scrawny neck. A lady lawyer called Maître Renée Jardin was assigned to the case by the court. In spite of her horror of the way Weidmann had lived, this pretty great-granddaughter of George Sand found much that was compellingly attractive in the virile German murderer.

The trial was covered by some of France's most famous crime reporters and journalists. Fryn introduced me to Géo London, ace-reporter of *Le Journal*, and I was able to introduce her to Madame Colette, who, stockingless in sandals, had come as a special reporter for *Paris-Soir*.

Eugene Weidmann was born in Frankfurt in 1908. He came of a good, law-abiding middle-class family. But, from the age of sixteen, when he committed his first theft, it was evident that the boy was both work-shy and had criminal tendencies. His life was one long series of arrests for petty crimes; but inevitably, when brought to justice and incarcerated in prison, he sought, and obtained, the respect and admiration of his jailers by his dedication to study. Besides his native German, he was fluent in French and English, and had, as well, a good smattering of Portuguese.

He was a most practical murderer. None of his murders, as has been said, had any sexual overtones. His neat little notebooks showed that he murdered only for gain; each time he took a life, a new initial appeared in his account book, specifying the exact amount taken from his victim.

Weidmann was a virile and impressive male, whose effect on certain women must certainly have been devastating. At one point, when he was analysing the motives that had led him into the hideous and bloody paths he had chosen, Fryn passed me her binoculars—the press box was a long way from the prisoner's stand—and I trained them on him. Although he was certainly not looking at me in particular, the intense stare of his yellow eyes— the cold gaze of a bird of prey—seemed for a moment to have a numbing effect on me. There was certainly a hypnotic quality about him and I could understand how little Jean de Koven, fascinated by her unusual companion, had gone merrily to her death at his hands.

The cameramen and cartoonists had been given a box with a good view of the accused. They sat opposite us, sketching busily. Fryn pointed out that one of the artists was concentrating on the people in the press box.

'I know him,' she said. 'He's a Swiss artist of great talent. I'd love to see who he is sketching.'

During an interval in the court proceedings, we went out to sit in a café with a number of other journalists, some of whom had met Fryn at other notable trials. There was much merry badinage about the curious vanities of famous murderers. Halfway through an anecdote about the finding of Crippen's wife's body, Fryn hailed the Swiss artist and asked him to join us. This was my first meeting with Géa Augsbourg.

I did not, at that moment, pay much attention to the chunky young man in the badly cut tweed suit and clumsy boots. I was, however, aware of the beauty of his large, innocent, intensely blue eyes and was surprised that in spite of his youthful, unlined face, the shaggy hair that tumbled down his forehead was streaked with grey.

His sketches of Weidmann were very fine. In one of them he had portrayed the murderer as a bird of prey, with the small, mangled body of a woman dangling limply from his claws. I was impressed by the bold line drawings which showed great command, discipline and *maestria*. Laughing, Fryn asked him to show us the sketches he had made of the occupants of the press box.

Géa looked embarrassed, but obediently flipped back a few pages to reveal a number of sketches, among them some of Colette and of Fryn. The rest, six in number, were of me. Fryn instantly offered to buy the originals when his paper had finished with them, but Géa shook his head, tore out the sketches and gave them to her. He did not address a word to me.

The trial ended in a verdict of 'guilty' and Weidmann was sentenced to die on the guillotine. As Fryn was unable to attend the execution, she asked me to deputise for her. I had no stomach for such spectacles, but felt I owed it to her to do as she asked. Even now I can hardly bear to think of the dreadful raree-show in Versailles that night before the execution.

People who were probably descendants of those who brandished pitchforks and cudgels at the King and Queen of France as they stood on the balcony of the château de Versailles now came flooding into the town to watch the guillotine being erected; others lined up in the street, near the little jail where Weidmann was incarcerated. All night music blared, and the crowds ate and drank in the cafés.

When, in the early hours, the murderer was led out, the crowd fell silent. Monsieur de Paris, as the city headsman has always been known, stood waiting. Even the descendants of the *tricoteuses* clustered round *la veuve* stopped laughing and chattering, as the murderer came walking down the road in the cool of the morning. He walked steadily and fearlessly, his cruel yellow eyes scanning the horizon.

It was all over very quickly, but many of those who attended this execution were so horrified at the crowd's barbaric behaviour that, within a few weeks it was decreed that all future French executions should take place in private.

*

A week or so later I was sitting in bed, eating breakfast and reading the papers, when my maid came in with a large buff envelope.

'The post is very early this morning.'
'This did not come by post, Madame.'
'Then it came by hand?'
'In a manner of speaking, yes.'
'Give it to me, Perrine, and stop being so coy and mysterious.'

I opened the thick envelope, and out fell Géa's first love-letter, twenty-six pages of prose, illustrated by thumbnail sketches of himself and his friends; the margins were illuminated with tiny drawings of mythical birds, beasts and flowers he thought might fire my imagination. It was an *extraordinary* letter, and as I read through the pages, written in an exquisite legible script, I had a sense of rising excitement. Here, I thought, is an unusual man, one who crashes through all conventional barriers to get where he wants.

I questioned Perrine. 'Is there someone waiting for a reply?'
The girl tortured her apron. 'I thought Madame knew.'
'Knew what?'
'That Monsieur Augsbourg spent the night in the study. Naturally, we thought Madame had given him permission.'

I had been living on my own for only a few months. I still do not know how Géa had gained admittance to my flat, and imagine he must have bribed the concierge; when I asked him outright how he had got in, he laughed and said Cupid is an astonishingly able locksmith.

Géa's letter and those that followed were a revelation. Slowly, I became intrigued and then attracted by a mind so different from mine, a mind in some ways so limited, and so protean in others. Also I was flattered at his likening me to a captive princess in a tower who must be delivered from bondage. He said I had the makings of a real poet, which is what I had always hoped to be and never became, in spite of having published, at my own expense, a 'slim volume' of *pastiche* poems about the agonies of unrequited love.

In his own fashion, Géa was to understand me very well; once having translated my melancholy disease into his own idiom, he tried to prescribe the cure he thought might heal my wounded heart, and help me to recover from Chris' desertion and death. Although he was intensely jealous and possessive, he was never jealous of my love for Chris, whose image he himself cherished from my descriptions, incorporating Chris' features into many of his drawings and paintings, until, finally, the face in them of Chris, and that of Arthur Rimbaud, whom we both loved, became one and indivisible.

Géa was jealous only of the living, and in the early days of our affair would follow me about with all the ponderous subtlety of the St Bernard dog he resembled. At first I was astonished and slightly irritated at finding him patiently waiting outside whatever shop, flat, museum or art gallery I had gone to. He never questioned me, but simply clumped along beside me in his great boots, grinning at having found me again.

Fortunately this inane phase did not last very long. I became so bored with being followed that I told him if he continued to shadow me, I should leave him for good. He realised I meant it and from then on, I was able to go about as I wished.

No sooner did the Baron discover that Paul Churchod, of whom he disapproved for being in 'trade', had been superseded by Géa, than he began his old game of trying to scare him off.

I had told Géa the tangled story of my marriage and involvement with Chris, explaining that my husband and I were separated and that I hoped to get a divorce. Since the conventional rules regulating normal marriages meant nothing at all to Géa, my having left the Baron simply meant to him that I was a free agent. So he was startled and annoyed one evening when we returned together from a preview to my flat for supper to find the Baron installed in the drawing-room, playing the piano with verve and assurance.

I was amused, but Géa was both uneasy and irritated by the Baron's nonchalant air of still being the master of the house. He poured the drinks with courtesy and made trivial social chit-chat with charm. I waited for him to leave, but the Baron refused to budge, and finally, conscious of the indignation of my cook, who took her craft seriously, I was obliged to invite my husband to dine with us.

During dinner, the Baron discoursed merrily on the subject of his ancestors and their foibles. Géa remained glum and silent. By the time we had arrived at the dessert, I was furious with both my guests: with the Baron for being so maliciously unchivalrous as to make my friend uncomfortable, with Géa for being an unsophisticated boor.

We had coffee in the study, where I made strained conversation, longing for both men to leave. Finally, at ten o'clock I got up, and to their utter astonishment wished them goodnight, and took myself off to my own quarters, carefully locking the doors between the master-suite and the rest of the flat.

It was not until some months later that Géa and the Baron told me how the evening had ended. When they discovered I had no intention of returning, they sat on grimly, playing chess and drinking my Cognac. Finally they went off together, to Fouquet's in the Champs-Elysées and then to a nightclub in Montmartre, where they spent the rest of the night drinking and discussing my shortcomings. The Baron warned Géa that I was difficult to live with, being both spoilt and independent. Géa, who always became sentimental, if not downright maudlin, under the influence of alcohol, promised the Baron, with tears, that he would instruct me in the realities of life. The Baron merely remarked dryly there would not be enough time for such an undertaking.

He also made a special point of telling me that if I continued to see Géa, I should end by being barred by the *right people*, the people of his world. He said that while he had no quarrel with the man himself—for Géa's reputation as an artist was great—he was uncouth, ill-dressed, had no small talk and was certainly not a gentleman. Prolonged contact with such a one, said the Baron, could only end in social suicide. It was immediately after this conversation that I made up my mind to go and live with Géa.

*

Our first trip together, one of many that gave depth and interest to our relationship, was a jaunt on a barge down the canals of Belgium. Géa had many Belgian friends, all connected with the arts; as he had always wanted to go down the canals, he asked one of his friends to hire a barge for him. It was called *Joli-Cœur* and was the prized possession of a poet. For the first few days, I shared Géa's pleasure in the cosy galley with its roaring (and suffocatingly hot) stove; like him I was entranced by the neat little lace curtains at the windows, and by the bright geraniums and shining brass which adorned the confined space of our living quarters.

Our journey gave me little time for introspection. I was expected to clean and cook, and take a hand with opening the locks. Géa was a good guide and a great believer in adopting the *customs* of the country in which he was travelling. When in Rome he did exactly as Rome does and this scrupulousness extended to food and drink. Beer is Belgium's national beverage, so we drank beer, which was potent and did absolutely nothing for my figure. One of Géa's ex-girl friends had married the owner of a restaurant to which we were invited for a sumptuous meal. Edith later initiated me into the mysteries of making *pape*, a favourite Belgian peasant dish. It was made of hot, sour milk, with crab apples floating about in the liquid. It made me gag, and Géa said he preferred sausages.

The main object of our journey to Belgium was for Géa to visit one of the last of the great impressionist painters who was still alive. James Ensor lived at Ostend, and since we were taking longer to get there than we intended, we jettisoned the barge, and took the train to Ostend, arriving there one wet and windy evening.

I had a cold and felt tired, crumpled and irritable. My hair needed attention. It was difficult to be well groomed when living on a barge. I was certainly not in the right mood for what Géa referred to as our 'little honeymoon'. I was even more chilled when we were shown into our bedroom in the little hotel Géa had chosen. I vividly remember a large brass double-bed with a sagging mattress, an art-deco lampshade, and a varied selection of rickety pieces of furniture. A sleazy old porter-handyman dumped my beautiful Vuitton cases on the bed, and departed mumbling at the paucity of Géa's tip. Géa was a poor tipper, for he always said tipping had been invented by *aristos* to make everyone who served them feel inferior. I was equally certain that tipping had been invented by the working classes for the sole purposes of exploiting the *aristos*—one of the many issues on which Géa and I differed.

Looking round the sleazy room with its unattractive wallpaper, which smelled of damp and drains, my spirits sank to zero. Sensing this, Géa tried to revive them by pulling aside the dusty velvet curtains to reveal a sad immensity of steely ocean. Flinging myself on to the bed, I burst into tears and sobbed loud and long into the duvet. Géa was uncertain as to how to deal with this delicate situation, so, after a few tentative pats on my bottom, he sat on a rickety cane chair and lit his pipe. The smell of the sweet, honey-scented mixture he used, and which, as a rule, I liked, now infuriated me. Rearing up like a cobra, I screeched, 'Where are your manners? Don't you know that one does not smoke in a lady's bedroom?'

Unable to cope with this display of temperament which bore out the Baron's direst prophecies about my uncertain temper, Géa beat a hasty retreat, and I flopped back on to my now damp, tear-sodden duvet. It was not an auspicious beginning to our 'little honeymoon'.

Later we dined in a restaurant in which Géa met some of his friends. I was, at first, puzzled as to why he introduced me as 'my little English friend'. Finally I realised that having an *English* mistress was, for some reason, the ultimate status symbol in the artistic and literary circles in which he moved. An English mistress was the final accolade for a Continental artist, like winning the Prix Goncourt, or the Loterie Nationale.

I also soon discovered that in Géa's circle, mistresses were not, as a rule, expected to express their views too freely, or in any way to hog the conversation. Wives were left at home to tend the children and prepare meals for the return of the breadwinner. In principle, wives and mistresses never met, though in some cases the mistress moved into the house or flat of her lover for economic reasons, and there was a civilised *ménage-à-trois* which worked quite well as long as the wife was not jealous or possessive.

Géa assured me that if his friends were not, like the Baron, tailor's dummies, they were, for the most part, the most talented of mortals, and it was just a question of time before they found fame and fortune.

Géa had purposely not told me much about James Ensor. He wanted our visit to be a surprise. The old artist lived, as he had always done, over his parents' shop. The family business, which stocked tropical shells, aquariums, and all manner of objects associated with plant and marine life, as well as souvenir pincushions, and photoframes decked with shells, was housed on the ground floor, where everything was kept just as it had been during the lifetime of Monsieur and Madame Ensor, though trading had stopped long before at the death of the old couple.

As the door into the shop opened, a distant bell tinkled, but nobody came forward. In the sub-aqueous gloom, stuffed fish and marine monsters smouldered away in their cases on the walls, their glass eyes resting indifferently on a sad jumble of children's fishing-nets, buckets and spades.

The artist lived and worked above the ghost shop in a vast, untidy studio, whose great north window framed the seascapes and skyscapes which were both his inspiration and his despair. Like many of the Dutch and Belgian painters, and like the Impressionists, the quality of light was of paramount importance to his work. Later, Ensor told me that while the sky of the Ile de France was pure and delicate, he personally could not capture its particular quality, and preferred to live in his own country and in his own climate. He said that often to him, sea and sky became one, producing an iridiscent shimmer like the inside of an oyster.

From time to time while he was talking, he broke into prolonged cackles of laughter, for he was a jokey, ironic old soul, who saw the humorous side of life. His lifelong passion, apart from his native land, was a search for the truth, and far from seeking it at the bottom of a well, he looked for it in the eyes of his contemporaries, peering deep and trying to penetrate the masks they wore. Ensor was, above all, a painter of human passions, vices and follies which is seen in his sly and often terrible 'mask' figures.

Ensor inherited certain grotesque and bizarre elements from Bosch and Breughel. At first glance, his work, with its light, gay colours and rich texture, has an air of *kermesse*. Masked faces crowd his canvases; but they are more disturbing than amusing, for they are an ironic comment on human frailty and falsity.

Ensor stands out from his contemporaries by virtue both of his great talent and of his isolation—he spent most of his life in his native Ostend, keeping himself apart from the schools and movements of his time. He began as a watercolourist and developed into a brilliant painter in oils. He was one of the founders of Surrealism, and while Picasso was working out an abstract art in flat-pattern cubism, Odilon Redon was producing surrealist pastels, and Marc Chagall and Giorgio di Chirico were showing surrealist pictures in the Salon des Indépendants.

'Surrealistic' was also the word used to describe Ensor's extraordinary painting, 'L'Entrée du Christ à Bruxelles', a nightmare of masks and skeletons, which was to become one of the most important pictures of the Surrealist Movement. It was their trump card. Painted in 1888, this picture is now in the Musée Royal des Beaux Arts at Antwerp.

The old painter himself bore a marked resemblance to a satyr. It was obvious that age had not diminished his pleasure in looking at and fondling flesh, for he constantly touched my bare arms, and occasionally give me sharp little nips on the bottom. Since I hate being touched, unless it is by the partner of my choice, I was extremely irritated by the great man's attempts to fondle me; but it soon dawned on me that there was nothing personal in his approach. In his own way, he was saluting what he had most enjoyed: a fine piece of female flesh. Indeed, he congratulated Géa on having found a woman whose pearly skin tones and hair-colouring might have aroused the interest of his old mate and painting companion, Auguste Renoir.

And all the time he was touching me, and talking, the old man was guiding us from one stack of canvases to the other, until I became quite giddy at the sight of so much colour and so many manifestations of erotic glee. He showed us some sketches made for his famous painting, *Les Masques Scandalisés*, and the memory of the scandal he had provoked with this canvas tickled him so much that he rocked about with laughter, as he described the reactions of those he called the '*bourgeois* bladders of lard'.

James Ensor was pleased to see us. I think he may well have been lonely, for he did not want us to leave, and made us some surprisingly good tea, accompanied by very soggy biscuits, a present from an English relation. Ensor was the son of an English father and of a Flemish mother and he finally adopted Belgian nationality in 1930 and was created a Baron.

I believe it was his habit to celebrate the visit to his studio of any passably young and attractive female by writing and illustrating a little poem in their honour, rather as Horace Walpole had done for his guests at Strawberry Hill.

Ensor wrote his poem on the spot and presented me with this most charming tribute to my youth. This poem, alas, together with all our pictures, lithographs, signed engravings and autographed first editions, vanished from our flat in the rue Jacob during the Occupation of Paris.

On reading the poem I was greatly flattered to find that the maestro had described me as *Une fleur des tropiques aux yeux de sirène*. This was heady stuff, and I began privately to compare my looks with those of Baudelaire's ravishing mistress, Jeanne Duval, until I was told she was a mulatto with long night-dark tresses.

*

Our next port of call was Brussels, where Géa had made appointments to see various people whom he thought might become contributors for a new literary and artistic magazine he was hoping to launch. It was to be called by the odd name of *La Ruche* (*The Beehive*), a title which met with incredulous dismay, or great hilarity, on the part of the contributors. The magazine was to be financed by a wealthy Swiss banker, patron of the arts and collector of Géa's paintings, and his moronic wife who had given the magazine its incongruous name. Géa was always used by his wealthy and successful friends to bring a little culture into their lives. Although most of them would have hated to change places with their artist protégé, there was, nevertheless, always a lingering thought in their minds that he was getting more fun out of life than they were, and that possibly the rigid, conventional existences which they led might be depriving them of some great moral or spiritual experience. So they jostled one another in an effort to get a piece of the action, and participate in Géa's magical Bohemian world.

Géa, who was utterly gullible, never realised that he and his contacts were being used so that bored rich men could say complacently that Pablo had agreed to illustrate a new edition of Rabelais or whatever, put out by the particular press they were

Murder was His Business

sponsoring. Knowing Géa was also an excellent excuse for a 'business' visit to Paris, without Madame.

I was always delighted by our forays into the thickets of printing and publishing, for although the new magazines, papers or reviews with which we were concerned did not always come into being, there were great compensations, such as endless sessions in restaurants and cafés, with poets, writers and artists.

At one of these sessions I met two of Géa's closest friends, the playwright, Jacques Audiberti, who looked like a member of the Bonaparte family and whose talent amounted to genius, and Gaston Bonheur, a poet of some repute, who was to become a great editor. Another time I dined with Ballard, editor and founder of the influential literary magazine, *Les Cahiers du Sud* which was published in Marseilles where he lived.

It was to Ballard I owed the discovery of a man who must surely have been one of the few remaining persons alive to have known the poet, Arthur Rimbaud, when they worked together as clerks in the Bardey offices in Aden. One of my main reasons for wanting to spend some time in Brussels was to continue my research on the monograph I was preparing on Rimbaud's peregrinations. This was to be a coffee-table type of book, to be illustrated by Géa and issued by a Swiss publishing house.

I had already written several chapters of this work, which was to be called *Rimbaud le Voyageur*. Chapter One was to deal with my first visit to Charleville, Rimbaud's birthplace. I did not want to share my first experience of *finding* Rimbaud with anyone, not even Géa. So I slipped out of the flat in the rue Jacob early one morning and went off to the station in a mood of great elation. At this time, my sense of responsibility was minimal, so I left no word of my destination or when I should return. Before leaving, I peeped in at Géa, who was rolled up in his blankets, but I was careful to make no noise which might awaken him.

Charleville, in the Ardennes, is a provincial little town which has little to recommend it beyond the fact that Jean Nicolas Arthur Rimbaud was born there in 1854. His home was in the rue Napoleon (now rue Thiers). It is in Charleville, too, that the poet is buried in the family plot, his grave sandwiched between his mother and sister, possibly the only two women who meant anything to him in the course of his brief, brilliant life.

His neat conventional grave would have sent young Rimbaud

into one of those cold, calculated rages which so provoked not only his family but also his tiresome drink-sodden lover, Paul Verlaine, another of the greatest of French lyric poets. Fortunately only Rimbaud's mortal remains lie under the bead-wreaths and bunches of dusty *immortelles,* for the poet's wild spirit still flies about the world, spreading the legend and poetry of the man who had invented the colour of the vowels.

I did not tarry long in Charleville; but I did go down to the river, to sit in a rowing boat similar to the one in which the sixteen-year-old poet had drifted down the sluggish waters, transforming the world about him by his genius, into a multi-coloured foam of words.

> Jai vu des archipels sidéreux! et des îles
> Dont les cieux délierants sont ouverts au voguer:
> Est-ce en ces nuits sans fond que tu dors et t'exiles,
> Million d'oiseaux d'or, ô future Vigueur?

I got back to Paris at about eight o'clock that evening, and hurried along the platform to the barrier, where, to my amazement, I saw Géa waiting. Since I had not told him where I was going, or even that I was going anywhere, I thought he might perhaps have come to meet a friend. But, as I passed through the barrier, he took my hand, and said gently, 'I knew where you were, and when you would return. It was right for you to go alone to your first meeting with *Rimb*; here, I drew this for you,' and he handed me a sheet of paper covered with sketches of me sitting on the banks of the river at Charleville, and in the rowboat with Rimbaud and a crew of Indians, sailing off into the mysterious jungles of the writer of *Le Bâteau Ivre.*

*

I was never in love with Géa. I admired and respected him, and he taught me many important lessons. Among them that a man may not lean on the achievements of his ancestors, no matter how noble or meritorious. Though one was certainly conditioned by one's environment, one was, he said, entirely responsible for the success or failure of one's adult life. This was a contrast to the Baron's conviction that anyone without thirty-six quarterings intact, without family heirlooms and who did not belong to the Jockey Club was indeed an inferior being.

The subject of family heirlooms particularly provoked Géa's ire. 'Heirlooms are *loot*,' he would thunder, 'and nobody looted more successfully than the great French families who owed their titles and possessions to the bounty of the monarchs they served. *They* were the royal lackeys,' he used to say, long before I had heard of the 'lackeys of the imperialist règime'. Though Géa was a communist, fundamentally he was not a political animal. His main preoccupation was to recapture in his work something of the purity and innocence of his childhood. He had a firm conviction that men who worked on the land and craftsmen of all kinds were innocent, open and loving.

Géa was a great draftsman. His drawings had the clarity and directness of some of the works of Picasso and Cocteau. I used to watch him at work, marvelling at the dexterity and assurance with which he tackled his subjects.

'It looks so simple.'

'It is simple, when you have twenty years of *métier* in your fingers.'

Géa had many childlike qualities. He was direct to the point of rudeness, and always told the truth. When he wanted something, an object or a person, he went after it with total concentration and lowered brow, like a great bull. Sarcasm had absolutely no effect on him, as I discovered when we first lived together.

Géa Augsbourg came of humble stock. His father was an employee of the Swiss National railways, a station master whose whole life was spent moving up and down minor stations of the Valais. When the old man finally retired, he bought a flat overlooking a railway. He used to sit on his flower-decked balcony watch in hand, waiting for the great express trains to thunder through on their way to Russia and Turkey.

Géa's paternal grandparents came from the Engadine, where they owned a farm high up in the mountains; it was they who brought him up until it was time for him to go to school. Géa never forgot the days he spent in the high pastures as a goat-herd, for it was during this time that he became engrossed with the perfect detail of the delicate wild flowers which grew in profusion all about him.

His mother came from St Gall, of an old and respected family, which owned a lace-making enterprise. She soon realised she had hatched an eaglet whose talents demanded special lessons. His father, in the traditional manner, wanted only that his son should grow up to be a good Swiss bureaucrat. Géa's first exhibition in a Lausanne gallery at the age of sixteen brought his work to the attention of the critics, who predicted a brilliant future for the lad who had poured his soul into a series of drawings and paintings of farm machinery, specially wheels, for always Géa was obsessed by wheels, belt-buckles and door-latches.

The good station master was puzzled and irritated by the laudatory articles in the newspapers about his boy's work. When Géa presented his father with the finest of his canvases, the old man tugged at his white moustache, and then hung the painting upside down in his tiny hall.

Géa's affection for his father was tinged with exasperation, for old Augsbourg was solid bone all through. His thoughts, like his beloved trains, moved on rails, and he made it plain that anyone earning a living by painting or drawing must be either dishonest or lazy. The fact that Géa became famous merely annoyed his father. Yet there were moments when old Augsbourg would look from Géa to the photograph of his late wife, whom their son resembled, and the corners of his mouth would turn down, making him look like an old sad baby. Their strongest bond was their love of Géa's mother.

'My mother,' he said to me one day, 'was one of those rare human beings who understand everything instinctively. I was sixteen when she took the first of her mysterious journeys to Geneva. She never said why she was going; but I remember one time she held my hand very affectionately, almost wistfully, though we were not, as a family, much given to outward manifestations of affection.

'My father and I got along as best we could without her. But we missed her. We welcomed her back, not effusively; we were not effusive. She looked tired and worn, but told us she had visited her cousins, and had brought me a paintbox. She went off again in the autumn, and when she came back she was more silent than usual. She worked hard in the house, and it seemed to me that she was melting away. Now I reproach myself bitterly for not having helped with those chores which must have exhausted her. Le Pé and I took her for granted. She had always been there, and the life of the household revolved about her.

'Then, suddenly, I became aware of a great unease about the

house. Twice a week she took the train to Geneva. She always wore her best hat, a rusty black straw, with big white bird-wings to brighten it up. Le Pé, during that year, was also unusually silent and brusque. He knew that mother was dying of cancer, but she had begged him not to tell me, because she did not want me to be unhappy. The cancer took a long time to eat her up; but she never complained. As the months passed, she became frailer and more shrunken, and finally it was like looking at someone down the small lenses of a telescope.

'We had a little chalet up in the mountains. She asked to be taken there. One afternoon le Pé went out early. I was out too, sketching some farm carts in a neighbouring farm. I came back and found mother lying on an old sofa, she who never in the whole of her busy life had ever stretched out except in her bed. She was wearing her best black silk dress. Round her neck was the gold chain le Pé had given her when I was born. A little gold locket dangled from it, and in it was a curl of my baby hair, and a picture of me at six months.

'She made room for me next to her. I took her hand. The windows were wide open over the valley beneath, and the scent of mountain thyme was strong in the pure air. She did not talk, but looked at me with profound love and pity, yes, pity in her eyes. We sat there for a long while. Occasionally, the tinkle of cowbells would shudder high above us in the mountains. I was afraid she would get cold; but when I got up to close the window, she pulled me down beside her again. I held her thin, work-roughened hand in mine, and looked deep into her eyes. They were large and blue. They looked very young in her pain-weary face. I thought that once she must have been very pretty. Strange, that in all my selfish life, I had accepted her loving and devoted ministrations as my due, without ever thinking of her as a woman needing love and reassurance, the kind of love and reassurance she had always given me.

'Under my fingers her hand was hot and dry, and I felt the worn gold band of her wedding ring. Something of my strength was flowing into her now, just as her life had flowed into me when she was carrying me. My love was keeping her alive. The colour of the sky was reflected in her eyes; the whole changing magnificence of the sunset, and then, there was a little light in her pupils, a light that burned strong and unwavering, like a small hopeful candle. As long as that light burned clear and steadfast, I knew she was there with me; and then, even as I watched, the tiny flame began to waver uncertainly, and suddenly, as if a wind had blown it out, the light was quenched, and she was no longer there.

'When le Pé came back, I took him into her room. I had laid her on their bed and closed her eyes. He stood there, hunching his shoulders as he looked down on his wife. I left him and went and sat on the sofa on which she had died. My mind was numb. I closed the windows and pulled the curtains, shutting out the night and the mountains. Le Pé came in. His face was expressionless, only I noticed his hands were shaking.

'He said, "Come, son, let us go into the kitchen." I followed him there. He went over to the dresser where there was a great dish piled high with new-laid eggs. Carefully and deliberately, while I heated the copper frying-pan, he broke twenty-four eggs into a bowl and then vigorously beat them with a fork. Then he poured the foaming mixture into the pan. When the omelette was golden brown, he cut it in half. We sat, one at either end of the scrubbed kitchen table, eating. Through the open door I could see their room. Le Pé got up and very deliberately closed the door. Then he sat down again. He was wiping up the remains of his omelette with a slice of bread. The froth of the omelette creamed on his heavy moustache. His face was puckered, and his eyes were wet. "Tonnerre de Dieu," he said, "one must still eat," and then, "Claudie would have wanted it this way." It was the first time I had ever heard him call my mother by her Christian name.'

I have no idea what Géa did at the Lycée. He learned to read and write, but little else. He had a theory that if one wanted to preserve any kind of mental originality, one should read only the Bible. At the same time, he had a passion for the sophisticated company of poets and doctors. Fortunately for me, whose intellectual diet was incomplete if I did not manage to swallow at least one book a day, poets, writers and doctors loved and admired Géa, and when I went to live with him, he introduced me to a wide circle of friends, most of whom are, today, revered mandarins of literature and medicine.

Géa always retained something of the naïf candour of a lad from a mountain hamlet. He was innately Swiss and homespun from the soles of his big clumsy boots to the top of his shaggy head. But, like his counterpart, the great ugly actor Fernandel, Géa's soul had wings, and he could be both sensitive and subtle.

He had always led a hand-to-mouth existence. Material possessions mattered little to him, and he was perfectly happy living in an attic-studio, with a *pot-au-feu* or a *fondue* bubbling on one of those suffocating French stoves that were an integral part of the fixtures and fittings of all French studios at that time.

Géa thought my daily baths a strange Anglo-Saxon perversion, and indeed, when we first moved into the flat in the rue Jacob, the large, rambling apartment had three *cabinets de toilette* and one *vater* and an altogether charming conservatory, decorated in art-nouveau style, and which overlooked a paved courtyard. There was no sign of a bathroom, and cockroaches gambolled happily in the dark kitchen. But I loved the rue Jacob. It was a famous street which had once been part of the grounds of the Abbey of St Germain-des-Prés. According to Colette, who began her married life with Willy in this same street, the sculptor Pajou, a king of Denmark, and the actress Adrienne Lecouvreur had all lived at one time in the rue Jacob.

We moved in with a few bits of furniture picked up at the Flea Market, which at that time was a real Aladdin's cave. I bought a marvellous bed, obviously designed for an imaginative courtesan, in the shape of a troika. Some of the gilt and plasterwork had been knocked off, but the bed had panache, and I enjoyed sleeping in it. Most of Géa's best pieces of furniture had been given to Louisette, the pretty model who had been his mistress and with whom he had lived quite happily until I came into his life.

At first the novelty of leading a Bohemian existence, with Géa as Rodolphe and myself as Mimi, enchanted me, but Géa was less enchanted with me when he discovered that I was totally undomesticated, and that although I was a good cook, I refused to spend my time preparing the good nourishing soups, *rushtis* and peasant dishes for which his Swiss stomach craved.

Our backgrounds were so totally different that there were moments when I came around to the Baron's way of thinking, that living with a peasant can only be of interest to another peasant. Some of the habits of my artist lover irritated me, such as the way he lapped up his soup, and dunked everything dunkable in his coffee. Furthermore, he infuriated me by adhering obstinately to his principles, about never in any circumstances whatsoever lowering his standards. More than once when we were practically penniless, he was asked by various manufacturers to decorate chocolate boxes; to design packaging and even to paint Christmas cards. The fees for such work were high, and living as we sometimes did on an almost permanent diet of tomatoes, when they were in season, I simply could not understand Géa's shocked reactions to those who asked him to 'prostitute' his art.

His reply to my outbursts when he turned down these offers was typical. He said that if I was so dependent on material things, I should go out and earn my own money. He maintained that my inability to become a mature human being derived mainly from my financial dependence on my Papa and subsequently on my husband. To keep his respect, I was obliged to refuse all offers of help from my family. Even what was left of Tante Regine's legacy was suspect, since it came from 'the other side'.

Whenever a cheque did arrive for what Géa called his *legitimate* work, there was great rejoicing. Once he appeared with a long box containing the first vicuna coat I had ever seen. It was biscuit and cream in colour, and fluffy, and I created a sensation whenever I wore it.

We had not long been settled in the flat in the rue Jacob, when a disastrous run of bad luck reduced Géa to penury. A publisher, for whom he had worked all one summer, failed and our cash flow dried up almost overnight. While I was out shopping in the neighbouring market in the rue de Buci, the bailiffs moved in, and when I came home with all the ingredients for *bœuf bourguignon* nothing remained in the flat but the troika-bed and a chair. Géa, surrounded by umbrellas, was stretched out, snoring loudly, on the floor. He was abysmally drunk.

Suddenly I was disgusted with the squalor of my *vie de Bohème*. I packed a suitcase and went off to stay with Maggy and Tamar. After a few days of luxurious living, I began to worry about Géa. We had no telephone, so it was difficult to contact him unless I went back to him. Finally, I missed him so much that I thanked my kind hostesses, and laden with expensive gifts they had given me to stock my larder, I rushed back home.

I banged into the flat and knew at once that Géa was out. This annoyed me. I went to the studio which, though devoid of furnishings, was unusually clean and tidy. When I opened my bedroom door, I stood staring in astonishment at the walls. Géa had furnished my room by painting a series of murals depicting the most charming pieces of Louis XVI furniture illustrated in my book on Marie-Antoinette's private apartments in the Palace of Versailles. This was a masterpiece of *trompe l'œil*. I went through to what was destined to be the drawing-room when we could afford to furnish it. Here too my artist had been busy. This room was decorated in austere medieval style, and was impressive, with its realistic coffers, complete down to the heavy ornamental locks, and long refectory table and monastic-looking benches. Géa had obviously worked throughout the days and nights I had been away to complete this labour of love.

Every room in the flat, and there were many, had been transformed. Even the dark kitchen had been painted white, and on the walls were painted a whole range of copper pans and saucepans as well as a cuckoo clock. On the wall, near the window, was a wicker-cage in which sat a white dove with a pink ribbon round its neck.

With eyes streaming with tears I went to look for Géa. I found him sitting on the terrace of the *Deux Magots*. When I looked into his candid eyes that were as blue and deep as one of his native glaciers, I bent down and humbly kissed one of his stubby, paint-stained hands.

*

Hoping to stabilise our shaky finances, I got myself a job. It was not a very grand one, for I was employed by Isadora Duncan's brother, Raymond, to sell hand-crafted Greek-style sandals in his shop in the Boulevard St Germain. The sandals were a good idea, for they were well made, and whoever had designed them understood the anatomy of the human foot. The trouble was that few of my customers had ever worn sandals, or gone barefoot, as I had, and while they were quite interested in the theories earlier developed by Isadora, and carried out by Raymond, the French element particularly had no reason to be proud of their feet, for, men and women alike, they had bumps, lumps, corns and deformed toes—not to mention a variety of offensive odours which made me feel faint.

Géa was interested in my reactions. He thought sandals a waste of time, and said so to Raymond, who was extremely irritated. I agreed with Raymond that it was of the utmost importance for people to care for their feet, and that the best way to do so was to wear properly constructed shoes or, in the event, sandals. So Géa and I had an argument in which everyone sitting on the terrace of the *Deux Magots* joined enthusiastically. Selling footwear in a heatwave is not the ultimate in job satisfaction, so I gave in my notice, and Raymond kindly presented me with a pair of sandals, which I wore happily until they fell apart.

Raymond Duncan was a strange man. Among his other interests was the academy he ran in the rue de Seine. The curriculum included courses on the many aspects of love. These seminars were eagerly attended by American matrons, with blue rinses and diamanté-studded glasses, all anxious to get a new angle on love and on culture from Isadora's brother's lectures.

Raymond wore a long hand-woven tunic, which, with his greying beard and sandals, was calculated to give him the look of an apostle. His constant companion was a plump lady of Russian origin, who also wore woven robes and a nunlike coif around her face. I believe she gave lessons in weaving.

Raymond had many disciples, who, with their offspring, lived in and about the building where he lectured. He and his flock were supposed to be vegetarians and teetotallers, which is as may be, although Géa and I often spied our robed and sandalled friends in a restaurant we frequented, eating heartily and washing down great plates of *biftek garni* with carafes of house wine.

At the end of the long hot summer, Géa and I went to Switzerland to see his publishers. When we returned, Paris was agog at the revival of *Cyrano de Bergerac* at the Théâtre français, costumed by Christian Bérard, an old friend of Géa, to whom he presented two tickets for the première, a munificent gift, since they were as rare as tap water in the desert; the background to this colourful production was a depressing dose of news making it clear that war was just around the corner.

I am ashamed to say that, at this point in my life, my notions of war were a tissue of romantic nonsense culled from books, plays and films, embroidered with glittering threads of the exploits of such legendary heroes as Marlborough—the Malbrouck of the French nursery rhymes—and Napoleon; of Romain Rolland's great saga and of Erich Remarque's *All Quiet On the Western Front*, and of *Journey's End*.

I had hazy remembrances of Papa in French uniform. He was hit in the back by a Boche bullet, wounded when fleeing from the enemy, we said as a tease. This tease annoyed him, but even the display of his war-medals did not turn him into a war-hero in our eyes.

Dimly too I remember the sound of firing. 'It is Big Bertha protecting us,' Lala said comfortingly, as I lay in my cot in the apartment near Paris she had taken for the duration, watching her dressing to go on duty in the nursing uniform that became her so well. One of her favourite photographs showed her surrounded by a group of maimed *poilus*, whom she had helped to nurse.

Certainly the rumours of war were on the increase. There was war talk in the cafés and in the shops; some of it singularly well informed. Many of our friends were political journalists who had contacts with men in high places. They had sure and secret sources of information.

Certain names and catch-phrases recurred so often as to become warning messages.... Hitler the Jew-hater, concentration camps, Goering and his fancy uniforms studded with medals and with his *colossal* airforce, the might of the German army, the jackboots preparing to march, Allied unpreparedness, the impregnable defence of the Maginot Line, and, camouflaging all the fears like flowers strewn on a death-bed, the garlands of spring and summer; the lilies-of-the-valley scenting the May mornings, and the haunting beauty of Paris at dawn, by day and at night.

In Search of Vincent

I have always had a passion for the paintings of Vincent van Gogh. My enslavement began in my student days, when I used to pass an art dealer's which specialised in the works of the Impressionists on my way to the Sorbonne. In those days, even masters such as Cézanne did not command really high prices, and it was possible to buy a Gauguin or a Van Gogh for far less than a Poussin, a Fragonard or a Hubert-Robert.

The gallery had acquired a canvas by Van Gogh, 'A branch of white lilies—white, pink, green—against something like black Japanese lacquer inlaid with mother-of-pearl'.[1] This painting was, of course, far beyond my meagre means, but it haunted me and I longed passionately to possess it. I never forgot those flowers, and read everything available about Vincent. The great exhibition of his works in the Petit-Palais gave me the excuse I needed to go off on what Géa called my literary pilgrimages. This time, however, I did not go alone for Louis Piérard, having just completed his comprehensive and masterly biography of Van Gogh, offered himself as a guide to the places where the Dutchman had worked and prayed.

I had imagined that the Borinage, the Belgian coal-mining district, our first port of call, would be dirty and unprepossessing. It was not: 'This country,' Vincent had written, 'is very picturesque; everything speaks and is full of character. The houses are very small, and might be called huts; they are scattered along the hollow roads, and in the woods, and on the slope of the hills.'

Here Vincent in his new career as an evangelist had prayed, taught and comforted the poor and the sick. I visited the bleak hall he had rented for his religious meetings. It was not difficult to imagine the gaunt figure of the lay-preacher standing there, his

---

[1] A letter, dated March 1886, from Vincent in Paris to his brother, Theo. From *Dear Theo*, autobiography of Vincent Van Gogh edited by Irving Stone, Houghton Mifflin Co., Boston, 1937.

red beard jutting from his pale face, as he addressed miners and charcoal burners.

'And they listened attentively when I tried to describe what the Macedonian was like, who needed and longed for the comfort of the Gospel and the knowledge of the only true God . . .' Vincent wrote.

The painter attempted to help the miners by divesting himself of all his possessions. But neither they nor the authorities in Brussels understood his motives. The miners had been made uneasy by his violent professions of love for them, and the Church authorities thought Vincent had lost dignity in trying to share the miserable and poverty-stricken existence of his flock; so they recalled him, to his utter astonishment and despair.

Before leaving Petit Wasmes, we visited its oldest inhabitant. He sat before a tiny coal fire, warming his hands and feet. Piérard questioned him. Did he remember Vincent van Gogh? The old man was deaf. The question was repeated close to his ear. He shook his head. 'Monsieur François,' I said, 'do you not remember the evangelist, the young preacher? His name was Vincent and he had a red beard.' The old man looked at me in silence for a while, then his dark, deep-set eyes lighted with malice. He chuckled, 'Vincent, bien sûr que je me souviens de lui. C'était un quasi fou avec une barbiche rouge, qui marchait dans la neige sans manteau . . .' and that was all he could remember—a madman walking in the snow with no coat. The old man might well have been the recipient of one of Vincent's few pathetic bits of clothing. As we left the village I saw, as Vincent must so often have done, lines of washing fluttering in the breeze, and in a tiny garden an almond tree was in delicate pink flower.

If one examines a chronology of Van Gogh's life, one is struck by the *leitmotif* which underlies all his actions. 'Dismissed from position, and begins again.' That in a sentence was the shape of Vincent's exterior life. He was dismissed, and he started again, without bitterness, filled with humility, anxious only to succeed.

My next visit was to Arles. We motored through the South of France, through Avignon and Tarascon, and all the small sun-drenched villages which had so rejoiced Vincent's sun-starved senses. When he came to Arles he came in quest of the absolute. The grey dreariness of the Borinage, the opal tints of Holland and Belgium, the grey mists of England, all, all were washed away by the brilliant sunshine. It flooded his being, and for a little while he was happy. His letters were enthusiastic. . . .

> Today I brought back a canvas of a drawbridge with a little cart going over it, outlined against the blue sky—the river blue as well, the banks orange-coloured, with green grass and a group of washerwomen in smocks and many coloured caps.[1]

It was about this time that he received his first letter from Gauguin, who, finding time hanging heavy on his hands in Paris, suggested he might come South for a bit to paint with Vincent. The Dutchman was delighted at the idea of working with a companion and immediately began to look for accommodation. He had always wanted to found a commune where artists might live together, sharing all expenses, and living and painting in peace and amity. He rented a house in the Place Lamartine, in Arles. The house was yellow outside and painted white inside. The rent was fifteen francs a month.

I went to the house, only to find it had been turned into a café, and the proprietor had no interest in Vincent or his works. I asked if I might see the room Vincent had occupied. The *patron* shrugged his shoulders, and said he was too busy to act as a guide to all the crackpots who came to see the spot where another crackpot had done himself a mischief. However, he showed me the staircase and left me. I ran up the narrow stair to the first floor. There was a long tiled corridor and many doors. I opened one of them; it was a cluttered boxroom. The last door revealed a homely bourgeois bedroom filled with large pieces of furniture and a plethora of photographs of the *patron*'s very plain wife and family; but the window overlooking the place was open, and outside was the very same plane tree that Vincent had painted. This then *was* the famous room. Mentally, I stripped it of its present furnishings, and restored it the way Vincent had described it.

> The walls are pale violet, the ground is of red tiles. The wood of the bed and chairs is the yellow of fresh butter, the sheets and pillows greenish lemon, the coverlet scarlet, the basin blue, the doors lilac. The broad lines of the furniture must express inviolable rest. Portraits on the walls, and a mirror. . . .[1]

[1] Ibid.

It was in front of this mirror that he had stood staring at his distorted face, razor in hand, and blood streaming down from his mutilated ear; and Gauguin in a frenzy of fear had rushed through the streets of Arles, screaming, 'He's mad, he's mad!'

Later, I decided to continue my quest for Vincent by going to Auvers-sur-Oise where the painter had spent the last months of his life in the care of Dr Gachet. I knew the doctor was dead but that his son was still alive.

I arrived at Auvers at four o'clock in the afternoon, and put up at the inn in which Vincent had stayed. I then sent a note to Monsieur Gachet, *fils*. An old gardener brought me a reply, a card, written in a beautiful copperplate hand. Would I wait upon Monsieur Gachet at 6 p.m. exactly for a glass of porto? Auvers is a typical little French village set against a background of gentle hills. Through it runs the murmuring Oise. Monsieur Gachet's house was at the end of a winding lane, set solidly in a gently sloping terraced garden. I pulled the bell on the gate. A figure appeared on the terrace, walked down the steps, and with a great clanking of keys, opened the gate. This was Douce, Monsieur Gachet's old servant. Like the house, she was solid and old-fashioned. She wore a white apron with a bib, and on her grey head a cap with long streamers.

She led me up the steep stone steps, pushed open the front door, and ushered me into a narrow hall, lined with framed sketches made on brown wrapping-paper. Some of them were still crumpled, for Dr Gachet had rescued them from the wastepaper basket to which Vincent had consigned them.

Monsieur Gachet, *fils*, received me in the drawing-room which has been immortalised on canvas by many of the great painters who came to his father's house for rest and treatment. My host was already an old man with soft white hair and clear blue eyes. He had lived for many years in the Far East, and wore a cream-coloured drill jacket buttoned up to the throat. He was small, neatly made and courteous, and all his gestures were precise.

We sat in rattan chairs, also a legacy from his former life, and all about us were the wondrous paintings he had inherited from his father. Little Monsieur Gachet was well aware of their value, but since he had lived with them most of his life, he was no longer overwhelmed with excitement as were those seeing them for the first time.

All about us were canvases by Cézanne and Pisarro, sketches by Buryas and Lautrec; and over the mantelpiece the famous portrait of Docteur Gachet, painted by Van Gogh.

> I am working at his portrait [Gachet's], the head with a white cap, very fair, very light, the hands also light flesh tint, a blue frock coat and cobalt blue background, leaning on a red table on which are a yellow book and a foxglove plant with purple flowers.[1]

Over in the corner was the piano at which Vincent had painted Mademoiselle Gachet,

> Yesterday, and the day before, I painted Mlle Gachet's portrait, which you will soon see, I hope; the dress is red, the wall in the background green with an orange spot, the carpet red with a green spot, the piano dark violet. . . .[1]

On the piano was the blue, blue opaline vase that Cézanne had immortalised.

The maid brought in a tray on which stood a bottle of porto with a plate of sponge fingers. Monsieur Gachet talked about his father and some of his patients and mainly about Vincent.

'Few people,' he said, 'have understood the tragedy of Vincent. He was one of the loneliest men in the world. I realise this now. I was only sixteen when he first came to Auvers to consult my father, so of course I observed him only with the severe and critical eye of the adolescent. Genius meant nothing to me. My father said Van Gogh was a fine painter, but then father collected painters. My sister and I found them tiresome. They cluttered up the house with their canvases and their nervous ailments. There was always some daft fellow or other having a fit, or falling into a trance in the sitting-room. Father gave his guests or patients— whichever you want to call them—the run of the house, so we never had much privacy.

'So far as I was concerned, Van Gogh was a gaunt, red-bearded, shabby Dutchman, with uncouth table manners, penetrating green eyes and a badly mutilated ear. Father loved and admired his work. He said that those who did not understand his pictures

[1] Ibid.

must be insensible to light and warmth and to the life force which emanated from Vincent's brush.

'Vincent was a loner. He had a passion for Japanese prints (a passion shared by most post-impressionist painters) the first of which was introduced into Paris in the form of packing paper around crockery sent from Japan. He used to go for long solitary walks. He seldom smiled. Once, when his brother Theo came down to see him he was in great spirits. He was full of gaiety. I never saw him like that again.

'During the long summer days, he painted and painted until the brush almost dropped from his hands. He and my father got on well. They both loved argument, paradoxes and painting.'

One morning Vincent came to see Docteur Gachet about his treatment, and flew into a passion of rage because the good doctor had left some Pisarro sketches lying unframed on the floor. The doctor, amused at Vincent's indignation, burst out laughing, until he saw in the mirror that the Dutchman was holding a revolver behind his back. Before he could stop him, Vincent had stalked out. He went into the cornfields and there, where he had recently painted a billowing sea of golden corn, he shot himself through the stomach.

I asked where young Gachet had been when Vincent shot himself. 'I was at home, on holiday. It was a hot day in July. Father was out on his rounds, and I was just about to go fishing with friends—there's capital fishing in the Oise—when one of the men came rushing in from the fields to tell us that the artist from Paris, the one who had the injured ear, was lying dying amidst the corn. By this time a farmer had organised a horse and cart, and Vincent was transported to the Hotel Ravous in the Place de la Mairie. I met the cortege halfway. I could see that Vincent was very badly injured.

'A posse of people had gone off to track my father down. While they were looking for him I sat in the tiny bedroom with the dying man. I was very young and had never seen anyone in this condition. Outside, it was high summer, and people were going about their normal daily pursuits. My friends had gone off fishing without me. I felt nervous and inadequate.

'Vincent lay very still. From time to time he would open his eyes, and ask whether his brother Theo was coming, for Theo had immediately been sent for. Finally, when I could hardly sit still on my hard chair for tinglings in my behind and up my legs, Father arrived, looking much wilder than Vincent had ever looked in his maddest moments. He was obviously distraught at the negative result of his treatment, and also, although I did not know this then, he blamed himself severely for not taking Vincent's revolver from him when he had seen it in the mirror that morning.

'I was sent home, and Father told me later that Theo van Gogh reached his brother before the end. Insensitive little brute though I was, I was glad, for I felt that Vincent would have kept death at bay until he had taken a last farewell of the only being who was ever really close to him. I think Theo knew why Vincent shot himself. His, Vincent's last words were, 'Zoo heen kan gaan' (I want to go home).

'The following day I accompanied my father to pay my last respects to Vincent. He had been laid out on the billiard table in the Ravous' café. Lying there he looked grim and noble. But the sight I have never forgotten, and which, even today, so many years later, is like a blow in the belly, was the impact on me of Vincent's canvases which had been stacked all around the billiard table. There they were, the shining beauties, the masterpieces, the sun pictures, as golden and glowing as his sunflowers; the strength and love that had been contained in that poor man's heart radiated outwards carrying the message he had been unable to communicate during his lifetime. Father wept, and even I sniffled a bit. So that was that. Theo van Gogh looked as if he had been turned to stone. Indeed, he only survived his brother by six months. They are up there in our little churchyard.'

Next day I walked to the top of the hill on which stands the church. Far below was the village ringed by its ocean of cornfields. A flight of crows rose high into the sky. Higher and higher they circled, and then dipped in salute over the two graves by which I stood. Twin graves with plain granite head-stones bearing simple inscriptions:

Vincent Van Gogh, born March 30th, 1843—Died July 29th 1890

and on the other:

Theo Van Gogh, born 1857—Died 1891

There were jam jars full of wild flowers on both graves.

16
The Writing on the Wall

With the exception of the deaths of Lucy and Chris, I had never taken anything really seriously, and my heart never bled for anyone but myself. Superficially, I was, of course, moved by the plight of the weak, by injustice, by cruelty and unkindness; but never until their deaths had I equated real hardship or risk with myself. It seemed to me that the world was indeed a stage, and that I was an extra in some great and mysterious production, just one of the crowd repeating parrot-like, 'Rhubarb, rhubarb, rhubarb!' with the rest of them.

The atrocities of the Spanish Civil War had certainly moved me, but again only superficially. I was not involved. Though many of my friends and one of my first cousins went to Spain, the whole terrible affair might have taken place on another planet, and my reactions were similar to those I experienced recently on seeing the landing of the first man on the moon. It was exciting, extraordinary, fantastic, and sensational, but had nothing to do with my little life.

Obviously I was not of the mould from which heroes or even dedicated war-correspondents are made; for once I had read the papers and been to the newsreel theatre, I returned complacently to my normal avocations, my ears stopped with the wax of cliché-conversations to the warning cries of those who could clearly foresee the magnitude of the horror about to overwhelm Europe and the world.

I had never given much thought to what the word *patriotism* meant, or tried to analyse my feelings in regard to the countries of my birth and adoption. The sound of the *Marseillaise* made me frantic to rush to the barricades to defend a country and a way of life which had given me so much joy; and whenever I heard the sound of the laughter of Africans, which is the national anthem of their country, I would yearn for my native land. Both France and South Africa were important to me, but, as I was soon to discover, most important of all was to be the fate of those who had come from that distant homeland I had never known: the Jews were my people, and their destruction was to strike at the very roots of my being.

*

During this time of waiting Pablo Picasso used to come regularly to the *Flore*, the café next to the *Deux Magots*, with one or two close friends. With the exception of a few stray tourists who sat transfixed, rudely staring at the great man, nobody bothered him. There were a few memorable occasions when he came and sat for a moment with our group, poised, like a bumble-bee, which in his velvet jacket he resembled. His dark brilliant gaze settled for an instant on the faces at our table, computing and filing away any detail which interested him.

Once, we were all sitting at the *Flore*. Picasso was explaining something to one of his friends. Impatiently, he pushed away the clutter of saucers and glasses on the marble-topped table. Then, taking a piece of charcoal from his pocket, he illustrated what he was saying with a lightning sketch. I was too far away to see what he had drawn, but a hawk-eyed American who had been watching every move made by the master, waited until he had left; then, dashing over to the table he had occupied, he sat there triumphantly, until the waiter padded over to remove the dirty glasses and to take his order.

All those in the immediate vicinity fell silent as they listened to the American asking how much he wanted for the marble-topped table. The waiter was polite but incredulous. The American, speaking very loudly, repeated his question. The waiter stared at him. Very slowly, and in bad French, the American repeated that he wished to purchase the table. The waiter looked stunned, and finally asked whether he had heard aright?

'Did Monsieur really wish to purchase this table?'

Monsieur nodded his head violently, and took out his wallet. The waiter then asked why Monsieur wanted this particular table? Monsieur said it was because of the little old sketch by Picasso. The waiter looked affronted. 'Did Monsieur mean that he wished to purchase the table, because Monsieur Picasso had doodled on it?'

Monsieur waved a sheaf of hundred-franc notes. Yes, this was why he wished to buy the table.

With a flick like a serpent's tongue, the waiter erased the sketch with a dampened napkin. The American let out an agonised screech.

'You dumbo, you. I *told* you that was a drawing by Picasso!'

'If it were by Michelangelo,' said the waiter stolidly, 'the *patron* wouldn't have sold you his table. It's real quality marble. None of your ersatz modern stuff, this here is quality marble.'

*

Two years earlier, in 1937, Géa had had some success with an album of drawings on the life of Serge Lifar, the dancer. Géa had much enjoyed watching the ballet master and first dancer of the Paris Opéra at work. The artist sat in the prompt box, making quantities of sketches which he later worked up into the final drawings for the book published by Correa.

For months Géa had lived in the shadow of the Opéra, and he told me many anecdotes about the lives and loves of the pretty little creatures who formed the *corps de ballet*. He also told me that these tiny fragile girls who appeared to the audience to drift like snowflakes across the stage sounded to him below like a herd of buffalo stampeding across the boards.

As a result of his contact with Serge Lifar, Géa remained interested in all aspects of the ballet, and took me to the preview of the magnificent exhibition, *Ballets Russes de Diaghilev*, organised by Lifar and staged at the Louvre. The exhibition covered the years 1909–1929, and was a dazzling success. All Paris flocked to see the costumes and scenery created by artists of the calibre of Picasso, Modigliani, Utrillo, Chirico, Braque and Marie Laurençin, when they were still struggling and unknown.

With us on this occasion was Marie Laurençin who had become a friend after I had interviewed her for an article I had been commissioned to write about her famous lover, the poet Guillaume Apollinaire. It was Picasso who brought Apollinaire and Marie together. She, like the young poet, was illegitimate. He was born in Rome of a Polish-Italian mother and a Swiss-Italian father. He was baptised Guglielmo de Kostrowitsky and spent most of his childhood in Monte Carlo, where his mother was an *entraîneuse* at the Casino. Apollinaire, besides being a poet, was also an art critic, short-story writer and leader of *avant-garde* movements in the painting and literature of the early twentieth century. It was from him that the Dadaists, then at the height of their powers, borrowed the word Surrealism. Marie became his great love. Having once met her he refused to be parted from her and it was he who introduced her to the painters and poets who, like herself, would become famous.

In her youth Marie was tall and slim, with almond eyes and frizzy hair. Her mother hailed from Normandy and her father from Picardy. She attended the Lycée Lamartine and studied painting at the Académie Humbert with Braque.

Her liaison with Apollinaire lasted from 1904 to 1911, during which they both worked hard. When war with Germany was declared he immediately enlisted and proved to be 'a steady, trustworthy soldier, cheerful amid rats, lice, mud, cold and danger, and he made friends among officers and men'.[1] He was wounded above the right temple by shell splinters. After some elementary surgery, the surgeons ordered a trepanation to relieve pressure on the brain. He went into the operating theatre, a brilliant, joyous lively human being and after the operation his friends reported, in tears, that Guillaume was a different man. He was irascible, egotistical and dull. He returned to civilian life and continued his literary life, but he was far from well and in 1918 he went down with an attack of pneumonia. He seemed to recover from this, only to die suddenly of an epidemic of influenza.

Marie Laurençin, when we met, was a brisk, lively creature, who seemed at first to be a typical French *bourgeoise*, interested only in her home, her cooking and her pets. She did not seem to care much for travel, and adored Paris as much as Madame de Stael, who, when in exile, sighed for the gutters of the rue du Bac.

Marie's house was old-maidish but charming. It was filled with books, flowers and cats. She was very short-sighted. She ate fast, read quickly, and painted very slowly. She spent the week working, closeted in her studio in the rue Vaneau, but consecrated her Sundays mainly to walking about Paris with her faithful maid, Suzanne.

Until one came to know Marie really well, there was little to connect the bustling housewife with one of the most successful

[1] *Apollinaire* by Francis Steegmuller (Rupert Hart-Davis, London).

women painters of her time. She was already famous in 1918, and throughout the course of her long life her paintings were in constant demand all over the world. Her models were a curious breed, 'bred out of illusion by Drian . . . half woman, half flower, half siren, half butterfly'. Her doe-eyed beauties clad in swirling, diaphanous pastel-coloured draperies carried bunches of flowers, or were accompanied by milk white hinds; groups floated by leading ponies, or leaning dreamily against tropical trees, while doves perched on their bare shoulders, and fluffy poodle-dogs capered about them. Marie never lost the key to the magical door to childhood that Alain Fournier had also pushed ajar.

*

In retrospect, I think I was happier at this time than ever before. I could, at last, write truthfully to my parents that I was settling down; a statement made to relieve them of the anxiety caused them each time one of their friends (specifically invited to contact me) returned home to say that they had indeed seen me, looking well but shabby, and in the company of a motley crew of unwashed Bohemians.

Certainly the young writers, poets and artists we mixed with were not models of sartorial elegance. Most of them were very poor or lived on a meagre pittance from their families; but they gave me their friendship and their trust and I rejoiced at being part of an intellectual community which had so much to contribute to life and letters.

I had found myself an interesting job in a news agency which operated from an office in the rue de la Paix. It was an international organisation and certainly broadened my horizons by sending me out on all manner of interesting assignments, which included interviewing political figures passing through Paris at this time.

For some unfathomable reason the French were in euphoric mood. Chamberlain's 'peace in our time' agreement seemed to have given the Parisians a shot in the arm and I covered a series of extraordinary parties. One of them was Lady Mendl's Circus Party, at which this astonishingly frail old lady did agile handsprings.

Count Etienne de Beaumont, one of the leaders of elegant society, surpassed himself by giving a great ball to celebrate the tercentenary of Racine. His guests were invited to come dressed as characters from the plays or the period of the playwright, and walking among the 'tout Paris' on that occasion was a stroll through the past.

Wherever I went I met the dumpy Elsa Maxwell, whose long reign of master-minding the social life of the international set was on the slide, for the simple reason that the whole of her gay glittering careless world was just about to be blown to hell.

I don't remember how my rugged, unsophisticated genius of a lover first became enmeshed in the trap from which he had sprung me. Suddenly, he was polishing his nails and his boots, changing his shirt daily, and worrying about the set of his woollen knitted tie. I began to wonder who was responsible for this change in my sea-green incorruptible. I cannot say I was even mildly jealous, for jealousy did not enter into the curious composition of my relationship with Géa. I was, however, sufficiently curious to want to meet my rival, and was staggered to find that Géa was fast losing his integrity to a *man*; to one of those silver-tongued socio-political animals that he had so often reviled as being hypocrites and parasites.

This charmer is now dead, and is certainly not in Paradise, but may well be in Hades with his friends, Hitler, Goering and their band of merry men. Thus, for a brief while, Géa and I became part of that elegant, glittering sink of corruption which had brought together pro-Fascist society hostesses, politicians, actors and actresses and a smattering of writers and painters. Géa's new friend had made him think that by joining this particular group his talents might be used to help avert the threat of war. Géa was flattered. He was an artist. He drew satirical cartoons and portraits of suspect politicians, and high-ranking military men and ministers. Géa became the fashionable artist of the moment. He was *their* pet artist; and not until the last moment, until the Germans were actually on the outskirts of Paris, did Géa realise that he had been duped. When he did, his anger was great, and he rejected his new 'friends' as speedily as he had joined them. Géa's elevation to the corridors of power had not gone unnoticed by his mates, who were intensely irritated and surprised by what they bluntly called his 'treachery' when they saw his cartoons and drawings published in the anti-semitic, anti-British magazines and newspapers owned by the powerful pro-Fascist faction.

At first I tagged along in Géa's wake, enjoying the cocktail parties, dinners and grand receptions and was most impressed by the perks that seemed to go with the great. I was a passenger on a trip in a private train laid on by Anatole de Monzie, a minister who invited us to his country house where Géa was to meet a man who was to publish a book of political cartoons which were part of the insidious fifth column campaign meant to confuse, weaken, and ultimately demoralise the French nation.

It is not for me to pass judgement on the men and women who later opened their homes, and their legs, to the invader. Some of them paid the price of treachery. Others had to live with their conscience, with the knowledge that they had compounded horrors such as the rape and destruction of the village of Oradour-sur-Glane; and of the deaths of the thousands of men, women and children who perished in concentration camps or by torture at the hands of the Nazis. I feel bitter when I read the memoirs of those who managed to slip through the net of the avengers, and who, by pouring gallons of whitewash over their dark deeds, have been reinstated, and, as cherished public figures, as sacred monsters so dear to the French, are once again seen strutting on the stage of public life.

*

In the meantime, ordinary folk, discounting scare headlines and the seismic shocks which periodically shook them out of their complacent lethargy, were planning their annual holidays in Austria, in the Black Forest and in the South of France. Long-legged, bronzed, butter-blond *wandervögels* with staff and knapsack, wandered the length and breadth of France, using their sharp eyes and wandering innocently in the neighbourhood of factories, airfields, and military installations.

The usual rush of tourists, British and American, came swarming into Paris; everything was slightly frenetic. We seemed to talk faster and to laugh louder and more readily. Never, in all my experience, had Paris looked more tranquil and more beautiful than in that April 1940. I walked to work each day, rising earlier, because I wanted to have the pleasure of strolling through the Tuileries Gardens which I had known and loved since my childhood.

In the offices of my agency, rumour was rife. The Germans had been halted by the Maginot Line: they had *not* been halted by the Maginot Line. Hitler had flown to England to see the King: Hitler had been murdered by a Jewish Charlotte Corday. . . .

To monitor the news, and to raise French morale, the Government had created a Commissariat-General for Information. Such was the euphemistic title given to the equivalent of the British Ministry of Information. This organisation was put under the control of the eminent writer Jean Giraudoux, who had more control over his fictional characters than over the motley bunch who served under him. The Headquarters of the C.C.I. were at the Hotel Continental, in the rue de Rivoli, together with the Press Bureau of the Quai d'Orsay, which had also been moved there. The offices were scattered amongst the bedrooms, bathrooms, pantries and public rooms, awash with potted ferns and dusty palms.

No manuscript with any kind of political or religious bias was supposed to get into the hands of a publisher until it had been vetted by an official of the C.C.I. I was engaged in editing the memoirs of a number of famous foreign politicians, and when my job was completed, I trotted along with the manuscript in my brief-case, only to find that I had to queue with my colleagues who had come on similar missions. The French are not queue-minded, and soon there were fierce interchanges of Gallic nastiness between literary hacks who tried to huff one another out of the queue. One, I remember, announced that as he was the recent winner of a literary prize, it was his right to see the Director before anyone else. This remark led to an ugly scuffle, with many of those present immediately forming themselves into pro and anti factions; in the ensuing mêlée, I managed to slip between the vociferous gentlemen and to get into the presence.

One of the manuscripts on which I had worked with the author caused me grave unease and misgivings. It was the autobiography of Otto Strasser who had once challenged's Hitler's power. He and his brother Gregor played an important part in the birth and development of National Socialism between 1920 and 1932.

Gregor, the elder brother, was a chemist by trade. He was sentenced with Hitler after the putsch of 1923 to prison, but was soon released after his election to the Bavarian Diet in May, 1924. In December he was sent to the Reichstag, and at once was in charge of the Nazi Party organisation. Next to Hitler, Gregor

Strasser was the outstanding figure in the movement until he fell out with his chief in 1932. He then retired from political activities, but Hitler's hatred followed him wherever he went, and he was assassinated in the purge of 30 June, 1934.

Otto Strasser worked closely with his brother. Otto was a publicist. He was a Socialist writer and editor and in 1923 followed his brother into the Nazi Party; he had a sharp and brilliant mind and he edited its National Socialist Letters, and during 1926–1930 was a director of the Nazi Kampf-Verlag, a publishing firm in Berlin. One of Otto's assistants was a young Doctor of Philosophy of the University of Heidelberg. His name was Paul Joseph Goebbels, and he became Gregor's private secretary when Heinrich Himmler elected to join Hitler in Munich, where the latter appointed him a little later, Gauleiter of Lower Bavaria.

In 1930 Otto clashed with Hitler and founded a more revolutionary group known as the Black Front with members of the party who had openly broken with Hitler. Among these were the youths of the Steel Helmets, the Young Deutsche Order, the Peasants' Revolutionary Movement and the Werewolves.

As soon as Hitler assumed complete power in 1933 he turned the full force of his wrath on Otto Strasser, who fled from Berlin to Thuringia. He then went to Vienna, but the Nazis were already strong in the Austrian capital, and the S.A. had special orders to hunt down the leader of the Black Front. Strasser next took refuge in Prague, but here too Hitler's long arm reached out to destroy him, or bring him back to Germany.

Deprived of his German citizenship, he fled to France, to Great Britain and finally to Canada. He returned to Germany in 1955. His book, *The Structure of German Socialism* written in 1932, and others written in war-time, *Hitler and I*, *Germany Speaks* and *Germany Tomorrow* had a wide readership.

My instructions at this particular time were to deliver Otto Strasser's very important manuscript only into the hands of the Great Monsieur Giraudoux himself. Each time I went on this mission, the Director was 'engaged in conference' or out. In the meantime, Herr Strasser, who was not the easiest of men to cross, was agitating to get his manuscript passed by the French authorities, so he could send it to the United States, where a publisher was waiting for it. Strasser intended following his manuscript as speedily as possible, for he had good reasons for not wanting to be around, if and when Hitler's Nazis took Paris.

Herr Strasser and I can hardly be said to have established a close friendship during our brief, but significant, encounters. There was something about his quiet, glacial insistence on getting his own way which chilled my blood; nor did I much care for the way he tried to order me around. Our 'vibes' were certainly not in harmony. Whether or no Otto Strasser shared the views of his erstwhile friend, Hitler, on the *final solution* for those who got in his path, I do not know, but it was with considerable relief that I returned his manuscript after it had been vetted, with a polite farewell and the ill-founded hope that I should never set eyes on him again.

17

Frère Jacques, Frère Jacques

If I have not yet mentioned the part played in my life by my brother Jacques—known to the family as Lino—it is because he was some years younger than myself and was being educated, first in South Africa, and then, briefly, at an English public school, from which, much to his chagrin, Papa plucked him to do his military service in France.

By the time I had left the Baron, lost Chris, and moved into the rue Jacob with Géa, my little brother was almost a man, and, as his visits to Paris grew more frequent, so did the bond between us tighten. At that stage, however, he was too busy learning about life to question my somewhat unconventional liaisons, but if he disapproved of them, he never said anything, for he was well aware that I did not exactly welcome criticism.

My brother was important to me. He remained always the little *Metoo* of my childhood, who had clung so trustingly to me, to the Big One, who to him then was the fount of all wisdom, wit, and experience.

Now, having done some of his *service militaire* in France, he was, at the outset of the war, stationed at Sospel, a village high in the mountains. He was serving in the 157 Regiment d'Artillerie à Pied. His safety was a cause of constant concern to me, and added greatly to my anxiety as the German advance swept across France.

In a letter to my family in South Africa, which I wrote from Paris early in June, I said:

Today for the first time since the beginning of the war, I am panic-stricken because of Lino on the Italian border, and because I've not seen him for a month. When I do he always reassures me, but when we don't communicate I get really worried.

I don't know whether you see the *actualités* in the local bio, but if you do, you will understand that everything we most dreaded is happening, right here, near us, and that the realisation of death has swept over me for the first time.

I am not afraid for myself, that would be doing the enemy too much honour; but should anything happen to me, I would like you to know how much I have thought of you, and loved you, although you may not always have known this, and thought me very selfish and uncaring.... I am staying here because I love this France. Lino is not with me, so I must stay near him in case he needs my help.

On Monday 10 June, I wrote again to my parents:

This is probably the last letter you will get from me for some time. The Germans are twenty-five or thirty miles from Paris, and everyone is scooting to safety as fast as they can. The Government is on its way today; that should give you some idea of the rats leaving the sinking ship.... No panic on my part, but a strong determination to get out before *They* get here.

Lino managed to phone me. He is well and fairly happy. As long as Italy stays out of the war he is in no danger, for the time being, anyway. I believe the Agency are making plans to go to Biarritz or Bordeaux, in which case I shall try to join them wherever they are, so long as it is in France.

The face of Paris in danger is extraordinary. People fleeing as if the Furies were after them. There is no transport, and the trains could be filled ten times over. I am still in the office, having walked from the rue Jacob in the scorching sun. I've some papers to destroy and some letters to sign. I wonder whether they will ever reach their destination? Business as usual is the motto in the office. A good thing too. It keeps our morale up. All my books and papers are in the flat, together with Géa's sketches and paintings. How to take one's beloved possessions away?

On 11 June, I wrote in my diary: 'Canada, Australia, New Zealand, South Africa and India, have declared war on Italy. The newspapers here have ceased publication. There is only one daily broadsheet available.

'Impossible to find a taxi or a bus. Where on earth have the great lumbering things gone? My powerful friends, ministers and such are withdrawn, silent and gloomy. At last they too can see the writing on the wall. At luncheon at *Paris-Soir* everyone was terribly pessimistic.'

On 12 June I wrote: 'I've just spent two hours walking the streets. It is probably the last time for years that I shall ever walk through this most beloved of cities. In the gardens around the Louvre, the grass has grown almost waist-high. Today an aged gardener was busy bedding out some plants. I stopped to chat with him. He told me his son was fighting "somewhere out there", and that it was a pity he had not bedded his plants out earlier. "We need a splash of colour to boost our courage," he said. "Now there may not be time."

'We stood silently staring at the magnificence around us. A surge of love for Paris swept over me. When I looked down, the gardener was on his knees patting the soft earth. The nape of his neck was old, vulnerable, pathetic.'

I went back to the flat, going from room to room, and tried to collect my thoughts, tried to make a list of my most precious belongings. Following me were Frau Muller, sniffing, and Tabou, the Siamese cat who usually ignored humans, living an entirely narcissistic existence. Now the panic in the air must have communicated itself to his feline soul, for he kept close to my heels, occasionally giving an eerie, banshee-like wail.

All the time the telephone was ringing, with friends asking me my plans, telling me theirs, asking what I intended doing, saying where they were going, and how we must meet the *minute* the scare was over. Some time earlier the Bureau Chief had called the members of his staff together, and told us that if it became necessary to quit Paris, our plain duty would be to get ourselves down to the premises leased by the Agency in a village called Cap Breton, about twelve miles from Bayonne. Free accommodation would be available for any member of the staff who reached the villa 'Les Lauriers'; the general idea being, it seemed, that the Agency should continue to function out of Paris for as long as possible.

The thought of an ultimate refuge was comforting, although I had no idea of the hazards we should encounter before reaching the comparatively peaceful haven that was Cap Breton. Nothing in my pampered existence had conditioned me to facing up to a situation in which all the rules that govern civilised living have ceased to exist; where the amenities one takes for granted—heat, light, telephone, and law and order in the streets—no longer function.

At that moment there was only one law in Paris, the famous *Système D.*[1] which operated in a multitude of ways, some of them later incorporated both into the Resistance and into the functioning of the Black Market.

Unasked, Frau Muller busied herself with wrapping all my jewellery in Géa's old underpants, which she then carefully packed in an empty Huntley and Palmer biscuit tin. She then addressed it to me, care of my parents in South Africa and, irony of ironies, registered the package at the Post Office, the last bastion of the empire of the *ronds de cuir*.[2] Needless to say it never reached me.

Her next errand was to the station to get tickets to Bordeaux. She returned dishevelled and grim-faced. 'Impossible to get within a mile of the booking-office. There's pure pandemonium. The exodus is in full swing,' and she began to cry, with great snuffling sobs.

At that moment there was a loud banging on our front door, and in came the concierge, panting and out of breath. 'Madame's husband, Monsieur le Baron, is on the way up.' From the gleam in her wily little eye, I knew she was enjoying what she supposed would be her moment of triumph at my discomfiture. She had always suspected me of living in sin with Géa, and now Renaud's bold statement that I was his wife had confirmed her worst suspicions. I thought Renaud's visit ill-timed and when he came bouncing in, my greeting was anything but warm.

Renaud was wearing the uniform he had worn all too infrequently when he had joined up in 1917, and was attached to his father's regiment. Renaud's war record was less than spectacular, not because he was a coward, but because he was incapable of conforming to discipline, and must have been one of the very few officers in the French Army to have been an interested observer, wearing blue silk Sulka pyjamas, at some of the famous and bloodiest actions of the crack regiment to which he had the honour of belonging.

Renaud always told me he never had sufficient time to dress. As his toilet took him about four hours, he may well have been

[1] *Système D.: Se demerder,* getting oneself out of the sh-t.
[2] *Ronds-de-Cuir:* bureaucrats.

right. Later, when he returned to civilian life, he managed to miss Madame Mère's funeral, because he had miscalculated the time it would take him to have his monthly bath.

In spite of his age, the Baron's vital statistics were still those of the young officer who had had his uniforms tailored by Anderson and Shepherd. It still fitted him perfectly, and he looked very dashing and romantic, standing there, with a flash of grey at the temples, and a breastful of medals, the like of which I had never seen outside a museum.

These medals—he was not entitled to wear any single one of them—were part of a collection accumulated through the centuries by his family who were renowned for their valour in battle. Neither Goering in his heyday nor President Idi Amin was more be-medalled than my estranged husband, the last of a noble line, as he stood there, clanking loudly in the flat I shared with my lover.

He had, he said, come to save me from the Germans by smuggling me out of Paris in an ambulance borrowed from a fleet of cars provided by the Marquise and an American millionaire's wife for the use of a group of well-intentioned society women formed early in the phoney war. Our destination, it seemed, was to be a convent in the Ariège, whose abbess was Renaud's first cousin.

I was touched. So was Géa. So was Frau Muller who, wildly polishing her pince-nez, peered at the affecting scene from a distance. The concierge, halfway down the stairs, was craning her neck upwards and straining her ears, hoping to hear the *dénouement* of a reverberating scandal.

Seeing that I was, as ever, resolved to go my own way, Renaud said, 'God go with you, *ma très chère*,' and having kissed my hand, clattered off with great dignity. It was all I could do not to rush down after him. I think at that moment, and for the first time, I loved and respected my husband. I never saw him again.

*

'You had better get going,' I said to Géa. 'Time is short, but you may still get a train going to Switzerland.'

'I'm coming with you,' he said, 'part of the way, anyhow! In the meantime, I'll nip round to the *Deux Magots* to say goodbye to the mates.'

'I'll meet you there.'

I crammed all I could into a hold-all, and into Tabou's basket I put the cat, his food bowl, and the French flag, which we used to hang from our window on the 14th of July and on other suitable occasions. Carrying the basket, I went out into the sunshine. I saw our concierge and a number of others sitting outside their buildings on hard kitchen chairs. While it has always been the habit of the French concierge to take the air in this fashion, I had never before seen a whole covey of these crones busily knitting away; the click-clack of their needles was, again, horribly reminiscent of the *tricoteuses* of the French Revolution.

My concierge always had the last word. 'Where shall I send your post?' she called, as I walked past. This sally was greeted with a great burst of laughter.

'We'll be back to pick up our luggage,' I replied coldly.

On my way to the *Deux Magots*, a taxi drew up beside me. In it were Géa and Pierre Lemoine, a journalist and a close friend of his. The two men hauled me into the cab as if they were kidnapping me.

'This is the last taxi out of Paris,' said Pierre. 'We've got to get ourselves to Tours.'[1]

I stared at the nape of the driver's neck. I noticed the way the grey hair straggled down the shabby collar of his jacket. He bent forward, releasing the brake. 'On-y-va, alors?'

We were off. I knew that I should weep, display some emotion; but I was numb and my only wish was to go, to get away quickly from the dying city.

Pompeii must have been as Paris was that day, just before the great, the final, flow of lava engulfed the whole population.

---

[1] I did not, of course, know that all through the night of 11 June, the Government had been driving south. 'The decision to establish the Government at Tours was a compromise. De Gaulle and Reynaud believed that the French Army should retreat to the Breton Peninsula and hold out until British shipping could transport thousands of Frenchmen to North Africa. To Weygand, the idea of a "Breton redoubt", was "preposterous". The French Army, he said, might only be able to hold out for two or three days. In the end, still hoping to go to Brittany later, but hedging his bet, Reynaud compromised, and decided on Tours, a hundred miles south-west of Paris, and almost midway between Bordeaux and Brittany'. (From *The Week France Fell* by Noel Barber. Macmillan.)

People were rushing madly to and fro in the streets, as in the early Mack Sennett films. The houses seemed to be made of cardboard, and the chestnut trees of green wood-shavings, like those of the Noah's Ark I owned as a child. Nothing was real. Tabou, incarcerated in his prison, mewed like a seabird. I opened the lid a trifle, and he pushed his funny, indignant little face up into mine.

Clutching Géa, I squealed, 'What about our luggage? It's in the flat. We must go back.'

'Impossible,' said Pierre. 'You'd have done better to jettison the cat, and to bring your clothes.'

The taxi raced through the familiar streets. Géa and Pierre each lighted cigarettes.

'Best way is through Rambouillet,' said Pierre, who seemed to have taken command of the itinerary. 'We can kip down there for the night, and get a train south tomorrow.'

'No trains will run again, friend. We must make Orleans, and as quickly as we can.'

'In this taxi?' I asked.

'Why not?'

'Is the driver willing?'

Géa tapped on the glass partition dividing us from the chauffeur.

'Will you drive us to Orleans?'

'Sorry, Monsieur, I can't leave Paris. My wife is in hospital. Besides, I haven't enough petrol.'

'Name your price,' said Pierre, who was always loaded. 'We've *got* to get to Orleans.'

The chauffeur was Russian, and a fatalist. He shrugged his shoulders.

'I want four francs a kilometre, plus my return fare and danger money?'

'Done.'

'In that case I'll do my best to get you to Orleans.'

'What's your name, old boy?' asked Pierre.

'Nicolai.'

'I expect you were an officer in the Prabojensky regiment?'

'Right,' said Nicolai. 'That's exactly what I was. Now shut up, and let me concentrate on my driving.'

We laughed, and exchanged the old joke about Russian princes and taxi drivers. The car bounded forward. At the Porte d'Italie we swam into a traffic jam of unbelievable proportions.

'They simply can't all be going our way,' said Géa, but they were; and each and every vehicle intended getting a head start. We edged delicately into a stream of traffic which spread and swelled while Nicolai urged his car forward. We babbled madly about matters which yesterday had concerned our daily lives, and were now utterly unimportant. We could not yet grasp the immensity of the horror that was overtaking us.

I said, as if we were going off for the week-end, 'Remind me to get that picture from Leroux, he said it would be ready by the end of the week.'

'You may never . . .' murmured Géa.

*

Nicolai was a brilliant driver. He knew all the secondary roads, and managed to hare ahead of the long, desperate traffic jams on the main road. We stopped at a small estaminet which had already been cleaned out by the militia. We managed to get six hard-boiled eggs, two stale *croissants*, and ten packets of Caporal cigarettes. Nicolai ate ravenously, with one eye on the clock.

Night fell. A scented June night. The roof of the taxi was rolled back, and I was reminded of driving in the Bois on other summer nights. The cat was becoming increasingly restive, and much to the annoyance of Pierre, who was allergic to cats, was allowed out of his basket.

We seemed to have been on the road for days; but had, in fact, covered barely fifteen miles. Conversation had dwindled and died. Nicolai's shoulders were hunched over the wheel. Behind us was a long serpent of light. A couple of large vans had pulled to one side. They belonged to Maggi and Hachette.

The roar of the D.C.A. guns startled us out of our apathy. We sat up and listened attentively.

'Must be an air-raid over Paris,' said Géa.

'As we're only a few miles from the city, we'll probably get the full benefit of a bombardment.'

My legs began to wobble. I had thoughts that in a moment of crisis I should be brave and ice-cold, but I could not control my shaking legs. A motorcycle, throttle wide open, tore past. A loudspeaker blared, 'Make way, make way for the Minister...' and a long black limousine shot by, leaving us far behind.

Suddenly there was a concerted shout. '*Alerte, alerte*, put out your lights.'

Nicolai pulled up with a jerk. We got out, as did most of the occupants of the other cars. In a second, the lighted serpent was dark, save for a motorist at the end of the queue, who raked the sky with his headlights. A deep growl shuddered through the crowd.

'Make him put his lights out, break his bloody neck. It's the Fifth Column, he's guiding the planes.'

A shot rang out. There was total blackness. Total silence.

I had often wondered how I should behave in a real emergency. This seemed to be one. I thought of the Playing Fields of England, of stiff Upper Lips, of Nelson's last heroic message... but my unworthy Jewish knees banged together like castanets. Géa grabbed my arm, helped me jump a ditch and sat me down under a tree in the middle of a field. The cars looked a herd of mastodons in the gloom.

We lifted our heads. Here they were. The enemy planes flew with a jagged roar. We strained our eyes, staring up at the sky. There was nothing, nothing to be seen. Only that menacing roar. So death might come like this, slyly, a bullet out of the night.

Nicolai had had enough of us. 'I wish now to return to Paris,' he said.

'Impossible.'

'But Monsieur, my wife?'

'Sorry old chap, but you're stuck, as we are. Even if you wanted to, you couldn't turn back now. Every single road leading to and from Paris is jammed.'

It was the longest night I had ever known. I sat huddled in a corner of the taxi, longing for the dawn. Twice, the call '*alerte, alerte*' sent us scuttling into the fields, where we lay flat in the grass on the stones. During one of these scampers into the landscape, Tabou leapt out of my arms.

Dawn broke like a spray of water. The fields were smothered in a grey cotton-like mist. I took out my mirror and tried to smooth and comb my hair. The car had moved only a few yards. I opened the door of the cab, and there, beside the running board, was my small taffy-coloured cat. He jumped into my arms, digging his claws into my neck and purring with pleasure at having found me again.

Nicolai, Géa and Pierre were scruffy and heavy-eyed, their faces smeared with five o'clock shadow. I wanted desperately to go to the lavatory, but dared not wander away; besides there was no toilet paper. We were inching towards Orleans. Again the alert sounded. We were sitting targets in the daylight. The cars stood out strongly on the white road. I wriggled into a ditch, and watched the planes dipping lower and lower. There was the rattle of machine-guns. The planes dipped, dived, and then winged wildly away. I crawled out of my ditch and looked around. Everything seemed calm. Then, halfway down the long line of cars, we heard the sound of piercing cries as one of the cars began to burn. Great whips of flame shot up into the sky. There was no way of getting to the occupants of the stricken cars. We had to go on as the queue moved forward.

At 6.30 a.m., we reached Orleans, Joan of Arc's city. The Maid herself was absent from France on that day. We made for a café. It was crowded. We got out again, and found another which seemed to be less full. It was an oasis in the universal bedlam. The waitresses were young, clear-eyed and competent, and did not seem unduly upset by the arrival of a weary crowd of refugees clamouring for coffee. Bread had not yet arrived, but there were baskets heaped with great mounds of golden Madeleines.

Géa rushed out to buy a paper. 'The whole thing stinks,' said Pierre forcibly. 'Don't you understand, you two, the whole fucking country is rotten to the core, rotten', and tears dripped down his cheeks into his *ersatz* coffee.

At the next table, a platinum blonde hooker, with a bored expression and a chic little hat crushed over one eye, toyed with her cigarette lighter. Her long red nails were like talons. Nicolai, having eaten a hearty breakfast and collected his cash, seemed more relaxed. He shook us all by the hand, wished us well, and left. He was a couple of thousand francs to the good. We hoped he would get back safely, and that his wife would be delivered of a fine boy.

'Now,' said Pierre, rising like a giant refreshed, 'what about trying to get on to a train?'

The platinum blonde also got up, dazzling us with a pair of

long Dietrich-like legs. We followed her out of the café, into the roadway, expecting her to climb into a limousine; but, to our amazement, she tucked up her skirts, and straddling a bicycle, pedalled away.

The station was crowded beyond belief. We picked our way over soldiers lying prone, their heads pillowed on their *bardas*; through countrywomen sitting stolidly on benches, their baskets at their feet. Babies wailed. Mothers held their little ones out to pee over the rails. We managed to struggle to the ticket office where a harassed official gave us three tickets to Tours.

'I'm not sure that there will be a train,' he said, handing us the tickets. 'You'll just have to be patient.'

When, eventually, a train did come into the station, a great cheer went up from all those moiling about on the platform. Pierre and Géa heaved themselves and me into a carriage already bursting at the seams. There was hardly enough room to move one's arms. An old peasant woman sat nodding and talking to herself. Seeing me looking at her, she cackled with laughter.

'What is so amusing, Mother?' asked an elderly gentleman. 'What is there to laugh about?'

'I'm laughing at you lot,' she said, 'poor boobies, thinking you're going to Tours. This train only goes to Norwens, six kilometres from here. It always has and it always will, in spite of your war.'

'Pardon me, Madame,' said the old gentleman furiously, 'the guard told me distinctly that this *was* the train to Tours.'

'I don't care what he told you. He was wrong. I've taken this train for twenty years or more, and I tell you, sir, that you will have to change at Norwens for Tours.'

A spirited argument involving everyone present was cut short by the arrival of the train at Norwens, where everyone was thrown into confusion by the guard shouting at the top of his lungs, 'All change for Tours.'

Tours was black with people, like flies on a wound. Pierre knew someone at the Hotel de l'Univers, and we went there to see if we could get rooms, but an irritable and haggard concierge said there wasn't a single bed and that people were already sleeping in the baths. Wave upon wave of tense and weary refugees broke on the town, besieging restaurants and hotels. We passed by the Centre d'Accueil, where, on wooden benches, exhausted travellers to nowhere sat munching bread and drinking wine or coffee. The market-place was a scrapyard of old cars piled high with luggage, furniture, baskets and even crates of protesting livestock.

We finally managed to get a meal in an old-fashioned hotel in a back street. Pierre went off to see what was going on in the press world. He went to the Hotel Metropole in the Place Jean-Jaurès, which had been requisitioned by the Government. He was told that the Ministry of Information had been set up in the rue Gambetta. Everything was in a filthy mess, but he decided to claim a desk there and to remain in Tours for the present. Géa and I had made up our minds to press on as soon as we could and to make for the little village of Percemont where we had friends.

'What are you going to do?' Pierre asked me.

'Close the file on Paris and go home.'

We stood in the hot sun waiting for the local bus. Everyone seemed drained and listless. In the queue was a French colonel with one leg. His breast was covered with ribbons. Finally the bus lurched to a halt in front of the stop sign. The people in the queue fought to get aboard. In the rush the colonel was knocked down. Géa got him to his feet and hoisted him on to the bus and yanked a spotty-faced yokel out of his seat to make room for the officer. There were mutterings and growlings from the lad's mother who glared malevolently at Géa and myself.

We rattled through the green and peaceful countryside, through wooded valleys and along country roads. Suddenly the bus came to an abrupt and screeching stop. There was a roadblock ahead. From the bushes sprang a dozen or so soldiers in German uniform. Panic flooded through the bus. The Boche captain, swinging himself aboard, ordered us to hand over our passports. The colonel refused. 'First show me your mandate?'

The young captain lost his temper. 'Give me your passport at once. I have orders to inspect the papers of everyone on this bus.'

'I refuse absolutely.'

The officer's voice rang out. 'Aux armes, aux armes!'

We sat there transfixed with fear. Other soldiers appeared from the bushes, and in a moment the bus was surrounded. The French colonel hobbled away demanding to be taken to the German commanding officer. It then transpired that our 'German' aggressors were Belgians. Deeply relieved, the passengers then blamed the colonel for their enforced delay.

'If the *sacre militaire* hadn't lost his rag, we'd be well on our way home by now.'

Shortly afterwards, the colonel, now escorted by a smiling and deferential Belgian captain was returned to us, and the bus bumbled off again. The farmer behind me tapped my shoulder and said, 'Even if they had been Boches, there was nothing we could have done. Those chaps were armed to the teeth. A live pig is better than a dead hog I always say.'

At which the colonel ground his teeth with rage at this exhibition of defeatism.

Percemont lay happily sprawled in the sunshine, a tiny village in the heart of the countryside. We found an estaminet in which I waited while Géa went off to phone our friends, only to return with the news that they had already left for the South of France with their small children, but that their parents were expecting us.

The *patron* offered to drive us to the château. Our kind hosts proved to be a distinguished and hospitable middle-aged couple, who welcomed us with great warmth. They had lived here most of their lives and had no intention of being driven from their property by the Germans.

We dined quietly at a table set with fine napery, silver and crystal glasses. The conversation was cultured. Nobody mentioned Hitler, or the Nazis. While we were having coffee, the Squire excused himself, and went to join his gamekeeper, and the other villagers, on their nightly 'Parachute Patrol'.

My bedroom, decorated in blue and white was fresh and feminine. The charming little Empire boat-shaped bed was comfortable. On the night-table was a *carafe* of orange-flower water to calm the nerves. I opened the window wide on the jasmine-scented night. The fields were silvered under the moon. I heard the short, staccato bark of a vixen away in the woods. Then, the château was wrapped in silence. Climbing into bed, I said my prayers and fell asleep at once.

We spent two days at the château. Two precious days in which to rest, collect our thoughts, plan the next step and replenish our nervous energies. The Squire had given refuge to a number of Belgian peasants. They worked in the dairy, making butter and cream from the milk of a famous pedigree herd.

In the evening, in the salon, we listened to the radio. The Germans were steadily advancing.... Reynaud had appealed to America. America would save the day.... She did last time.... The King of the Belgians had betrayed his country, he had fled with his mistress; down with the King.... The bewildered Belgian refugees refused to believe this news. They said, 'Our king was so good, such a kind man, and so fond of his Queen, poor dead beautiful Astrid.'

We sat waiting for Reynaud's final speech. The polished wood of the furniture and the panelling reflected the light that shone through heavily fringed shades. The shutters were tightly closed, and the velvet curtains drawn across the shutters; for the château with its pepperpot towers would be an easy target.

The first three bars of the *Marseillaise* announced an important message: 'Reynaud is going to speak', said a voice, then the voice trailed away. We sat leaning forward, waiting. We sat silently until three o'clock in the morning when a weary voice came over the ether. 'I have asked America for help, but, at the moment, she cannot help us. But we will fight, we will go on fighting. We will struggle on until the end. France cannot die, must not die....'

The sad, defeated voice was silent. The Squire's eyes were wet. This was the end and we all knew it.

*

By six o'clock next morning, Géa and I were on our way. He had managed to get transport, and we embarked in a lorry filled with passengers like ourselves. One was a young school-teacher on her way to Poitiers, where she had an aunt. She sat thumbing through a dog-eared paper-covered book containing the prophecies of Nostradamus in which she had great faith. He said that the Germans would be halted before they got to Poitiers and that France would be saved from the Germans. We hoped she and Nostradamus were right.

I had always wanted to see the châteaux of the Loire, but had never thought to glimpse them from the back of a lorry, haring across the 'garden' of France, with a load of garlic-scented refugees, with dirty feet and smelly breath. Like a moiré ribbon the Loire threaded its way through an enchanted landscape, starred with the magnificence of the great châteaux whose names were like a litany.

The sun boiled our brains as the lorry shuffled along. We were tired and hungry. It was difficult to keep one's dignity, when being bumped along, like a load of cattle bound for the abattoir. As we reached Poitiers, sirens sounded and we tumbled from the lorry, scuttling like ants, looking for shelter. It was a short raid, but suddenly I *knew* that we must leave Poitiers before the Luftwaffe returned to finish off the job they had begun.

I was standing on the street corner, looking at the endless stream of traffic, and wondering how on earth we were going to get away this time, when someone grasped my arm. It was a Belgian diplomat, a great friend of Géa, who had always hoped that our friendship might develop into a more intimate relationship. He did not waste time in gossip.

'You must get away from here as fast as you can.'

'I know, but I also know that there are no trains until 4 a.m. Géa has just checked.'

'The ministerial train from Tours will be passing through here in ten minutes. Get aboard.'

'I won't be allowed into the train.'

'Come with me.' Bellowing loudly for Géa, I hurried off with Leopold. Géa, carrying Tabou's basket, was pushing through the crowds to get to us. He had been sketching a group of exhausted refugees lying in a huddle on the platform. He and Leopold fell into one another's arms. Leopold dashed away, returning in a trice, with two first-class tickets, obtained, goodness knows how, since the queue snaked out of the station and halfway into the town.

Leopold positioned us on the platform, and sure enough, just as he had said, a long train flashed into the station. It slowed down for the space of a minute, which gave us just enough time to fling ourselves aboard. This train, it appeared, was packed with privileged, high-grade civil servants on their way south. In a moment we were roaring out of the station. The next day I heard that at 3.30 a.m. there was a raid on Poitiers. The station was pulverised, and hundreds of people were wounded and killed.

*

It was impossible to sleep. The train kept stopping, but the night was still, and there was no sound of enemy planes. A young nurse attached herself to me. She had worked in a hospital near Liège. After the bombing that destroyed her hospital, she had managed to squeeze aboard a truck. She possessed nothing but the uniform in which she had escaped. She said she was hungry so I burrowed in my pocket, where I had secreted a lump of stale bread and a piece of cheese as iron rations. These I gave her. We were thirsty, but there was no way of getting anything to drink.

At 9 a.m. we reached Bordeaux, capital of the Gironde, a great seaport, which boasts Montaigne as its most distinguished native, and some of the finest of the French château vintages, of which Château Yquem was always my favourite. The city was packed. Hundreds of people had spent the night in the streets. The smell of hysteria and panic was in the air, for here in Bordeaux were the two consulates, Spanish and Portuguese, both swamped mainly by Jews, all trying to get their visas to get over the border into Spain and then into neutral Portugal.

Here, at Bordeaux, Géa and I decided to part. I knew it was high time for him to get back to his own country, where he had orders to rejoin the unit in which he would spend most of his war service. I knew too that I would greatly miss the reassuring presence of my big warm bear; but in a strange way I wanted this adventure to be mine alone.

I sat on the terrace of a café, waiting for Géa to come back with a newspaper, and the times of departure of our respective trains. He returned with the news of the bombing of Poitiers, and with the glad tidings that he had found someone with a car who was going 'in the direction of Switzerland'. I knew that my Papa had, for many years, had business dealings with a famous wholesale company of wine-merchants in Bordeaux. I had met the head of the firm when he came out to South Africa to visit the vineyards of the Cape. I remembered him as a pleasant old man with flowing white whiskers. I thought it might be wise to try to establish contact with him, so that he could, if necessary, get a message through to my family.

I found the address of Messieurs Burdigala et Cie in the *Bottin*, phoned, gave my father's name, and asked if I might call immediately. I went straight to their offices where I was greeted by a pretty young secretary who seemed totally unaware of the pandemonium outside; finally I was taken into the sanctum of Monsieur Edouard Burdigala.

Sadly, my Papa's old friend had been gathered to his fathers, and there reigned in his stead a pale dark young man with eyes like prunes in cream behind a pair of unbecoming pince-nez. He was helpful and sympathetic, and when I asked him to cable my family to tell them my whereabouts, he agreed at once. This cable took three weeks to reach Johannesburg. There is no doubt that without the financial support of 'Monsieur Edouard', I might well not have survived the ordeal which lay ahead.

Géa took me to the station, kissed me warmly, promised to write as often as possible, assured me that he would love me all his life, begged me to change my mind and accompany him to Switzerland; and at last, left me with tears. I sat on a bench and howled, in concert with Tabou.

*

Night had fallen by the time the train arrived. I had my usual monthly cramps and dizziness. I got into the train to find that each and every carriage was packed with tired and irritable refugees. At last I found a seat, but gave it up to an old nun who was escorting a rabble of unruly children who were being taken to a place of safety deep in the Landes.

In the middle of the night, dazed and weary, I was shovelled out of my carriage, on to yet another platform, to wait for yet another train. I could smell the sea and the aromatic scent from pinewoods, and was comforted by these pungent odours which seemed like a signal of hope from nature itself.

Unbelievably, a small local train, known as *la correspondance*, was actually waiting to take passengers as far as Labenne, where the station-master informed me that Cap Breton was still eight miles further on and possessed neither railway station nor train. He said flatly that there was no way of reaching Cap Breton that night. I asked if he could recommend an hotel, at which he shrugged his shoulders, and pointed to the station clock. However, a tip produced a change of manner. Flinging open the door of an empty second-class compartment on a siding, he invited me to enter, and to make myself comfortable. There was, of course, no light. I took off my shoes and with Tabou in my arms, tried to sleep. Although I was exhausted I remained wide awake. A frieze of people churned through my brain. I remembered the expressions on the faces of those around me when the sirens had signalled an air-raid; the wide eyes of a baby, glimpsed over its mother's shoulder; the slack mouth of a terrified old man. Everywhere was pain, bewilderment, fear. How had this great nation been forced to her knees? Why had she given in so easily? Who was responsible for her defeat? Finally, I slept uneasily. I missed my companion.

*

Cap Breton was no tourist paradise. It was a fishing village which, like so many others, had been taken over by townees who had built ugly holiday villas near the beach. There were wide, pale, windswept sands, a few pretentious hotels, and some solidly built fishermen's cottages. In a café, overlooking the stone quays, the fishermen gathered each day to listen to the radio, and exchange items of news.

My Chief had not yet arrived, nor had any of my colleagues. I spent my first night at Cap Breton in the 'best' hotel. The only palatial thing about this establishment were the prices charged by a canny management prepared to cash in on the plight of the refugees. The hotel was packed with them, wandering about with set faces, wondering where to go and what to do. None of them, so far as I could see, ever went to the beach or looked at the ocean. I made up my mind to find cheaper and cosier accommodation as soon as I could.

Just off the market-place, I discovered an inexpensive little restaurant. The *patronne* wore trousers and had a mop of pink hair, crowning a crumpled, painted clown's face, but she was an inspired cook. Watching Madame Andrée among her saucepans made me feel that in spite of the appalling news, so long as there were cooks of her calibre, French culinary traditions would survive.

There was nothing much to do while waiting for the others to arrive, so I took to sea-bathing, and in the cold salt water purged my body of the grime and fatigue of travel. Watching me from the beach were some small pale children, evacuees from Paris. They were typical *Poulbot* kids, born in the shadow of the Sacré-Cœur, and stood there, shivering in the cold wind, as sad and homesick as sick monkeys in a zoo.

The Chief arrived late one night. He was the bearer of ill news.

Bordeaux had been bombed, and the Germans were rapidly cutting a swathe through all of France. Soon, he said, they would reach Cap Breton; before that happened, he had to go to Bayonne and Biarritz on urgent business.

The graceful bridge that spans the turgid waters of the river Adour was solid with cars. So was the town. The hotels had closed their restaurants, as there was no longer enough food to go round. One dish, and one only was the order of the day. Meat had completely vanished, as had all fancy bread and pastries.

Bayonne had become the meeting-place of all those anxious to flee. Patriots, it seemed, were in short supply. Rolls-Royce, Hispanos and Delage automobiles lined the pleasant square framed by its fine trees. There was only one subject of conversation. How to get one's visas? From 5 a.m. long queues lined up in front of the Spanish and Portuguese Consulates. Wealthy men and women offered large bribes to enable them to jump the queues. An American passport was a great prize; the British refused to trade their passports. Nobody seemed anxious to have any other kind, except Swiss passports, which rated as highly as American.

The Chief dashed around making arrangements for a V.I.P. who had to leave as soon as possible. I kept his place in the queue, while he went off to see important contacts who might help. Few people had thought of taking their umbrellas when fleeing the enemy, and the rain poured down soaking the elegant ladies and dandified gentlemen who were crazed with anxiety to get the precious bits of paper that would ensure their safety.

Finally the consulates were closed. *Fermé, geschlossen*, for the day. The Chief and I hurried to a café, where we sat steaming, in our bedraggled clothes. When the rain let up a little, we went down to the quays to have a look at the ships. The Chief had an appointment with a man who knew someone who could pull the necessary strings to procure a passage. A little yellow-faced rat of a fellow in a dirty raincoat inched up to us. He whispered that it would cost around 15,000 francs to get a Spanish visa (the usual charge was about 12 francs) and he wanted cash in advance. In dollars, if possible. He also said he wanted the passport for which the visas were needed. The Chief refused to hand over his friend's most precious document. Unabashed, the rat sloped off to find another victim.

The rest of the day was spent listening to false rumours; in talking to people who said they had 'important contacts' who could get us the visas. We had luncheon in Biarritz, and I wondered what the Empress Eugénie, who had made this the most fashionable watering place of the Third Empire, would have said if she could have seen her country in such sad disarray. Yet I was shaken by the sight of so many smartly dressed men and women strolling calmly in the streets. Furthermore, the Biarritz branches of both Hermès and Lanvin were open, and business was as brisk as usual in the summer season.

Late in the evening, tired, and without the much desired visas, we returned to Cap Breton. The B.B.C. news was bad. I had found new lodgings in a fisherman's house on the seafront. The landlady was kind-hearted and liked animals; she allowed Tabou and myself to camp in a tiny room filled with horrendous bits of furniture, moth-eaten mats, and artificial flowers. The view from the little window over the sea was soothing; Tabou was allowed to run about in the little garden. Only once did I take him to the beach to relieve himself, but finding himself in the biggest sandbox of all time, which he obviously felt he had to fill, he became hysterical and totally constipated.

The Chief and I dined together. He was spending the night in the villa he had leased for us, a gloomy place into which I refused to move. But after dinner I walked him home, and as he opened the gate a dark figure surged out of the night. Both the Chief and I stood frozen, as the figure raised a torch to reveal the face of Herr Otto Strasser.

Strasser and the Chief went into conference. This lasted all night. Early next morning the Chief came to find me. I was to take charge of Herr Strasser, who must be spirited away before the oncoming German Army got to Cap Breton. I was to ship him off on the last of the mystery ships due to sail from Bayonne that day. The Chief, seeing the revulsion and rebellion in my face, patted my cheek and offered me his car.

At the last village before Bayonne, the French militia halted us. Herr Strasser handed them a forged passport stamped with every imaginable visa. He had, in fact, been of great assistance to the French Government in the preceding months, and they had not neglected to give him every potentially useful document to assist his departure. I did not care for this man at all, and although he was loud in his protestations of hatred for Hitler, I remembered all too well how close he and the Fuhrer had once been.

The mystery ship was due to sail on the four o'clock tide. The Captain had told Herr Strasser to bring with him stores and water for a journey which might last four to five days. We scoured every provision shop in town for tinned food, but there was nothing to be bought, even on the black market; Herr Strasser began to look both glum and hungry.

Finally, leaving him sitting moodily before a cup of acorn coffee, I went off and managed to discover a *confiserie* which dealt solely in the delicious *pâté de fruits* for which this part of the world was renowned. The sweetmeats were made in every shape, form and flavour; having collected a basket of mixed sticky sweets and two bottles of Vichy water, I went back to the café, where I found Herr Strasser writing a letter. I gave him his food parcels, paid for his coffee, and we left.

It was raining again. The quays were dark with people running hither and yon. Many were Jewish. Their faces were grey and gaunt. They knew, as well as I, that the arrival of the Germans was a matter of hours, and were frantic to get away. Like lemmings they dashed to the edge of the quay, trying to force themselves aboard the mystery ship.

Suddenly a man detached himself from the crowd, and came towards us. Taking Herr Strasser's arm, he led him quickly to the gangplank. For a moment Strasser stood and looked at me with his cold pale eyes. He said nothing. Then, a faint smile at the corner of his lips, he stiffly inclined his head, and rapidly marched aboard.

It did not take long for the ship to swing away from the quay. She was loaded to the gunnels. I stood there, watching with the refugees, as their last hope moved away out to the open sea. A young Jew flung himself into the water and swam wildly in the wake of the vessel. A siren blasted the air and a small boat was lowered to go to the rescue of the swimmer. As he was dragged into the tiny craft and then hauled aboard the parent ship, a great sigh of relief went up from those watching. The rain was pouring down my face, mixing with the salt of my tears.

*

The following day, the Chief sent me off again in his car, this time to deliver some important files to a 'contact' at Hendaye on the Spanish border. At Ciboure, a postcard village with brightly coloured houses, I came upon a quarter of a kilo of butter and a few kilos of magnificent ripe peaches. At Hendaye, which was also swarming with refugees, all loudly complaining of the shortage of food, I found my 'contact', handed over my files and began the journey back.

It was a soft and beautiful day. The countryside was green and peaceful. I felt calm and rather somnolent. All my problems had receded into the background of my mind. I wondered what sort of crossing Herr Strasser was having, and I hoped it was a rough one; I also thought of Géa and wondered how he was faring. I stopped the car, got out, and with my back against a sun-warmed rock lit a cigarette. Then far away on the white road, I saw a sight which quite literally froze me to the spot. I saw a long dark column snaking towards me. The Germans! Of course it was the Germans on their way back from the Spanish border. As they came closer I could see that the armoured tanks and cars were filled with soldiers in grey-green uniforms, their steel helmets coming low over their eyes, making them seem even more terrifying and inhuman. Many of them, riding high in the armoured cars, wore goggles. Like a great dark wave, the column pressed on, totally ignoring the woman sitting by the roadside.

When the first shock of seeing Hitler's army in front of me had worn off, I began to cry with rage. I could not bear the thought of the enemy here in this land, in this, my beautiful serene France. That they should ride thus, victoriously through the lovely summer afternoon, their arrogant faces betraying nothing of their pleasure at effecting yet another rape! When the column was well away, I got back into the car, and drove slowly towards Cap Breton. The farmers and village folk were out in full force, all along the road, silent, abashed, and in tears.

By the time I reached Bayonne, the Germans were everywhere. The town was almost devoid of civilians. They had prudently retired behind their shutters, all of which were closed in mute protest. Unconcerned, the German officers swaggered through the streets, while the soldiers stopped, now and again, to stare at the shop windows.

I arrived at Cap Breton in time to see the German flag being flown from the mast at the Mairie, which had suddenly become the *Kommandantur*. Cars and tanks filled the Place. Certainly the Germans were fast and efficient operators.

When the Chief and I finally met at the Café de la Paix, we found a heated discussion in progress. Everyone was waiting to hear a State of the Nation broadcast over the radio. We sat around debating what this message could possibly be. When it came, it was brief and shocking. Negotiations were in progress with a view to an Armistice with Germany. Dismayed and confused, we all stared at one another.

'What about England?' cried one old sailor. 'England would never accept such a shameful arrangement.'

'Never mind the English,' cried another. 'Do you think our French soldiers, our boys, would allow an Armistice with the Boche? Never, I say, never!'

When they heard that the Armistice had indeed been signed, their anger was terrible. It was not possible, they said, that their old Marshal Pétain had betrayed his soldiers, the men who had fought so gloriously with him in 1914.

'You heard what the traitor said,' the sailor said. 'Peace with honour,' and then, as the *Marseillaise* rang out, all present bowed their heads in their hands and wept with grief and shame.

*

Food supplies were becoming increasingly scarce. My scarecrow of a landlady thought up an ingenious scheme by which she agreed to cook any food we brought in; thus managing to feed both herself and her aged old crone of a mother, who looked like Popeye.

Most of the refugees were practically indigent, and although Committees and relief organisations did what they could to supplement the meagre rations, the population of Cap Breton, swollen to six times its size by refugees, was famished. Yet never once did I hear a local inhabitant grumble at the problems the 'Parisians' had brought with them.

I enrolled in the Soup Kitchen as a helper, and stood for hours doling out hot soup and bread to refugees and their children. Each day brought more people and soon it became impossible to find them sleeping quarters. Groups of whey-faced Parisians, with their scared children, sat with their backs to the beach.

Early one morning I was woken by the sound of loud voices.

The Germans had arrived; they were in running shorts and vests, making for the beach. Tumbling into my clothes, I rushed down into the street, to join the rest of the population who stood gawping at the blond, virile young Siegfrieds and Parsifals on their way to take a dip in the ocean.

Not all the soldiers were in shorts. Some of them were in uniform. They marched down to the beach, took over the beach huts, occupied them, and shortly reappeared in bathing trunks. They did not leave their clothes in the beach huts, but, for some reason made neat little piles of their clothes and boots on the sand. Once in the water, they swam about as gracefully as dolphins or young seals.

A shrill whistle called them back and they assembled to do gymnastics on the beach. Some of the young men had purchased large and expensive bottles of toilet water, which they splashed over themselves. After putting their clothes on again, answering a roll-call and giving a salute with a loud, Heil Hitler, they smartly re-embarked in their trucks.

The soldiers billeted near us were not fine physical specimens, but all the very young men seemed to be in peak condition. One of them approached me in the street, and asked in bad French where he could find a sewing-machine. I said I had no idea, and we stared at one another. An officer came up and asked the soldier what he had said. He was sent off with a flea in his ear.

The officer sauntered down the street with me, subjecting me to a barrage of questions. (Later I discovered that all Germans asked the same questions in France.)

'Do you think we are barbarians?'

Averting my profile, I said, 'No, why should we?'

'Why do most people look through us when we come close to them?'

'They are not used to invaders.'

'Do you think the English have let you down?'

'Certainly not.'

'Then you are wrong. They have betrayed you. You have been told lies about us too. We are here to help you. We will not take your food. We have food in plenty in our own country, and will be able to feed France when she has been bled dry by the British blockade.'

The French were icily polite to the Germans. In the shops they served them, swiftly, but unsmilingly; but at night, when the shutters were tightly closed, dozens of rebellious faces and damp eyes gathered round the radio to listen to the only link with reality, the B.B.C.

Many of the younger fishermen talked of joining de Gaulle. For this reason, perhaps, because there were spies amongst us, they were not allowed to go out in their boats, and the beach was put out of bounds to the civilian population.

Soon we began to feel the 'bite' of the victor. The nightly radio séances in the Café de la Paix ceased. We listened to the B.B.C. in secret, in attics or in cellars. The Armistice became a fact. The Government made its headquarters at Vichy. The Chief and I had a long discussion on our future plans. He made it clear that he thought it no longer safe for me to remain at Cap Breton, and said I must try to find a way to return to South Africa.

To this end I went to Bordeaux to see whether I could obtain the two necessary visas, one for Spain and the other for Portugal. I also told Monsieur Edouard Bourdigala that my money was running out and I had decided to go home. I explained the difficulties involved in getting the two crucial visas. He asked me for my passport, and having handed it with a note to one of his clerks, took me out to luncheon. We had an excellent meal in a tiny restaurant. Monsieur Bourdigala was a thoughtful host. Afterwards, we returned to his office, where he presented me with my passport, duly stamped with both visas, and with a cable from South Africa which had arrived while we were out. It was from my Papa, and it was brief and to the point.

'I expect you return home with my son, your brother. Affectionately Papa.'

I showed the cable to my friend. He chewed his lustrous red lower lip.

'What will you do now?'

'Find my brother, and take him home to Papa.'

'*Bonne chance*,' said Monsieur Edouard; 'rather you than me.'

*

Monsieur Bourdigala's loan paid for the car I bought. It was an old banger; but it still had plenty of fire in its aged belly. I drove back in it to Cap Breton, and told the Chief what had happened. He was worried.

'My information is that things have toughened up considerably. No young woman with your background should go back into Occupied territory. Why don't you change your mind? Your father will understand the danger of the situation.'

I was adamant. I knew my Papa. There was no point in returning home without the Patriarch's heir. I was surprised that Lala had not got into the act; but was told later that she had gone haring off to South America to 'find' me. She never could resist a long sea voyage to new places.

The Chief managed to collect some petrol coupons for me; one of my fishermen friends put a *bidon* containing five litres into the boot, 'in case'. I was told to drive to a town about twenty miles away from Cap Breton, where I should find fresh supplies of petrol at the *Kommandantur*. I spent another hundred francs of my loan buying sardines and a vast cheese which had just arrived and which the shopkeeper had no business to sell me, as I had heard him promising slices to all his regular black-market customers.

I set off early one morning with Tabou protesting violently at being incarcerated in his basket again. The landlady and Mrs Popeye saw me off.

My first stop was at Hossegor. The once gay little seaside town was dreary, and looked neglected. All traffic, save for a few vehicles driven by Germans, had been suspended. As I sat on the terrace of a café, drinking *ersatz* coffee, I was joined by one of my Parisian friends who was driving an ambulance to Dax. She told me she had been in Poland since the beginning of the war, and had watched the Germans advance in tanks which they drove over their own wounded and dying. She said that most of the base camps were filled with wounded French and German soldiers, all of whom were heartily sick of the war and of Hitler and his pack of lunatic advisers.

We went down to the beach where we watched German soldiers buying postcards and films for the cameras they all seemed to possess. They were great photographers, and the folk back home must have had a pretty good idea of what French towns, villages, monuments and tarts looked like.

My next stop was Dax, a small town famed for its hot-water springs and for the purity of the morals of its inhabitants. It too had suffered an avalanche of refugees; its narrow streets were jammed solid with cars, bicycles and handcarts.

At Dax I collected the people who were to come with me on the rest of my journey. The first was a young fragile-looking Belgian woman with a baby; the second was a French officer with a mangled arm in a sling. Both of them were sitting on the terrace of the café at which I stopped for a rest and a drink. Somehow I got into conversation with the officer. Hearing that I was making for Nice, he asked if he might accompany me, and whether I would consider taking the young woman and her baby as well. He had found her sitting on the pavement near a petrol station.

Claude Maeterlinck's story was similar to that of many of the refugees fleeing from the Germans. She had arrived at Dax the day before, dazed and bewildered by what had befallen her. She had left Brussels with her elder sister and her two young children. On the road, their car had been machine-gunned. Her nieces had died instantly. Their mother, crazed with rage and grief had refused to stop, but had driven on and on with her dead children in the car. At last, when her petrol ran out, she was forced to stop. Claude got out of the car with her baby and went to fetch help. When she came back, the car driven by the poor crazed woman with her terrible passengers had gone.

I who had hardly ever been in command of a situation was now the leader of my little troupe. They were hungry and tired, and it was, I knew, up to me to find lodgings for them. I ended by herding them into a room in an inn furnished only with a vast, broken-down settee, a truckle bed and four chamber-pots. I found milk for the baby, food for Tabou who was howling, and leaving the officer on guard, I went out to spy out the lie of the land.

A soft fine rain was falling. Dax was a small neat town of small neat houses. On the Place de l'Arsenal, the Germans had parked their cars, and I was able to examine at leisure some of the formidable ironmongery they had amassed.

The shops were full of German soldiers buying everything they could lay their hands on. In one store, the shopkeeper told me he had sold out of his entire stock of fountain-pens in one hour. The 'locusts' bought gold and diamond rings, suitcases, leather handbags and perfume for which they paid with a flourish, in marks, twenty marks to the pound. The shopkeepers were not always aware that these marks were worthless bits of forged paper.

One does not easily change one's habits, even in wartime and times of calamity. Having seen an exciting-looking bookshop, I went in to find it full of German officers buying maps and coffee-table albums of photographs of the French countryside, French furniture, and French paintings.

I walked to the back of the shop to look at the books. I took down a fine edition of the works of Rimbaud, leafed through it, picked up a book of Mallarmé's poems, read one of them and found I was crying. Fearing the *locusts* might hear, I sat down on a stool and buried my face in my hands. I felt a touch on the shoulder, and looking up saw the owner of the library, a dwarfish little man with a silky grey beard. Gently he mopped my face with a large, rather grimy handkerchief, and then wiped his own wet cheeks. Then he took my hand, and we sat for a moment, two mourners by the grave of liberty. I have never forgotten the unutterable sadness in his dark, red-rimmed eyes.

When I returned to our lodgings, the officer, Major Armand Renan, told me he had just heard that, as from the following day, no car carrying refugees would be allowed to leave Dax for the South of France. This put me in a quandary, for we had little petrol left, certainly not enough for the long haul to Nice.

We ate our dinner in a courtyard packed with Germans, laughing and guzzling. One of them was concentrating on reading a map spread out on the table. I only saw his face properly when he straightened up to pick up his wineglass. I recognised him instantly. He could not see me, for I was screened by a projecting trellis covered with vine. This young German officer had long frequented the Café de Flore in Paris, and we had had many flirtatious arguments together. I had often seen him with a plain young companion, who turned out to be an important member of the Fifth Column.

Later, in the room we all shared, the Major drew me aside.

'Do you still want to go to Nice?'

'Of course. I'm convinced that is where I must begin my search for my brother.'

'You do understand that your journey may be dangerous and that it will be even more so if you take us?'

'I understand.'

He smiled, a singularly charming smile, and I realised how attractive he must have been before the great and secret grief he carried inside himself had sucked all pleasure out of life.

'So be it then. I have lived in this part of the world most of my life, and I know someone, an important official, who is not afraid to risk his life to help us. So come on, before the curfew, we have to get forged papers and petrol coupons from him.'

The important official lived in a dignified old house not far from the *Kommandantur*. We were ushered through his office, up a flight of stairs, and into a comfortable, homely *salon*, filled with good old-fashioned furniture and family portraits. The official's wife was middle-aged, and very elegant. She made us welcome, and offered us real coffee and Cognac. I apologised for my informal clothes. I was wearing the cotton dress and sandals which made up my complete wardrobe.

The official was an ardent patriot, and his hatred of the Germans was obsessive. His father had been killed by them in the 1914 war. In his official capacity, he was obliged to deal with the enemy on a very high level. He was a fiery fellow with a twisted mouth. 'We're not allowed to possess firearms,' he said, showing me two magnificent Winchester rifles which lived in what appeared to be a broom-cupboard. 'They told me to take down the Flag. If it were daytime, I'd tell you to look out of the window, where you'd see it flying, as it always has until sundown. The other day, two Boche soldiers came and tried to take it down. I sent for them, asked them in, and then locked them into my office. I then sent for their commanding officer and asked him to remove and deal with two of his men who were harassing an important civilian who was doing his best to co-operate with the occupying power. He took his idiots away in double-quick time, apologising profusely for their stupidity. They're crass, I tell you, crass!'

Later we were taken along a corridor into a pleasant book-lined study. The official checked that shutters and curtains were tightly closed. Madame opened the door a crack to make sure nobody was lurking in the corridor. She then went over to one of the long bookshelves, and removed a fat volume. Slipping her hand into the vacant space, she pressed a button, and the wall of books slid aside to reveal a vast room.

This was filled with built-in cupboards and trestle tables heaped with piles of clothing, all of which had been sorted into neat heaps according to sizes. There were tables dedicated to warm clothing, to underclothes; others were used for trousers, skirts and shirts, while shoes, caps, and battered suitcases were kept, together with a large supply of tinned goods, on shelves in the cupboards.

Ever since the outbreak of the Spanish Civil War, Monsieur and Madame X had handed over food, clothes, papers and money to the refugees brought to them, and now they were doing the same thing for those who were trying to escape from the Germans.

They remained at their self-imposed post throughout the war. Theirs was a *safe* house, known to members of the Resistance, many of whom owed their lives to the official and his wife, who were nearly lynched at the Liberation by those who had accused them of collaborating with the enemy!

My Major was obviously an old and trusted friend of theirs; as I later heard, he was a man of great courage, who returned to Dax to work with the local Resistance. He died silently when he was found by a German patrol, preparing to blow up a bridge.

We got back to the inn, just before the curfew, with petrol and food coupons, and a suitcase full of curiously assorted garments which would have shamed the average scarecrow.

I found Claude trying to comfort my miserable little cat who had been taken ill, and was lying in a piteous huddle. He was obviously in pain, so I went out again to find a vet. This was not easy, as once curfew had sounded anyone on the streets was liable to be hauled off to prison.

I knocked on many doors before finding a doctor, a compassionate man who examined Tabou, said he had a gastric upset, and was in a highly nervous condition. He then gave the cat an injection, and me some tablets which I was to dissolve in hot milk, if and when Tabou became obstreperous. He refused payment for looking after his unusual patient and hustled us out on to the street.

After an uneasy night spent sharing the settee with the Major, we left very early, crossing the frontier between the Occupied and Non-Occupied Zones at about 7.30 a.m. The German guards scrutinised our passes and peered into the car. The Major had temporarily shed his uniform, and wore clothing given him by Monsieur and Madame X. Once we were well away from the frontier, we stopped the car and offered up a prayer of thanks that we were in Free France again, out of reach of those grey-green uniforms and hideous helmets.

18

Experience is What Happens to You

We got to Pamiers at eleven o'clock. The streets were full of anxious people, and a gendarme told us that we had better move on, since there was not a corner to be had in the district. It had just begun to rain, and the prospect of sleeping in the car was unattractive.

Suddenly, Claude Maeterlinck remembered that a friend of her sister lived in Pamiers, and leaving her baby in our care, she went off to find him. When she had gone the Major and I exchanged meaningful glances. We had both had the same rather uncharitable thought, that Claude might not return. Fortunately we misjudged her, for she found her sister's friend sitting quietly at home. She dragged him out to the car, and, touched by our plight and evident fatigue, he invited us to spend the night in his flat. He owned a small drapery shop, and he, his wife and mother-in-law lived over it.

Mattresses and blankets were produced; and soon we were all installed on the dining-room floor. Tabou promptly disgraced me by lapping up a bowl of milk that had been put by for breakfast. The draper had just returned from Dunkirk and told us a long, rambling and what sounded a very unlikely tale; but we all agreed that it was a miracle that he had managed to get home safe and sound to his loved ones. At this, the mother-in-law, who smelled strongly of camphor, burst into tears and said that it would soon be like living through the Siege of Paris, when everyone ate rats and elephants. The Major observed tartly that he thought that elephants might be in short supply in Pamiers, after which the family retired, and we all settled down to sleep.

After a good breakfast with our kind hosts, we got back into the car, which now represented my only security. There was little traffic, and we spun along at a great rate. The countryside was serene, and for the first time in weeks, we all felt as if an iron bar had been removed from our chests. We inhaled the fresh morning air, breathing deeply and thanking God for our freedom.

I was worried about Claude. She had become very silent and withdrawn, and once or twice I had seen her push her baby roughly away. The Major and I were afraid that she might do the child a mischief, so while I concentrated on driving he kept a sharp eye on her.

When we reached Carcassonne, we found the narrow picturesque streets were crowded with French soldiers, refugees and children. In the Place, grouped together like a herd of elephants, were the Paris buses which had left the capital a month before to bring troops and refugees south. They were camouflaged a dreary, battleship grey, but were, none the less, easily recognisable as Parisian buses. Besides, their conductors, waggish to the last, had left the original names indicating the vehicles' destination, and I read on the boards, MADELEINE ... PASSY ... ST GERMAIN-LES-PRES and NEUILLY. A wave of nostalgia washed over me, for Paris, and for the brilliant love-spangled days of my youth that were gone for ever.

We listened avidly to the radio, our only link with the outside world. We were sealed inside a pressure cooker of conflicting emotions and rumours. A communiqué told us that Britain was continuing the struggle alone. The names of refugees trying to contact their families and friends were read out like a litany. Madame S. of Blois, now at Carcassonne would like news of her daughter Solange, last seen at Tours station. Madame D. of Ville d'Avray, would like news of the whereabouts of her son, Lieutenant D. last seen in Rouen, and so on *ad infinitum*.

From time to time, French soldiers would pass the café. Most of them carried sticks or cudgels. They looked tired and shabby, but they smiled and waved at the young women. There was something ragged and defeated about their appearance; so must Napoleon's troops have looked, at the outset of the retreat from Moscow.

By now we had run out of food. The baby was teething. It was fretful and cried continually. It was by no means an endearing infant, with boot-button eyes, and a wizened grumpy little face. The Major's wound was suppurating, and I was afraid of gangrene setting in, but he would not hear of our stopping at a casualty ward in an hospital to have it examined and dressed. We made a grand tour of all the restaurants and food shops in the vicinity, hoping to be able to buy a tin of condensed milk or a loaf of bread, but nothing edible was to be had.

It was getting late by the time we reached Arles. We tried to find an hotel, but even the *Centre d'Accueil* was filled to capacity. I drove out into the countryside, fearing we should have to spend the night in the open. Luckily it was warm. It was not easy to find a resting-place in the dark. The Major went off on a recce, returning with the farmer who owned the acres of vineyards around us.

He took us to a big old farm kitchen where we were greeted by his wife and a number of big dogs, one of whom became frenzied by the scent of Tabou shut up in his basket. He was dragged away snarling and snapping. There was a fire burning in the hearth, and a steaming cauldron of soup made us feel faint with hunger.

Claude said she did not want any food but wanted to lie down, so the farmer's wife took her to a spare room in which there was a baby's cot. After we had drunk bowls of good, hot soup and eaten chunks of fresh farm bread with cheese, the farmer led us, the Major and me, across the courtyard to the stables.

I washed my hands and face at a tap in the yard, and made a makeshift bed on a truss of straw. I was dropping with fatigue, but when I heard a rustle, I thought of the rats and mice that must inhabit my quarters and, terrified at the idea, I jumped up and went out. The dogs barked wildly but I ignored them, and walked up and down, smoking a cigarette and reflecting on my plight. I could not really believe that Lala and Papa's delicate little daughter, the pampered wife of the Baron; Géa's exotic bird of paradise, should be bear-leader and provider for a wounded major, a manic-depressive refugee, a squalling baby and a schizophrenic Siamese cat. 'This be none of I', I quoted to myself aloud in the darkness, and almost jumped out of my skin when a tiny point of flame was thrust under my nose.

'This be none of any of us, but don't be scared; like you, I have insomnia. Let's walk a bit and I'll tell you who I am supposed to be.'

My companion who walked me back to the stables was a youngish Englishman in a military greatcoat. I thought it a bit odd to find him strolling about in this out-of-the-way farm, but decided that in view of the topsy-turvy world in which I was living, this was no time to be analytical. I introduced my Englishman to the Major, and left them to smoke, talk and drink together, for by then I was dying of fatigue.

Next day the Major told me that the young man had been invalided home after having been wounded in the Battle of Flanders. As it turned out he and the Major arranged to meet again in the course of time and by the grace of God they succeeded in making their way to England, where they then joined the French section of S.O.E., both of them being frequently parachuted back into France.

On the third day of our Odyssey, we swept into St Raphael, and into the familiar scenery of the Riviera. Instead of pressing on to my destination, I had to go in the opposite direction to deliver letters and cards in code to various contacts living in villas, shops and cafés in towns and villages along the coast. Nearly all the hotels and villas were shuttered and closed, and the streets and beaches were empty of tourists and holidaymakers. Ste Maxime was visited only by the Mistral, and St Tropez, except for its indigenous population, appeared to have gone into hibernation.

Outside Nice, the Major asked me to drop him off. He stood for a moment by the open window of the car, looking at me; then, kissing me hard on the lips, saluted, and strode away. I drove Claude and her baby to the house of the friends who had been expecting her, her sister and her children. I was glad to see how kindly they welcomed the poor demented woman. When she had been led away weeping to her room, I managed to whisper my fears to her host, who reassured me by telling me he was a doctor, and would see that she received immediate treatment.

I drove away in tearing spirits, happy to be rid of my passengers, who had become a source of worry. Now I was, once more, truly on my own. How, I wondered, would I find my brother? How long would it take to track him down? My euphoria evaporated and I felt tired and lonely.

I was in one of Nice's least glamorous districts. I saw a little bar. Pushing through the bead and bamboo curtain, I went in to see if a glass of wine would raise my drooping spirits. The bar was empty, save for a somnolent old man sitting in a corner. The bead curtain rustled in the breeze. I wondered when I should see Lala and my home again. The wine was heady. It seemed years ago since I had had my sparse *petit-déjeuner*. I began to feel drowsy. I closed my eyes for a moment. The *patron* leaned over the counter and tapped me on the shoulder. 'Now, now, you can't nod off here. That's what comes of having so many late nights; but I bet it was good, hein? Tell old Victor about it.'

I was conscious of someone looming at my elbow. I turned and saw my brother Jacques, looking bronzed, fit and furious. He had been seconded to the Chasseurs Alpins, and had, that very day, come down from the mountains. Once we had exchanged rapturous greetings, he told me that after a short, sharp skirmish with the Italian troops, and after the Armistice, his regiment had been sent down to Nice.

He gave me a brief but vivid description of the fight against the Italians. He made it clear to me, without saying so, that he was spying on the Italian Armistice Commission. I tried to draw him out about his activities but he refused to say anything.

I asked when he hoped to be demobilised and he gave me a quizzical glance. He was living from day to day, billeted in a barracks in the neighbourhood of the café in which we had met. He told me he had met two Jews who had managed to escape from one of the German concentration camps. One of them, he said, had the letter J branded on his forehead.

*

With the help of some of Jacques' contacts, I found a tiny flat in which I entertained many of my brother's fellow soldiers. I cooked for them, washed their clothes, and tried to give them some of the comforts of the homes they so sorely missed.

I was having trouble with Tabou. As a result of our peregrinations, he had become desperately insecure and neurotic, and was happy only sitting on a bed of cotton-wool in the bath-tub. Having to remove him to take a bath was a traumatic experience, for his claws were long and sharp. Finally, in despair, I phoned one of my friends who had a property at Cagnes. I knew she loved animals and that Tabou would be safe in her care. I took him to her in his basket, and the last I saw of my furry travelling companion was of him disappearing up a tree, where he sat on a branch, staring balefully down at me and emitting ear-splitting cries.

Many months later, when I was back in South Africa, I received a communication from Géa. When I opened the envelope, a lock of his hair fell out. His letter had been so censored, that only my name and his signature remained. When I rejoined him after the war, he asked me whether I had ever received this particular letter. I said I had, and had cried over his lock of hair. He roared with laughter.

'That wasn't *my* hair. It was a snippet of Tabou's fur, so you would know he was glossy and well-cared for.'

I had come to Nice to liberate my brother and take him home to Papa, and this I intended doing, no matter what obstacles stood in my way. I told Jacques this and asked him to arrange for me to see his commanding officer so that I could obtain his release from the Army.

'He will realise the importance of letting you go before the Germans get here,' I affirmed gravely. And again I saw the quizzical look on his face. But he said nothing. As my old banger was being serviced after the long trip, and any other form of transport was virtually unobtainable, I borrowed a bicycle, and rode off one fine morning, to keep my appointment with Jacques' colonel. I had not ridden a bicycle for years, and was none too certain of my balance. Gritting my teeth in an agony of concentration, I wobbled my way into the dusty, sunny courtyard of the barracks, and asked a soldier on guard-duty to conduct me to Colonel G.

He took me to a small office, where I was left to cool my heels before a po-faced portrait of Marianne wearing a Phrygian cap on her head. After half an hour, the Colonel's P.A., a young, pink-faced officer, was sent to conduct me to the presence. The baby-faced officer was obviously electrified at my *chutzpah* in demanding an interview with his chief.

Colonel G. was dark, suave and dapper, with thin, hairy wrists, and beautiful tapering fingers, with manicured, filbert-shaped nails. He had a dark crescent of moustache arched over moist, very red lips. He bowed over my hand, brushing it delicately with his moustache, and when I had explained my mission, he sat and considered me intently.

'Your brother is fortunate, Madame, if I may say so, in having so loyal, brave and affectionate a sister.'

'My visit to you has little to do with affection, *mon Colonel*. I am here, as I told you, on a mission. My father insists that I bring my brother home with me. Papa is a Frenchman, a patriot and an old man. He feels that since France has been betrayed, his son must help purge her shame by fighting elsewhere, with the British or with General de Gaulle, for example.'

The Colonel leant across the table and put a long finger against my mouth. '*Motus*, Madame, walls have ears these days; and while I entirely agree with your sentiments, and those of Monsieur your father, your brother is a French soldier serving in the French Army, and here he will remain until the end of all hostilities. Do I make myself clear? Of all *hostilities*. Now, if you will forgive me, I must leave you to attend a staff conference. Incidentally, desertion is punishable by death. I salute your courage and enterprise. Adieu, Madame.'

When I repeated the gist of this interview to Jacques, he patted me affectionately. 'I told you it wouldn't work. How could it? Don't worry about me. I'll make my own way out of this trap. But I must wait for the right moment. I want you to go as soon as possible. But as long as you are here, you are a liability; I couldn't vanish and leave you to face the music. One of us must get home to comfort the old man.'

The only place where I might obtain the visas essential to get me back to South Africa, was Marseilles, where I had many contacts. So, with a heavy heart, I gave up the lease of my flat, gave my car to Jacques, and packed my miserable little suitcase. He carried it to the station, bought me some oranges and a bottle of mineral water. He helped me struggle aboard the train and found me a place in a crowded carriage. Then, hugging me tightly, he jumped down on to the platform.

I managed to push my way to the window. I looked down at my brother, in his shabby, ill-fitting uniform, his beret jauntily cocked over his baby face, with the wide, shining grey eyes that were so like those of our mother, and I wept as I have never cried before or since.

As the train moved out of the station, I hung further and further out of the window, to get a last glimpse of Jacques. He looked so isolated, so young and so vulnerable. Finally, someone dragged me back into the compartment. It was a fat old farmer, with sweaty palms.

'*Allons, allons, jolie Madame,*' he said, in the aioli-scented accent of the Midi. 'You'll spoil those pretty eyes with all those tears; and anyway, take a tip from a wise old man. Just forget that little *militaire*, he's much too young for you.'

Index

Afrikaaners' and Afrikaans' language, 130–1
Aga Khan, 162
Alain-Fournier, Henri, 82, 171, 207, 257
Albaret, Celeste, 116
Almanach de Gotha, 28
Apollinaire, Guillaume, 255–6
Arles, 247–9, 295
Armistice with Germany and Italy (1940), 285, 287, 297
Armand, Antonin, 207
Audiberti, Jacques, 235
Augsbourg, Géa, 229, 236, 244–6, 263, 264, 284, 295; sketches at Weidemann trial, 225–6; his love letters, 227–8; travelling in Belgium, 230–5; draftsmanship, 237; family and early life, 237–41; life in the rue Jacob, 241–3; connection with pro-Fascists, 258–9; departure from Paris, 266–72, 274–8
Auvers-sur-Oise, 249–52

Bagnold, Enid, 216
Ballard, editor of *Les Cahiers du Sud*, 235
Ballets Russes de Diaghilev, exhibition, 255
Balzac, Honoré de, 29, 82
Barber, Noel, 268n.
Barnes, Sir Kenneth, 208
Barney, Natalie Clifford, 201–4
Bashkirtseff, Marie, 203, 207
Baudelaire, 23, 115, 166, 234
Bayonne, 281–5; arrival of the Germans, 284
Beauharnais, Josephine de, 71, 110
Beaumont, Count Etienne de, 257–8
Bellini, Mario, 80, 83
Bérard, Christian, 244
Biarritz, 281, 282
Bibliothèque Nationale, 17, 199
Blanche, Jacques-Emile, 114, 117
Blé en Herbe, Le (Colette), 34
Bonheur, Gaston, 235
Bordeaux, 278–9, 281
Borinage, the, 246–7
Boudin, Eugène-Louis, 96, 103, 155, 166
Braque, Georges, 255, 256

Bromfield, Louis, 121
Brontës, the, 215
Brooks, Romaine, 202
Brussels, 234–5
Budberg, Moura, 121–3, 216
Burgoyne, Sir John, 105
Burgundy, wine and wine-growing châteaux, 31–3
Bussy, Dorothy, 216–17

Cabourg, 155; Proust at, 115–16
Cahiers du Sud, Les, 235
Cap Breton, 265, 279–82, 284–8; arrival of the Germans, 284–6
Cape Town, 125–6, 146
Capri, 187–8
Carcassonne, 294–5
Carpentras, Marie-France de, 65–8
Carpentras, Thérèse de, 64–8; memories of Proust, 66
Catherine the Great, 112, 201
Cézanne, Paul, 190, 246, 250
Chagall, Marc, 233
Chambers, Sir William, 210
Chanel, Coco, 155, 162, 220
Charleville, 235–6
Cheremeteff, Count Boris Petrovitch, 111
Cheremeteff Palace, 111
Cheremeteff, Serge, 12, 22, 84, 108–13, 118–21, 185, 200, 201, 207, 216; and St Petersburg, 111; escape from Russia, 112
Chéri (Colette), 34, 165, 199
Chevakinsky, Savva, 111
Chirico, Giorgio di, 233, 255
Clairouin, Denise, 206–8; Denise Clairouin Foundation, 207
Close to Colette (Goudeket), 35n., 176
Cocteau, Jean, 34, 170, 202, 237
Colette, 32–6, 165, 178, 199, 202–3; her Institut de Beauté, 33–4; her suite at the Hôtel Claridge, 34–5; and Proust, 117; at St Tropez, 174–6; at Weidmann trial, 225
Commissariat General for Information, 260

Index

Concentration camps 10, 68, 259, 297
Connolly, Cyril, 210
Coppée, François, 189
Cost, March, 216
Courbet, Gustave, 166
Croisset, 97–9

Dadaists, the, 256
Dali, Salvador and Gala, 190
Dax, 288–92
Dear Theo (ed. Stone), 246n., 248n., 250n.
Deauville, 78, 103, 105, 162–3; Casino, 162
Deffand, Madame du, 198, 206
De Gaulle, General Charles, 268n., 287, 299
De La Minaudière, General, 28, 43
De La Minaudière, Baron Renaud Marie, 11, 13, 26–32, 78, 84, 86, 96, 103–8, 113–14, 122, 124–5, 127, 144, 147, 150, 153–5, 160, 167–70, 172, 183, 186, 191, 197–9, 217, 241, 263, 295, 297–8; family, 27–30, 42–4, 76, 78, 80–2, 144, 147, 155, 156, 167–9; courtship, 31, 37; engagement, 38–45, 50; plans for fishing fleet, 39–42; marriage, 27, 31, 53; typhoid fever, 55–8, 62; married life, 59–61, 64, 68–70; and Chris, 161, 165–6, 170; and Géa, 228–9; in 1940, 266–7
Délices des Quatres Saisons, Les, toile by Huet, 84
Dives-sur-Mer, 163–5
Doublet, Jean-François, 80
Dufy, Raoul, 162–3
Duncan, Isadora, 243, 244
Duncan, Raymond, 243–4
Duse, Eleonora, 188
Dusty Answer (Lehmann), 215
Dutton, Beatrice, 208
Duval, Jeanne, 234

Eliot, T. S., 41
Ensor, James, 230, 232–4
'Entrée du Christ à Bruxelles, L'' (Ensor), 233
Eugénie, Empress, 104–5, 109, 190, 211, 282
Evans, Empress Eugénie's dentist, 104–5

Finaly, Marie, 115

Flashing Stream, The (Morgan), 212
Flaubert, Gustave, 81, 82, 96–9; birthplace, 97; home at Croisset, 97, 98–9
Foujita, Japanese artist, 149–50
Fountain, The (Morgan), 211, 212
Francis, Robert, 171
French Resistance, 207, 266, 292

Gachet family, 249–52
Gauguin, 246, 248, 249
George VI and Queen Elizabeth, visit to Paris, 190
Geraud, Maître Henri, 224
Gide, André, 41, 213
Giraudoux, Jean, 260, 261
Goebbels, Joseph, 261
Goering, Hermann, 245, 258, 267
Golden Treasury of Verse (Palgrave), 142
Goncourt brothers, the, 82
Gordimer, Nadine, 130
Goudeket, Maurice, 35 and n., 175–6
Gourmont, Rémy de, 202
Grand-Meaulnes, Le (Alain-Fournier), 82, 171, 215
Grange aux Trois Belles, La (Francis), 171
Guillotining, public, 222n., 226–7

Hansford Johnson, Pamela, 123
Harwood, Tottie (H.M.), 208–10, 215
Heath, Neville, 209–10
Hemingway, Ernest, 148
Hendaye, 283–4
Himmler, Heinrich, 261
Hitler, Adolf, 245, 258, 260–2, 275, 283, 284, 288
Honfleur, 78, 80, 84–5, 92, 96, 154, 156, 160
Horizon magazine, 210
Hospice de Beaune, 32
Huet, Jean-Baptiste, 84
Hutton, Barbara, 46
Huysmans, Joris Karl, 189
Hyères, 176, 177

Illuminations, Les (Rimbaud), 171
Institut de Beauté, 33–4
Isle du Levant, 176, 179
Italian Armistice Commission, 297

Jardin de la Mère Toutain (Courbet), 166
Jardin, Maître Renée, 224–5
Joan of Arc, 97, 272

Johannesburg, 14, 15, 38, 53, 71, 126–7, 129, 130, 133, 136, 143, 186, 209, 279
Journal, Le, 225

Kennedy, Margaret, 216
Kew Gardens, 110
Korda, Sir Alexander, 122

Landru, Henri, 222, 224
Laurençin, Marie, 255–7
Lebrêton, Madame, 105
Lehmann, Rosamond, 215
Lemoine, Pierre, 268–70, 272–4
Lifar, Serge, 170, 255
Ligne, Prince de, 110
London, Géo, 225
Louis XVI, 28, 62, 83, 110, 226

Macaulay, Rose, 216
McCall, Marjorie, 208
Madame Bovary (Flaubert), 33, 97, 98, 104, 157; working notes and manuscript, 98
Maginot Line, 245, 260
Mallarmé, Stephane, 290
Malmaison, 110
Manoir de Rollo, 78–84, 102, 103, 113, 153, 154, 160, 170, 213
Marais, Charles, 174
Marie-Antoinette, 28, 54, 55, 63, 72, 73, 110, 226, 243
Marquet, Albert, 96
Masques Scandalisées, Les (Ensor), 233
Maugham, W. Somerset, 53
Maupassant, Guy de, 81, 114
Maxwell, Elsa, 258
Mdivani, Prince, 48
Mendl, Lady, 257
Miller, Henry and June, 207
Monet, Claude, 96
Montaigne, 82, 278
Montmartre, 184, 185, 229
Montparnasse, 148, 185
Monzie, Anatole de, 259
Moréno, Marguerite, 175
Morgan, Charles, 208, 210–12, 215; and Napoleon, 211; and France, 212
Moro-Giafferi, Maître, 224
Morrell, Julian, 216
Morrell, Lady Ottoline, 216
Munthe, Axel, 187–8

Naissance du Jour, La (Colette), 34, 176

Napoleon I, 189, 211, 244; at St Helena, 177
Napoleon III, 190
Nazis, the, 259–62, 275
New York Herald Tribune, 50, 63, 223
Nice, 296–8
Nicolson, Harold, 213–15
Nicolson, Nigel, 213
Nin, Anais, and her Journals, 207
Noailles, Charles de, 190
Noailles, Marie-Laure de, 170, 190
Normandy, 41, 81–2; *cuisine normande*, 91; tours of, 96
Notable British Trials series, 209
Nouvelles Littéraires, Les, 207, 208, 210, 219

Ode to France (Morgan), 212
Olivia, 216
Orléans, 272–3
Ostend, 230–4
Ouistreham, 38–42

Paris: life in a Pension, 18–22; literary figures; 22–3; historical Paris, 23; Faubourg St Germain world, 43, 45; Les Halles, 62; shops, 62–3, 193; Ile St Louis, 64; 'on the town', 184–5; cabarets, 184, 189–90; *salons de thé*, 192; and the German advance, 272–8
Paris-Soir, 225, 265
Pascal, Blaise, 82
Passy cemetery, 203
Paton, Alan, 130
Pepita (Sackville-West), 214
Pétain, Marshal Philippe, 28, 285
Philippe d'Orléans, 189
Picasso, Pablo, 123, 191, 233, 237, 254–5
Piérard, Louis, 246, 247
Pin to see the Peepshow, A (Tennyson Jesse), 209
Pissarro, Camille, 96, 250, 251
Plettenberg Bay, 144–6
Poitiers, 277, 278
Polnay, Lucy de, 20, 48–9, 60, 102–8, 147–53, 221; death, 152–3, 253
Polnay, Peter de, 153
Porquerolles, 176–82
Port-Cros, 176, 179
Portrait in a Mirror (Morgan), 212
Portrait of a Marriage (Nigel Nicolson), 213n.
Press Bureau, 260
Prisons et Paradis (Colette), 33n., 175n.

Index

'Profils Anglais', 208, 210–17
Proust, Marcel, 23, 64, 66, 96, 114–17, 127, 165; and Normandy, 114–17

Rastignac, Marquis de, 29
Rastignac, Marquise de, 28–31, 59, 70–7, 107, 198; and the Baron, 28–30, 38, 40, 42, 70–1, 73–7, 79, 102, 169, 172, 218; *l'heure bleue*, 30; the 'Swan', 30
Redon, Odilon, 233
Remarque, Erich Maria, 245
Renoir, Auguste, 190, 233
Reynaud, Paul, 268n., 276
Rimbaud, Arthur, 23, 162, 171–2, 228, 235–6, 290; birthplace, 235; grave, 235–6
Rodin, Auguste, 47
Rolland, Romain, 244
Rose-Macleod, Lewis, 211
Rouen, 96–9
Royal Academy of Dramatic Art, 208
Royer, Madame, 116
Ruskin, John, 96

Sackville-West, Vita, 213–16
St Helena, 176–7
St Paul de Vence, 186–7
St Petersburg, 111
St Siméon Group and the Ferme de St Siméon, 161, 166
St Tropez, 174–6, 296
Salon des Indépendants, 233
Sand, George, 99, 155, 171, 214
Schiaparelli, Elsa, 46, 155, 220
Ségur, Comtesse de, 84
Sévigné, Madame de, 163
Seychelles, the, 176
Shaw, Bernard, 215
Sido (Colette), 33, 34
Simenon, Georges, 39, 41–2
Sissinghurst Castle, 213–15
Sitwell, Edith, 216
Smith's tearoom, 72
Snow, C. P., 123
South Africa, 14–15, 18, 60–1, 77, 125–46, 153, 253, 278; attitude to the Africans, 130–1; effects of European civilisation, 131
Spanish Civil War, 253
Staël, Madame de, 221, 256
Steegmuller, Francis, 256n.
Stein, Gertrude, 190–1, 202

Stern, G. B., 216
Stowe Park, 110
Strachey, Lytton, 216–17
Strasser, Gregor, 260–1
Strasser, Otto, 260–2, 282–4
Surrealist Movement, 233, 256
Système D, 266

Tennyson Jesse, Fryn, 208–10, 212, 215, 221–2; and the Weidmann case, 209, 222, 224–6
Thérèse de Lisieux, Ste, 173
Thompson-Bywaters case, 209
Tolstoy, 143, 180
Toulouse-Lautrec, Henri de, 250
Tours, 273–4; French Government at, 268n., 274
Trefusis, Violet, 121, 213
Trouville, 103, 105, 106, 115, 155–6; Proust at Trouville, 114; Les Pins, 156

Van Gogh, Theo, 246n., 251, 252
Van Gogh, Vincent, 246–52; in the Borinage, 246–7; at Arles, 247–9; at Auvers, 249–52; grave, 252
van Hoorn, Elodie, 16–17, 23, 25, 29–31, 60, 70, 198, 200, 206; her books, 17, 198, 200, 206; musical soirées, 25–6, 31
Varenne, François Pierre de, 90
Venice, 187
Verdun, 28; battlefields, 31–2
Verlaine, Paul, 23, 236
Versailles, 54–5, 63, 222, 224, 226, 243; Trianon Palace Hotel, 54, 222; Petit Trianon, 54, 110
Vichy, 14; French Government at, 287
'Victims' Reception', the, 28, 29
Victoria, Queen, 109, 112, 190
Vie Parisienne, La, 69, 129
Villon, François, 22–3
Vilmorin, Louise de, 170
Vivian, Renée (Pauline Tarn), 203, 204
Voyage, The (Morgan), 212
Vray Cuisinier François, Le (de Varenne), 90

Walpole, Horace, 110, 234
War and Peace (Tolstoy), 33, 142–3
Waugh, Evelyn, 210
Weidmann, Eugene: his murders, 209, 222–4; trial, 222, 224–6; execution, 226–7

Wells, H. G., 122, 215
West, Rebecca, 216
Westminster, Duke of, 162
William the Conqueror, 163

Winter Palace, St Petersburg, 111
Within a Budding Grove (Proust), 115–16
Woolf, Virginia, 214